Between a...

Between Art and Science is both a celebration and a critique of contemporary psychotherapy. Jeremy Holmes is a practising psychiatrist and psycho-therapist in the NHS, who writes with infectious enthusiasm about the importance and usefulness of psychotherapy and its wider application within psychiatry.

He shows how psychoanalytical ideas can illuminate such clinical prob-lems as disturbances of personal identity, adolescent loneliness, obses-sionality, long-term mental illness, agoraphobia and suicide. Ilustrating his arguments with literary as well as clinical examples, Dr Holmes emphasises the importance of creativity in psychotherapy and the connections between the artistic and psychotherapeutic impulse. He stresses that psychotherapy is an important humanising force within psychiatry and contemporary culture, and that the psychoanalytical vision acts as an important bridge between the arts and the sciences, combining the intuitive and the rational, the narrative with the experimental approach. Looking at both the strengths and the limitations of the psychoanalytical approach, Dr Holmes suggests that contemporary psychoanalysis needs to escape from its esotericism by taking into account advances in cognitive science, family therapy and the realities of psychiatric work in a public health setting.

Between Art and Science makes a strong and persuasive appeal for an integrated approach to psychotherapy and in particular shows how analytic and family therapies can be reconciled at a theoretical level and can complement each other as part of an integrated 'psychological treatment service'.

Jeremy Holmes is a consultant psychiatrist and psychotherapist working within the National Health Service at North Devon District Hospital. He is currently working on a study of the role of Attachment Theory in psycho-therapy and psychiatry.

Between art and science

Essays in psychotherapy and psychiatry

Jeremy Holmes

Tavistock/Routledge
London and New York

First published 1993
by Routledge
11 New Fetter Lane, London EC4P 4EE

Simultaneously published in the USA and Canada
by Routledge
a division of Routledge, Chapman and Hall, Inc.
29 West 35th Street, New York, NY 10001

© 1993 Jeremy Holmes

Typeset by Ponting–Green Publishing Services, Sunninghill, Berks

Printed and bound in Great Britain by
Mackays of Chatham PLC, Chatham, Kent

British Library Cataloguing in Publication Data
A catalogue record for this book is available from the British Library.

Library of Congress Cataloging in Publication Data
Holmes, Jeremy.
  Between art and science : essays in psychotherapy and psychiatry /
  Jeremy Holmes.
  p.   cm.
  A collection of the author's essays originally published in various
  British medical journals.
  1. Psychotherapy–Philosophy. I. Title.
  [DNLM: 1. Literature–collected works. 2. Psychoanalytic Therapy–
  collected works. 3. Psychotherapy–collected works. WM 420 H751b]
  RC437.5.H65   1992
  616.89'14–dc20
  DNLM/DLC
  for Library of Congress   92–2377
                                                          CIP

ISBN 0–415–08307–9
ISBN 0–415–08308–7 (pbk)

This book is dedicated to the memory of my parents.

Contents

Acknowledgements

I am grateful to the editor and publishers of the following journals where earlier versions of many of the essays in this book first appeared: The *British Journal of Medical Psychology* for Chapters 3, 6 and 11; the *British Journal of Psychiatry* for Chapters 2, 5, 7, 13 and 15; the *British Journal of Psychotherapy* for Chapters 4, 10 and 12; the *Journal of Family Therapy* for Chapters 8 and 9; and *Psychoanalytic Psychotherapy* for Chapter 14. Thanks also to Seamus Heaney for permission to reproduce the extracts from his prose and poetry in Chapter 11, and to his publisher Faber & Faber, to whom I am also indebted for permission to publish the poem by Robert Lowell in Chapter 10.

The suggestions, support, encouragement and forbearance of colleagues, friends and family are essential ingredients in the making of a book. I am grateful to the following who have all, in different but important ways, contributed to the production of this work: Pat Bartlett, Anthony Bateman, Ros Holmes, Alison Housley, Sebastian Kraemer, Richard Lindley, Pat Millner, Charles Montgomery, Oliver Reynolds and Glenn Roberts.

My greatest debt, and also the most problematic, is to the patients whose stories form the backbone of these pages. To write meaningfully about psychotherapy I believe it is necessary to describe case-histories. Yet to do so is a breach of the confidentiality that is the prerequisite of a psycho-therapeutic relationship – and at worst can be a form of psychological theft. Of course, biographical details have been altered in an attempt to preserve anonymity, but a psychotherapeutic case-history remains a *roman-à-clef* and to read about oneself in this way cannot fail to be shocking. My current practice, which has evolved after many years of unease and prevarication about this issue, is to show my material to patients and to ask directly for permission to publish. I then face the consequences within the transference and countertransference as best I can. Since these essays were written over a period of nearly twenty years, there will inevitably be some patients whose permission I have not been able to ask: to them I offer my apologies.

Finally, a note about the perennial problem of personal pronouns in a post-feminist era. The majority of psychotherapists and their patients are female.

This psychotherapist happens to be male. I have decided to be consistently inconsistent about this issue, describing patients and their therapists as *he* or *she* in a random but, I hope, even-handed fashion.

Introduction
The eclectic psychotherapist

When I first entered psychiatry as a rather callow Laingian (Laing 1960) twenty years ago, I was advised it would be as well to choose what sort of psychiatrist I wanted to be. My mornings, I was told, would be spent on the wards of the mental hospital, but the afternoons could be devoted to psychoanalysis, research or golf. Since then there have been remarkable changes in both psychiatry and psychotherapy. The dissolution of the institutions has meant that most psychiatrists work not in mental hospitals but from District General Hospital units, as I now do, spending large parts of their day in the GP Practices, Day Hospitals and Community Mental Health Centres which comprise 'the Community' (see Part IV). At the same time there has been an explosion of interest in psychotherapy. It can no longer be seen as a gentlemanly, post-prandial pastime; nor, given the proliferation of different forms of therapy, can there be any simple equation between psychotherapy and psychoanalysis.

Nevertheless, the themes of that half-joking initiatory comment have not entirely disappeared. In the house of psychiatry there are many mansions: psychotherapeutic, biological and social. These are far less divided among themselves than they were, but there is still much mutual suspicion and misunderstanding. That division of the day into two halves epitomises the hybrid character of psychiatric work – and the difficulty of trying to combine a psychiatric and a psychotherapeutic vision persists (see Chapter 14). Similarly the psychotherapies show endemic fissiparity: it is not enough for one to be a psychotherapist: one must also establish whether one is a psychoanalyst, an analytic psychotherapist, a systemic therapist, a cognitive therapist or a behaviourist.

These tribal groupings within psychiatry and psychotherapy can either be seen as marking the confusion and uncertainty of disciplines still in the early stages of their evolution, or as reflecting an inherent richness and pluri-potentiality. It is worth noting that the divisions within both psychiatry and psychotherapy have lessened since an acceptable 'container' has been created – the Royal College of Psychiatrists and the United Kingdom Standing Committee for Psychotherapy respectively (see Chapter 2).

Polarisations are endemic within Western culture: artist *or* scientist, yogi *or* commissar, hedgehog *or* fox. Britain is handicapped by an educational system which produces illiterate scientists or innumerate artists (see Chapter 12). The election on the world stage of political leaders who are also artists is an encouraging but recent phenomenon. And yet many of the most important scientific and cultural advances, paradigm shifts in thinking, have come from the combination of differing perspectives. Within the field of psychotherapy these include Freud himself, who combined a deep commitment to nineteenth-century science with the traditions of German Romanticism (Gay 1988) and the Jewish mystical tradition (Bakan 1990); Jung's explorations of Eastern philosophy and psychoanalysis (Jung 1978); Bowlby's creation of attachment theory from the building blocks of ethology and psychoanalysis (Bowlby 1969); and Bateson's foundations of family therapy from cybernetics and anthropology (Bateson 1973).

I have always been attracted to systems of synthesis: Marxism with its Hegelian 'interpenetration of opposites'; psychoanalysis in which, according to Freud, in the unconscious incompatibles can coexist (See Chapter 10); and Zen Buddhism with its 'ecological' vision which emphasises the essential interrelatedness of all things (see Chapter 7). The essays that make up this book attempt to explore the connections between psychotherapy on the one hand and, on the other, developmental psychology (Part I), literature (Part III), and psychiatry (Part IV). Similarly, within psychotherapy this compulsive eclecticism has led me to explore the relationships between psychoanalysis and family therapy (Part II), and within psychoanalysis to try to find what seem to be the most useful contributions from a wide variety of schools: from the Kleinians the idea of containment and projective identification; from the middle group the emphasis on creativity and play; and from Bowlby and Kohut the idea of the importance of continuing attachment throughout life. A certain 'negative capability' is needed in order to sustain this eclecticism. I resist attempts to solve the dilemma of the status of psychotherapy by trying to prise it away from the sciences and characterise it as a purely hermeneutic discipline (see Part III), and the contrary tendency to ignore its moral and cultural contribution and to ask it to stand or fall by the same rigorous but limited scientific scrutiny of a drug trial (Holmes and Lindley 1989).

But eclecticism has its dangers. The eclectic can be a chameleon, moving restlessly from topic to topic in search of a secure base somehow lacking within himself. The results may be more a pretty but superficial collage rather than a true blending of hues or an original line. The dangers of being unable to tolerate uncertainty and so falling into dogmatism is ever present within a psychotherapy (Casement 1991) which lacks the external validation of the experimental method in science, or of public scrutiny in the arts. Equally, to see psychotherapy as a 'nomadic discipline' (Kohon 1986) lacking a secure theoretical base (and therefore inherently prone either to esotericism or assimilation) may be another avoidance of the necessary anxiety that precedes the establishment of firm roots.

Reality acts as a constraint on the inner world of thought, but is also in its sheer 'givenness' a source of security. The safe shores from which I have tried to build these bridges have for me been twofold: first the clinical encounter with the patient – despite the fact that the 'patient' whom one sees is inevitably influenced by one's theoretical perspective – and second the realities of practising psychotherapeutic psychiatry within the National Health Service. Almost all the essays in this book have been stimulated by a particular patient or clinical problem which has arisen in the context of trying to provide a psychotherapeutically informed psychiatric service. I hope their case-histories form a bedrock upon which its diversity rests.

For me psychotherapy has always been an essential humanising force within psychiatry, providing a moral vision without which psychiatry can all too easily become banal or brutalising (Holmes 1991). The combination of moral perspective, practical method of treatment and set of theories about psychological development and character formation make the psycho-therapies central to the practice of psychiatry. A psychiatry which lacks these psychotherapeutic perspectives is reminiscent of Rothschild's (1984) des-cription of his wartime work as a bomb-disposal expert. His first approach to an unexploded bomb would be to crouch behind a well-padded sofa, look intently at the device and, by a process of mental dissection, think very hard about the way it was put together. The great advances in psychiatry, for example our understanding of the biological and social aspects of schizo-phrenia, are the result of that sort of well-defended intellectual effort. This view of the patient as potentially explosive needs to be balanced by a complementary type of empathic thinking (see Chapter 11) that is the provenance of psychotherapy.

An illustration of these mutually enhancing viewpoints can be found by comparing two descriptions of trees by Gerard Manley Hopkins (1953). Here is his minutely observed prose view:

> Oaks: the organisation of the tree is difficult. Speaking generally no doubt the determining planes are concentric, a system of brief contiguous and continuous tangents, whereas those of the cedar would roughly be called horizontals and those of the beech radiating but modified by droop and a screw-set towards jutting points.

And here his poetic account, *Ash-boughs*:

> Not of all my eyes see, wandering on the world,
> Is anything a milk to the mind so, so sighs deep
> Poetry to it, as a tree whose boughs break in the sky
> Say it is ash-boughs ... May
> Mells blue and snow-white them, a fringe and fray

Of greenery: it is old earth's groping towards the steep
Heaven whom she childs us by.

In the poem the carefully and scientifically described tree of the prose version
is transformed into part of a nurturing, milk-giving nature-mother, honey-
sweet and blending ('mells' – miel, melding), who 'childs' the poet and
humanity in general. This capacity to make identificatory shifts from
observing adult to child, from self to nature, to invest what is observed with
feeling and meaning, can be compared with the psychotherapeutic capacity to
make imaginative identifications with the patient, with the ability to tackle
problems from the perspective of the inner world as well as the outside.
Eclecticism at its best can be seen as reflecting the ability to move freely
between each 'end' of the relationship between the self and its object that is
a mark of psychological health.

This raises the question of to whom this book is addressed: who or what is
its object? It will be obvious to any reader with a deep knowledge of the wide
range of subjects covered here that I am not a scholar. Nor is this the work of
a populist: it offers no simple message or 'answer'. It is perhaps aimed at that
important middle ground between scholarship and populism – the professional psychotherapist and psychiatrist who wish to reflect on wider
aspects of their subjects. But the true 'object' of the book is the very work it
describes. Each essay represents an effort to think about my own thoughts –
a form of 'metacognition' (see Chapter 1) based upon that benign internal
split between 'I' and 'self' which is a prerequisite of the craft of psychotherapy. It is also an attempt to celebrate, make sense of and show gratitude
towards the work I have been lucky enough to find and which continues to
fascinate, at times to confuse, to be demanding but never boring, and which
provides a unique and privileged window into that inner world – my own and
my patients' – which is an indispensable part of our humanity.

Part I

Analytic psychotherapy

Analytic psychotherapy
An introduction

Psychoanalytical thinking is for me the bedrock and font of my approach to psychotherapy. A central preoccupation has been the attempt to adapt the analytical approach to the realities of NHS psychiatry. Throughout my psychiatric career I have held a caseload of around half a dozen once- or twice-weekly long-term analytic psychotherapy patients. Most of the essays in this section (and the book as a whole) were stimulated or are illustrated by such cases.

But I am not a psychoanalyst. My personal therapy, supervision and training cases have never approached the gold standard of five-times-a-week (see Chapter 15), nor have I subjected myself to the full discipline and rigours of psychoanalytical training. While this is a matter of some regret and no doubt reflects an avoidant aspect of my makeup, it has also been a deliberate choice. I see my espoused version of analytical psychotherapy not as a watered down or alloyed (to use Freud's metaphor) form of psycho-analysis, but as a discipline in its own right, 'ecologically' adapted to the prevailing atmosphere of contemporary psychiatry and psychotherapy.

In my view there are three main areas, two theoretical, one practical, where psychoanalysis still suffers from the culture of secrecy and esotericism which, under the influence of Ernest Jones, was a feature of its early years in Britain (Pines 1991). The first concerns the advances in cognitive science which, stimulated by the search for artificial intelligence, have taken place in the past decade or so (Johnson-Laird 1983). Despite Freud's insistence that the essence of neurosis is a turning away from reality, psychoanalysis, with some notable exceptions (Peterfreund 1983; Bowlby 1980) has not incor-porated this 'Darwinian' model of the mind as a cybernetic self-regulating system, in which the function of mental structures, emotional and cognitive, is to adapt to the realities of the human and non-human world, but clings instead to one in which cognitions are seen as mere defences against the fundamental unconscious emotional forces which motivate and determine character. This leads to a teleological or 'Lamarckian' view of the mind, in which thought itself is a response to loss (Bion 1962), dreaming a response to the need to preserve sleep (Freud 1900), and exploration and creativity ways of overcoming depression (Klein 1950).

Although Dixon (1982) has shown from work in perceptual defence that there is no incompatibility between the idea of the unconscious and the findings of contemporary psychology, a general psychology which combines the psychoanalytic perspective with that of cognitive science has yet to emerge (but see Ryle 1990; Horowitz 1986). Cognitive therapy, while it has much in common with analytic psychotherapy, tends to be viewed with suspicion by psychoanalysts as a threatening newcomer rather than a fraternal member of the psychotherapeutic family.

A related area where exciting recent developments have taken place which have not been adequately incorporated into psychoanalytic thinking is in the field of developmental psychology. Despite the emphasis placed on infant observation, psychoanalytic theories of infant psychology are largely extrapolations from the pathological mental states of adults. Margaret Mahler's pioneering observations of normal and abnormal infant development have been extended and to some extent superseded by a new generation of researchers of infant behaviour (Stern 1985) inspired by the work of Bowlby (1988) and the development of attachment theory from ethology and linguistics. These studies have partly confirmed the 'object-relations' view of infancy in which the relationship with the mother is a vital determinant of personality development. They show, for example, how the pattern of attachment at one year old is a good predictor of how confident and socially skilful that child will be at six (Bretherton 1990). But in contrast to the Kleinian view of infancy which sees the baby as racked from the start between love and hate, doomed to a never-quite-to-be-achieved escape from the paranoid-schizoid into the depressive position, developmental psychology emphasises how, under reasonably favourable circumstances, there is a 'fit' between mother and baby. It sees pathology as a result of disruption or distortion of this relationship rather than being built into infant psychology.

A third area where, as a psychotherapist working mainly in the National Health Service, I see psychoanalysis as a prisoner of its own esotericism, lies in the practical questions of who is suitable for analytic therapy, how frequently and for how long they should be seen, and by whom. There tends to be an 'inverse care law' (Tudor Hart 1971) at work in NHS psychotherapy in which the most disturbed patients are often seen by the least experienced therapists. Despite the pioneering efforts of Malan (1963) and Balint (1959) it is still not clear how psychoanalysis can best be modified so as to provide adequate and relevant brief treatments that are applicable to the realities of NHS practice. Psychoanalysis has always claimed a place as first-among-equals among the psychotherapies. In one sense this is justified since any psychotherapeutic encounter can be understood and illuminated in terms of transference and countertransference, although the same may also be said of the systemic approach (see Chapter 7). But as a method of treatment psychoanalysis, in my view, must come to accept a pluralistic position within a Psychological Treatment Service alongside behavioural-cognitive, family, 'active' and Rogerian approaches (see Chapter 15). Only thus will the differing needs of the variety of patients be met (Holmes 1991).

It might be argued that psychoanalysis is a very broad church and that, for example, the division of the British Psychoanalytic Society into Freudian, Kleinian and 'Middle-group' streams is a good example of the very pluralism I advocate; that object-relations theory has contributed to and incorporated many of the findings of developmental psychology; and that, through such organisations as the Association for Psychoanalytic Psychotherapy there is a strong commitment to finding ways in which analytic therapy can be applied within the NHS.

The essays in this section are attempts in different ways to engage with these pluralistic and progressive forces within psychoanalysis. Each poses a question or points to a perceived gap in psychoanalytic thinking. The first chapter looks at how ideas of personal identity can be understood in the light of the new developmental psychology. This is followed by a chapter on dreams which contrasts modern psychophysiological ideas with the classical and Kleinian psychoanalytic accounts of dreaming. The following two chapters – on obsessionality and adolescence – try to marry the developmental approach of Piaget and Bowlby with psychoanalytic ideas. A chapter on supportive therapy shows how a modified analytic approach can be adapted to helping long-term, very disturbed patients. The final chapter in this section looks at the sibling relationship in therapy and acts as a bridge to the next section which explores the relationship between psychoanalysis and family therapy.

Chapter 1

Personal identity in psychotherapy

Surprisingly perhaps, problems of personal identity rarely present themselves directly to psychiatrists or psychotherapists. I have yet to meet a patient who thinks he is Napoleon; loss of personal identity only occurs in the final stages of dementia; fugue states are rare and usually short-lived. So too in psychotherapy: however confused or 'ontologically insecure' (Laing 1960) patients may be, they always know who they are and usually turn up for their own appointment, not someone else's.

It is true that in the course of psychotherapy patients may wrestle with the metaphorical question of who they 'really' are, and may struggle to 'find' themselves or lost parts of themselves. But even these are not issues which often occur immediately to someone seeking help, who is more likely to be conscious of feelings of unhappiness or self-dislike than self-estrangement. Psychotherapy *is* concerned with the self – its perturbations, constrictions and dissociations – but with problems not so much *of* as *within* personal identity. If psychotherapy's role within society is to help those whose socialisation has gone awry (Parsons 1951), then the central issue appears to be that of *belonging*, and the key question not so much 'Who am I?', but 'Where do I fit in?' In this chapter I shall try to show how closely related these two questions are.

The question of a 'fit', or otherwise, between an individual and his environment implies a relationship between a self and others that underlies the 'Bowlbyian' object-relations viewpoint of this book. In this chapter I shall review some recent ideas from developmental psychology about the origins of a secure and coherent sense of self, and look at parallels between these developmental models and some of the themes and processes of psychotherapy. I shall try to relate these to recent contributions to the philosophy of personal identity from Derek Parfit and Jonathon Glover (Glover 1988).

In the Bowlbyian (Bowlby 1988) version of psychoanalysis the distress which leads many people to seek psychiatric or psychotherapeutic help is the result of developmental difficulties which have impaired the normal processes of updating and revising 'internal working models' of the self and others. This leads to a self that is split between incompatible models, or dominated by outmoded models, and so cannot easily adapt to or 'fit in' with the environment. In this view the self is, from the start, a social and historical self, as Bretherton (1990) describes:

> Consider an insecure parent with an ill organised working model of attachment. Not only is such a parent likely to misinterpret attachment signals from an infant, they are also likely to provide misleading feedback, thereby making it difficult to 'get it right' ... a parent with distorted ill-organised working models of attachment will, in turn, interfere with his or her infants' ability to begin the task of constructing adequate well-organised internal working models of interpersonal relations.

Fonagy (Fonagy *et al.* 1991: see also Holmes 1992) has argued that *coherence* is the key feature of a healthy internal world, based on the capacity for self-reflection. He draws an analogy between mothers of secure infants, who can reflect on their own and therefore their children's mental states, and the process of psychotherapy in which a patient learns to become self-reflective through identification with the therapist's self-reflective responsiveness. I consider three facets of this process and its pathology which I call 'attunement', the development of 'autobiographical competence' or 'storying', and 'affective coupling'. Each will be illustrated by a clinical example.

ATTUNEMENT

Mothers of insecurely attached one-year-olds can, in comparison to mothers of securely attached children, be shown to have been less responsive to their babies in the preceding months: looking at them less, picking them up less when they cry, reacting less when they need stimulation and intruding more when they are happily playing (Bretherton 1990).

Stern (1985) sees maternal responsiveness in terms of 'affect attunement' in which the mother is empathic but not intrusive. She 'replies' to the baby's feelings communicated by crying, smiling, babbling, kicking, reaching etc., by mirroring not just the baby's facial expression but the *contours* of those expressions – their shape, duration and intensity – for example by making accompanying movements or sounds: 'Oooooh ... aaaaaah ...' etc. In this way, as Stern sees it, the infant begins to build up an 'inter-subjective self', the nucleus of a separate but connected identity. Stern, like Bowlby, Winnicott and Kohut, sees an unobtrusive but present mother who provides the security that underpins the developing sense of self:

> one may compare the need for the continuous presence of a psychologically nourishing selfobject milieu [i.e. attuning parent] with the continuing physiological need for an environment containing oxygen. It is a relatively silent need of which one becomes aware sharply only when it

is not being met, when a harsh world compels one to draw one's breath in pain.

(Stern 1985)

The development of a core self depends on a dynamic equilibrium with the parental environment. Pathologies of identity arise through either controlling intrusiveness or understimulation.

In psychotherapy, the therapist tries to reproduce this normal process of attunement and availability within the session, maintaining, in Vygotsky's (1966) phrase, a 'zone of proximal development' in which the patient's feeling states are continuously monitored and, by 'contouring' responses, enabling the patient to build up a continuous internal 'line of self':

> Tracking and attuning ... permit one human to be with another in the sense of sharing likely inner experience on an almost continuous basis. This is exactly our experience of feeling-connectness, of being in attunement with another. It feels like an unbroken line. It seeks out the activation contour that is momentarily going on in any and every behaviour and uses that contour to keep the thread of communication unbroken.

(Stern 1985)

The capacity to attune but not to intrude in this way is basic to the psychotherapeutic process:

> Despite marriage, parenthood, a profession, and a circle of good friends, Mrs A had reached her 50th year almost without any sense of who she was or what the meaning and direction of her life should be. In her social self she played the part of a cheerful and active woman constantly fighting off feelings of depression and the wish to end her life. In therapy she returned again and again to the question 'who *am* I?' She had been brought up in a 'progressive' children's home where her parents were the proprietors. She had always felt that her mother was 'so near and yet so far': she could *see* her, but was expected, from the age of three, to fit in and share a dormitory with the other children, and was not allowed to have any kind of special relationship with her. Her father was harsh, distant, controlling, and physically and sexually abusive. She dated the origin of the split between her 'social' and her 'real' self to the age of 8 when she had naïvely tried to disclose her father's abuse but had been disbelieved, and punished by him for what to her was quite inexplicable 'wickedness'. Any attunement between her inner world and the external one was fractured from then on. Peer Gynt-like, she complained that however much she peeled away the onion skin of her existence she could never find her real self, her identity. As therapy progressed she found the 'attuning' sounds of the therapist – the 'ums' and 'aahs', grunts, inhalations and exhalations – immensely comforting. 'They give me a sense that somehow *you know* how I feel, however much you appear

distant, rejecting or uninterested [all words she had used about her parents] in your verbal comments.' In fact it was extremely difficult to tune in to this patient who varied between desperate attempts to draw the therapist into her pain and misery, complaining ['Why aren't you *angry* about the terrible things that happened to me as a child?'], demanding ['I need to know that you *like* me'], and excluding him with a self-absorbed miserable monologue. [Nevertheless the fact that she *could* complain, demand and moan was, for her, in itself a considerable achievement.] She dreamed of the therapist gently putting his arm around her in a gesture of protection, not seduction, and phantasised that she would become so irritating to him that eventually she would provoke him into shouting at her, and that only then would she finally be led or jolted into a true sense of who she was and what she wanted.

Quite apart from any interpretations he or she may make, the therapist must attune to the patient so that she feels held but not squeezed, is given space in which to explore without feeling abandoned, while resisting the transferential and countertransferential forces which are continuously trying to disrupt this process.

On the basis of this pre-verbal attunement the patient begins to feel a sense of connectedness with the therapist, an intersubjective aliveness that is a precondition of the sense of identity. But attunement alone is not enough. The patient has to be able to build up a *story* of themselves, one based not just on responsiveness but also on loss and separation. A story is in a sense a recreation of what has been lost (Segal 1991), a model of the world as it was, transmuted into a form which can be stored, used and, when necessary, updated. Mrs A, although reassured by her therapist's grunts and exhalations, continued to feel self-estranged for most of the time. She was hopelessly tied to her therapist, desperately wanting him to say that he liked her, scanning his publications for some direction as to who she might be or what she might do. Her lack of identity, her feeling of inner emptiness, followed from parental rejection and abuse. But to become herself she had in some way to identify with those very abusing parents: to accept that she was the product of *this* intercourse, grew up in *this* family. The first step towards doing so meant an acknowledgement of the unwantedness and violence within her, of the rage and disappointment she felt. In her waking life she conformed and complied, but dreamed at night of herself as naked and shitty: rather be empty and false than face the rage and shit. She sought instead a new identification with the therapist. But how much could or should he be real to her? How much was her wish for him to be so an avoidance of the pain she had to go through to reach some kind of self-acceptance? Could he act as a bridge, a transitional identification between her present emptiness and a more solidly achieved identity? Was she ready to see herself as a separate person who could make her own decisions, who ultimately knew more about herself than any therapist? Could she survive the terrifying memories of her childhood aloneness and isolation which this evoked?

To have an identity is to feel *both* a sense of connectedness *and* separateness: the sense that one is active and autonomous and that the world will respond to one's projects, wishes and desires. This is how William James (quoted in Erikson 1968) describes this state:

> an element of active tension, of holding my own, as it were, and trusting outward things to perform their part so as to make it a full harmony, but without any *guarantee* that they will.

Identity forms along a line of fissure between the self and the world, and yet it is only when one has a sense that the gap can be bridged, as in Michelangelo's depiction of God creating Adam, that one really feels one's self. Glover (1988) quotes Richter's beautiful description of this flash of self-recognition:

> I shall never forget ... the phenomenon which accompanied the birth of my consciousness of myself and of which I can specify both the place and the time. One morning, as a very young child, I was standing in our front door and was looking over to the wood pile on the left, when suddenly an inner vision 'I am a me' shot down before me like a flash of lightning from the sky, and ever since it has remained with me luminously: at that moment my ego had seen itself for the first time and for ever.

In psychotherapy, then, we are trying both to align and attune ourselves with our patients, and at the same time to hold back sufficiently for a space to open out within which an identity can be forged.

AUTOBIOGRAPHICAL COMPETENCE

The root of the word identity is *idem*, the same. The more one knows what one is *like* the more one comes to know who, as a unique individual, one *is*. But, in a modernist or post-modernist world, one can no longer assume a personal identity that is congruent with the settled community of village, tribe or family into which one is born. A sense of identity is a psychological state to be *achieved*, a story one has to develop for oneself rather than taking for granted. Moreover, it is *gendered*, so that as adults we need to be able to answer the question 'What kind of a man (or woman) am I?'

A simple but effective technique in family therapy is to ask the family to draw a genogram and to characterise each member by a word or phrase which sums them up. Similarities often emerge that are surprising to the family members and that strengthen their sense of collective and individual identity. One discovers who one is by seeing oneself through the eyes of another, initially one's parents, later G. H. Mead's 'generalised other' (Glover 1988). To have an identity in this sense is to *recognise* one's self: to be born (*natus*) and then to be *re*-born through the vision of another. One's identity is prepared by the parents who *expect* and *name* one, through their hopes, fears and dreams. To become a person is to know one's *story* (Kraemer 1991): Miranda, at the start of Shakespeare's *The Tempest* lives innocently in a sort of Garden of Eden. Her origins have been concealed from her by her father in an attempt to protect her from the pain of loss to which, as a usurped king, he has been subjected. But once she has seen Ferdinand, she begs her father 'to tell me what I am' (Act 1, Scene 2).

As an example, consider the following psychotherapy session.

Mr B is a man in his late fifties, now in his second year of weekly therapy. He has a very strong presence: powerful, pugnacious, a self-made man who grew up in the Gorbals, he is now a ship's captain, away from home for long stretches of time. His problems are depression, marital conflict and suicidal feelings which have been present for many years but which came to the surface after the birth of his youngest child. He starts the session by talking about money. 'I'm like my father, always worrying about money. I'm feeling good today, I've bought a car cheap, and I've got some work.' But that means another break away from home and from therapy. A lot of therapeutic effort has gone into helping him recognise how he detaches himself from feelings of loss when he goes away. 'I used to pride myself on not bothering to ring home or to miss them when I was away – it's only two weeks, why make a fuss?' I take up the implication that in one sense therapy has made things more difficult for him now that he is in touch with feelings of loss and separation rather than cutting off from them. I remind him of the misery which he described when as a child he was evacuated to the country during the war, away from the bombs but also from his mother. 'Yes it was terrible. After a few weeks my mother came to collect me. *Did* she dote on me or what? Everyone says that she did, but I just can't remember.' He then goes on to list a string of incidents which we have already unearthed and discussed from his childhood: playing truant at the age of five without his mother knowing, feeling an outsider among his playmates, learning to establish himself through fighting – 'Who *is* that little boy, I just don't recognise him: *is* that me?' He jokes: 'Oh well, like my father used to say, nostalgia's like neuralgia.' I suggest that he can't piece himself together, can't identify with the little boy he was because his mother wasn't there to string the episodes of his life together for him, just as I won't be there when he goes off to work next week. He protests: 'But I can get what I like from women' and gives several examples to prove his point. I reply by wondering if he feels these women really *know* him, whether he feels that I know him, his wife knows him, his mother really knew his sadness and fear. Perhaps it was his vitality and strength that she doted on, like the women he can get what he likes from, not his vulnerability. He then recounted some new history about his mother's childhood: how she was illegitimate, the offspring of his grandmother's second 'husband', how his grandfather had been quite well off, loved opera (as he himself does) and had taught his mother to play the piano, how she had been only eighteen when she became pregnant by his father and they 'had' to get married. I suggest that his confusion about whether or not his mother 'doted' on him was perhaps because she was depressed during his infancy, confused in her new 'legitimate' identity, just as he had become depressed after the birth of his youngest child. There was a pause: it seemed that this had struck a chord. '*Click*: they always used to say what a difficult feeder I was as a baby. My father [the father who had always told this highly intelligent man what a dunce he was] had to buy special milk for me.' I said: 'So money goes to the heart of your identity. He worked to keep you alive, just as you see me working to keep you alive now.' He began to weep. I wondered if his sadness was to do with the coming break. 'No,' he said, 'It's gratitude – you seem to *recognise* what I am like.'

A mother will pick out her baby's cry from all others in the nursery: she recognises the pitch, timbre, tone and rhythm that identifies her baby (this also applies to sheep). The baby's sense of who he or she is grows in the inner nest which the mother creates inside herself: 'the place in her heart'. Meanwhile the baby builds up a sense of pattern, form and regularity which, around seven months, becomes manifest as attachment behaviour, when, in effect, the child begins to say: 'This is *my* mother.'

A sense of identity depends on this mutual knowing: 'I am known – seen, recognised, understood – therefore I am.' What seemed to be unravelled in the session was the patient's feeling of non-recognition (possibly on the basis of his mother's postnatal depression), and then an owning of his story, extending it back into his mother's childhood, and an acknowledgement of his *identifications*: an acceptance of his father's preoccupation with money (he bought him the milk he needed), a discovery of male tenderness, an understanding of his mother's worry and unhappiness, so that by the end of the session he could say: 'This is *me*.' The 'maternal' contribution to identity is to provide the psychological 'womb' from which this core self can hatch, which is then available for identifications with the father, grandparents and the mother herself. This suggests, in contrast to Hume's view, that personal identity depends on an experience over and above a particular set of perceptions and memories: that it requires a gathering of them together into a coherent story. There is an important connection between this narrative capacity, the fostering of which is an essential part of the psychotherapeutic process, and the sense of self-esteem and effectiveness which underlie a strong sense of identity. In order to know who you are, you need to know where you have come from, to be able to *own* your origins. Bretherton (1990) has shown that children who at one year old have been classified as securely attached to their mothers are, at ten, more likely to be able to tell a coherent autobiographical story of this sort than those who were deemed to be insecurely attached. Furthermore, the *mothers* of the securely attached children are more likely to be able to give a clear account of their *own* childhoods, however difficult, than the mothers of those infants who were anxious or insecurely attached.

AFFECTIVE COUPLING

Who we are seems most of the time to be solid and tangible, something we could shake hands with or embrace. But from the psychotherapeutic point of view we know this is not so. A person is not so much a solid mass as a pointillist painting: the closer we approach, the more we see that what appears to be solid is composed of many different elements. This is true both in space and time. Mrs A, through splitting, projection and denial, felt depleted and estranged from herself. Equally, although we have a sense of remaining a single person across time, there are also clear discontinuities. So, like Mr B, we can look back at our former selves and ask: 'Was that really me?' Derek Parfit (Glover 1988) has suggested that too much emphasis has been placed on unity in personal identity which he sees as a matter of degree rather than an absolute category. He sees the individual across time as a collection of serial selves, related to one another rather as members of a family might be. This view has been helpful in clarifying the question of 'deserts' in moral philosophy, looking, for example, at how much someone should be held responsible for crimes committed many years before. There is an obvious application of this to the excessive guilt which depressed patients feel about their past misdeeds in which one part of a person's 'story' dominates the whole narrative.

More relevant to our purpose is the question of how different internal 'selves' may cohere or be disconnected. Psychological coherence, I argue, depends upon continuity of affect across time. When we summon up remembrance of times past it is the feelings we experience that authenticate the recall: if, through affective remembering, we can *feel* the feelings that we had 'then', then we must 'be' the same person.

Parfit's approach to personal identity has much in common with the Buddhist viewpoint which sees the individual not as an entity but a *process*: the Buddhist term for individual is *santana*, a stream. A comparable idea is implicit in psychotherapy: Mr B felt more of a person when he began to think about his mother's childhood, to understand her difficulties and to connect up with the continuity of life across the generations. This is consistent with the Buddhist view that 'there is no birth and no death'. Identity is not a solid *thing*, but, rather like the banks of a stream, an envelope containing all the elements which go to make up a life. Self-estranged individuals have lost touch with the feelings associated with their former selves. One of the aims of psychotherapy is, through affective processing, to recouple these disconnected identities.

Ms C, a teacher in her thirties, had at the age of eighteen been the victim of a brutal sexual attack in which she was convinced she would die. She now lived with her dogs in unhappy solitude. She had had several relationships with men but they had always left her feeling used and second-best. She sought therapy 'to help me come to terms with being single'. She liked to go on physically adventurous holidays but often ended up feeling overstretched and (sometimes literally) out of her depth and frightened. About a year into therapy she returned radiantly from such a holiday. She had met a man whom she found attractive and, although nothing had 'happened', she sensed that her feelings were reciprocated. The turning point for her had come when they had gone for a walk on a beautiful deserted beach with their dogs. Hers were normally well-behaved but, under the influence of his more unruly hounds, they had set up a rabbit from the dunes and had chased it to the sea. There Ms C had found it, gasping and exhausted, and had held it until it died. She would have expected herself to feel very angry and upset about this, but to her surprise she had found herself accepting it as part of the elemental nature of the scene in which life and death teamed inexhaustibly and uncontrollably together. This incident seemed to release some of the rage and fear which she had been at such pains to suppress ever since her attack. She felt less threatened by the male aggression locked inside the dogs and felt herself less vulnerable. She could accept and value the feminine part of herself, symbolised in this dream-like episode by the power of the beautiful and never-ending sea. Her identity as a feminist, pacifist, vegetarian single person had not altered but it was no longer a sequestered defensive fortress but more an 'id-entity' which could enter into the wider stream of life of which sex and death were an inescapable part. She was no longer bound to her traumatised and terrified former self.

THE SELF AND ITS 'I'

In her song *Me Myself and I*, with its refrain, 'I came into this world alone', Joan Armatrading echoes William James' classical distinction between *I* as the knower, and *me* or *myself* as the representation of that which is known. I have tried to demonstrate the interpersonal nature of a *me* or a *myself*, the very antithesis of aloneness, and that to have an identity, to be a self, is to be in relationship to others. But what of the *I*? Who is the I that, like Mrs A, wails 'Who am I?'

Although the self may be a process, a stream, there is surely a unifying principle in our identity which makes Parfit's multiple selves less than entirely convincing. The search for unity, for coherence, for integration of the many parts that make up a person, is one of the central goals of psychotherapy. But this central reference point, the centre of our being, is unusual in that, as Hume pointed out, it seems to have no properties, for to describe it is to objectify it and thus to make it a *self* rather than an *I*. Wittgenstein suggested that it is like an 'eye' that can see but which does not see itself, an impersonal I. This I is beset with paradox. It is both a single Euclidean point, 'within' us, and at the same time is not bounded by the self, seeming to permeate the whole universe of our experience. It is integral to our bodies, and yet, like the Cheshire cat, it is not inextricably embodied, and is as much 'out there' as 'in here'.

The 'I' can be thought of as the centre of consciousness. A consensus seems to be emerging between contemporary philosophy and cognitive psychology in which consciousness is regarded, in Dennett's (1991) words, as 'the straightforward state of having a higher order accompanying thought that is about the state in question'. Johnson-Laird (1983) suggests that consciousness is the experience we have of our own executive processes. Consciousness in this view is a form of 'metacognition' – thought about thought – a product of the complexity and hierarchical organisation of the brain. The aim of analytic psychotherapy, making the unconscious conscious, can be seen as an attempt to widen the perspective of this I, to turn a blinkered, narrowly focused eye into one with a wider angle and depth of field.

Can we ever see with another's 'I'? In Bruce Chatwin's novel *On the Black Hill*, identical twin brothers who live together for a lifespan of eighty years can, when briefly apart, sense one another's feelings: when Louis has a heart attack out in the fields, Benjamin feels a thump in the chest as he is kneading bread in the house. At one level we know that this is 'magical realism' and merely a coincidence, representing an omnipotent phantasy of control and connectedness in the face of the threat of illness or death. But it also shows how, through empathic imagination, the boundaries of personal identity can be transcended to encompass those we love, the environment, and ultimately the whole universe. In Western culture this is the Romantic vision; in the East, the sober Buddhist viewpoint of the continuity and connectedness of all things. As Erikson (1968) says:

> The counterplayer of the 'I' therefore can be, strictly speaking, only the deity ... This is why God, when Moses asked him who he should say had called him, answered ... 'I AM has sent me unto you'.

The Romantic vision is a reminder of the creative 'I' that is contained within the confined self. The prototype of this experience is the empathic understanding of parent for child, of lovers for one another and, at times, of therapists for their patients.

CONCLUSIONS

The psychotherapeutic approach to personal identity sees the self as developing organically within the interpersonal culture of the family. I have picked out three elements – attunement, autobiographical competence and affective coupling – and suggested that these, among other processes, are needed in order to make a coherent and satisfying story, and hence a sense of self, out of one's attachments. Psychotherapy may be needed when these developmental processes are impeded or distorted. When psychotherapy is successful the patient emerges with a stronger sense of identity – a clearer 'I' and a more integrated self – and this is based on the empathic bond between therapist and patient.

Although this view of personal identity is quintessentially social, I have said nothing of the wider implications of identity. Yet identity embraces far more than gender and family: it includes a sense of social, occupational, geographical, ethnic, religious and national belonging. Perhaps some of the psychotherapeutic principles I have been advocating are also relevant here. There is a contrast between the identity of the 'identity card' or the prisoner's 'mug shot' and the developmental approach to identity implicit in psychotherapy. Contemporary history is dominated by an explosion of groups of peoples trying to express national identity in the face of the bureaucratic state. One can envisage a state which, like a good parent, is attuned to the aspirations of its people, values the many constituent ethnic and religious 'stories' that make up a nation, and gives full weight to the feelings (national pride, heroism, pain, grief, guilt and shame) they embody. The problems that such a state or 'world state', such as the UN, might encounter in trying to balance, reconcile and especially to control these differing voices, is not unlike that of the Freudian ego. Freud saw an individual as poised between the 'life instinct' and the 'death instinct', which might be seen in today's terms as a balance between cosmos and chaos, negative entropy and entropy. For psychological health a strong sense of individual identity needs to be balanced by the 'Parfitian' recognition that the self is formed of elements that are accidental and universal and which are constantly changing. A healthy individual will neither cling too tenaciously and neurotically to the past, nor, unlike Ozymandias, will they hate and fear the future inevitability of death and the extinction of personal identity. The same may be true of nations or even of humanity itself.

Chapter 2

The democracy of the dream

During the 1930s Kilton Stewart, a young American anthropologist, visited the jungle highlands of western Malasia (Domhoff 1985). There he met and studied members of the Senoi tribe. A handsome, striking figure, long-haired and bearded, known as 'Torso' by his friends, he was something of an early hippy, interested in dreams (he had had a few months of analysis with Otto Rank in Paris), hypnosis, travel, socialism and seduction. Later he spent time at the London School of Economics where he wrote a long thesis on religious practices among the Senoi. During the Second World War he established himself as a hypnotherapist in New York, and in 1951 published an article called *Dream Theory in Malaya*. In this he described the 'astonishing' Senoi tribal society whose cultural life centred around dreaming. The adults met regularly to discuss their dreams in primitive 'dream workshops'; each morning the children would discuss their dreams with their parents, who would instruct them in a method of 'dream control' that could influence the outcome of subsequent dreams, and lead to enhanced sensuality and reduced anxiety. Most remarkably, this society, Stewart reported, was virtually free from aggression, competitiveness and violence.

The article went virtually unnoticed at first, but in the 1960s it was taken up enthusiastically by the pioneers of the growth movement centred on Esalen in California. Stewart's ideas soon became part of the human potential *credo*: dreams are good for you, they can be controlled, they may even prevent war.

However attractive this theory may be, its factual foundations are, according to Domhoff, extremely shaky. Stewart spent only a total of a few weeks with the Senoi (on three separate visits) and not the months which he later claimed. He never learned the local dialect. What he took to be dream workshops were in fact interminable village meetings. In his account he failed to distinguish between daydreams and dreaming proper, or to notice that it was the shamans who discuss dreams (as they do in most systems of traditional healing), not the ordinary people. Nor are the Senoi as peaceful as he maintained: internal disputes and border conflicts with neighbouring tribes happen frequently.

How did the story gain such wide acceptance? Domhoff, a sociologist who had worked with the psychoanalytic dream researcher Calvin Hall, postulates a process of social wish-fulfilment analogous to Freud's description of intrapsychic wish-fulfilment, in which members of the counter-culture of a Vietnam-torn American society saw in Stewart's theories the answer to their own aspirations and difficulties. But Domhoff's account of social wish-fulfilment is very different from Freud's theory of 'dream-work' (1900). Stewart's personal desires were not disguised or distorted by the *subtraction* of meaning, but elaborated, added to, until a socially congruent, if partially false, narrative emerged.

For Freud, dreams were the product of a subversive unconscious, hidden messages smuggled through enemy lines, evading the censor by their bizarreness, throwing it off the scent with their metaphorical and metonymic transformations. The analyst is a cryptographer, able to decode and so reconstruct the disturbing wishes which started this game of intrapsychic Chinese whispers.

Modern neurophysiological dream theory, whilst still influenced by Freud's detailed observations, stands him on his head. Hobson's (1990) 'activation-synthesis' hypothesis agrees with Freud's view that dreams are meaningful; that they reveal the dreamers' guiding preoccupations, assumptions and phantasies, and that they implicate recent experience ('the day's residue') still uncommitted to long-term memory storage. Activation-synthesis agrees, too, with Freud's emphasis on basic affective issues in dreaming: fear, sexual arousal, and aggression. (Calvin Hall (1953) claims that Freud's own published dreams are atypical in that, unlike most males, including Jung, they contain a predominance of aggression towards women and affiliation towards men rather than the reverse.)

But, according to psychobiology, Freud was wrong in a number of important respects. First, he was wrong in his motivational and teleological account of the overall purpose of dreaming. As Charles Rycroft (1979) puts it, it is not that we dream in order to sleep (Freud's 'guardian' hypothesis), but rather we sleep in order to dream: it is not sleep as such that we need, but the Rapid Eye Movement component of it. Second, Freud's view of the brain as essentially inert unless activated by drives or desires seeking discharge has been superseded by a model of the brain as a self-activating, self-regulating self-powering system with low energy requirement. Third, dreams are not wish-fulfilments, but represent the attempts of the cortex to synthesise and make meaning out of the patterns generated by the spontaneous activation of midbrain circuits and their cortical connections. These patterns are unique to each individual and reveal the brain's inherent capacity for meaning-making.

This account is, if anything, nearer to the Jungian rather than the Freudian view of the dream as transparent rather than opaque, and not reducible to a few a priori symbolic categories. The bizarreness of dreams is not the result of the distortion and subtraction of meaning from a unique pristine text but a consequence of the way in which the brain processes and stores experience. Bert States (1988), a drama critic with an interest in neurophysiology, sees the dreaming brain as thinking on its feet rather like an actor improvising, shifting from image to image, and still making metaphorical, if not logical, sense. The dream is expressive, not repressive.

Neural network theory suggests that experience is stored throughout the cortex in clusters which are related to one another 'metaphorically' – that is to say, by arbitrary similarities rather than in a logical library-type filing system. All this leads to a democratic view of dreams which, like poems (Darwin, quoting Richter, called dreams an 'involuntary kind of poetry') (Rycroft 1979) have multiple meanings, no one of which can claim absolute privilege or superiority. Since Freud considered *The Interpretation of Dreams* (1900) to be his finest work, and dream interpretation to be the cornerstone of psychoanalysis, contemporary psychoanalysts face the problem of reconciling these shifts in the understanding of dreams with allegiance to their founding father. (It is worth noting that Freud himself was no slavish Freudian; his seminal 'Irma' dream is not particularly opaque, nor does he interpret it in terms of instinctual wish-fulfilment.)

> Consider, for example, a young man who described a 'delicious' dream in which he found himself able to fly. Nearby were three older men. He thought to himself in the dream 'Why don't I do this more often', finding that he could manoeuvre himself by a swimming motion – 'breast stroke'.
>
> (Freud, 1900)

A Freudian account would perhaps concentrate on the sexual symbolism of flying and the Oedipal aspect of the forbidden breast and its 'delicious' contents. A more Jungian perspective might see the dream as a message from the self to the ego about the importance of pleasure and escaping from the constraints of conventionality. The dream is so explicit, albeit in a metaphorical and punning way, that an expressive rather than a repressive model seems more appropriate: wishes are *revealed* in the dream – activated perhaps by unmodulated brainstem stimuli leading to eye movements which are then interpreted by the cortex as weightless movement or 'flying' – rather than concealed.

Independent analysts such as Rycroft (1979) have quietly cut loose from Freudian dream theory altogether, concentrating on semantics and seeing dreams as 'glimpses of the dreamer's total imaginative fabric', 'self-communings' between disparate parts of the self. Dreaming is simply one facet of the imagination which also generates daydreams, phantasies and art. The attraction of this approach is that dreaming (and art) become normal phenomena rather than manifestations of neurosis; but Rycroft's analytic pedigree is still evident in his reification of the imagination which, like the unconscious, becomes another machine-ghost, bent not on drive-discharge but self-expression.

While the Jungian approach is consistent with the activation-synthesis model in seeing the dream as self-revelatory, it too retains a teleological edge in which the dream is celebrated as a valuable message from the deeper self to the conscious ego. Activation-synthesis imputes no *purpose* to the dream, which is consistent with the fact that at least half the population fails to remember or to assign any significance to their dreams, and yet appear to be untroubled by this lacuna. The origin of dreams may be random, but, because of the narrative capacity of the brain, interesting stories are made which, like a Rorschach ink-blot, reveal important personal themes and preoccupations. This perspective encompasses Wittgenstein's objection to Freudian dream analysis when he pointed out that it would always be possible to create a meaningful, but not necessarily true, story out of a random collection of objects on a table. Even if the collection is random, the way someone weaves a story from them reveals their inner preoccupations. The dream is the cortex's 'reading' of the assembly of images, memories and stimuli presented to it by the midbrain. Dream interpretation, like the post-structuralist account of reading a text, is a collaborative effort in which dreamer and analyst each contribute their themes and theories.

Hanna Segal's (1991) Kleinian approach to dreams differs from Freud's in a number of important ways. She no longer sees the dream narrowly as an attempt at wish-fulfilment, but that 'the dream thought ... is an expression of unconscious phantasy and our dream world is always with us', rather as the stars continue to shine invisibly during the day. She emphasises the importance of the *form* of a dream, and the way it is narrated – in a parsimonious, evacuatory, or manic fashion – as well as its content: 'we must analyse the dreamer as well as the dream, otherwise we will miss manic, erotic, defensive ... aspects'.

Segal also acknowledges the inherent ambiguity of dreams and the importance of resonance and allusiveness in art: 'inferior art gives all the answers'. Unfortunately, Segal's evident intellectual powers, cultural breadth and therapeutic skills are imprisoned within her own theorising. Everything has to be reduced, in a procrustean way, to the basic formulae of projective identification and the depressive position. We are told that a child who could do multiplication sums, but not division, was suffering from an unmetabolised wish to dismember his mother's body. This curious explanation follows the Kleinian premiss that exploratory thinking – including mathematics – arises from the pre-Oedipal prohibition on exploring the mother's body, with its attendant anxiety and guilt, and that this leads, by displacement and overcoming of depressive-position disappointment, to the 'endowment of the world with symbolic meaning'.

Here too it is as if the mind has to be given a teleological nudge by unconscious phantasy if its intrinsic inertia is to be overcome. The more probable explanation that exploratory activity is an inherent biological property which we share with other animals (and that difficulties with maths are more likely to be due to faulty learning that faulty feeling) would entail Segal reading Bowlby and other non-Kleinian writers, and an abandonment of a Marxist-like wish for an overall explanatory formula. A similar objection can be levelled at Bion's (1962) notion of the origins of thinking out of loss and absence ('no breast, therefore a thought'), which is based on Freud's idea that the infant hallucinates the breast as a wish-fulfilment generated by its non-appearance. Segal notes this approvingly, ignoring the evidence that the brain intrinsically generates its own thoughts, and the evidence that REM activity – and so dream thought at least – is at its height during the prelapsarian bliss (the Kleinian story can be seen as a version of *Paradise Lost*) of intrauterine life.

Once the teleological components of Kleinian thought are discarded (we dream *in order* to preserve sleep; we think *in order* to compensate for the loss of the breast; we create art *in order* to make reparation) they are quite compatible with contemporary cognitive brain science. The idea that our precepts, choices and actions are in part determined by basic assumptions and phantasies of which we are unaware is now widely accepted. Hobson (1990), the neurophysiologist, might be quoting Klein when he says 'every act of perception is an act of creativity', for this is the idea that underlies the concept of projective identification. Conversely, when Segal states that 'unconscious phantasies are a series of hypotheses which can be tested by reality', she could be quoting from the father of cognitive therapy, George Kelly.

The essence of dreaming is that it is *not* subject to reality-testing: the brain is temporarily relieved of its duties of adaptation to the external environment. Segal views the dream as an attempt to synthesise a story out of the fragments of what has passed and what, except in memory, is therefore lost. This is one aspect of the overall process of 'reinstatement of the lost object' whose physiological basis could be the installation of memory-traces via metaphor, which she sees as central to emotional development. The function of the facilitating environment, whether parent or therapist, is to hold those fragments until they can be reassembled. The Kleinian dichotomy of paranoid-schizoid/depressive positions, if translated into catabolism/anabolism, fragmentation/assembly, or activation/synthesis points to fundamental psychophysiological processes without requiring any particular psychoanalytical articles of faith.

Segal's Kleinian approach works best in her discussion of the biographer, whose role is akin to that of the psychoanalyst as not-quite-an-artist. She quotes from Richard Holmes's (1989) *Footsteps* in which he recalls his youthful identification with Robert Louis Stevenson and his attempts to repeat his *Travels with a Donkey in the Cevennes* (1879) in Southern France. Holmes describes his idealisation and identification with Stevenson, and his disillusionment when he has to face the reality that his subject will always remain elusive, irredeemably separated by time, however much he inhabits the same places. But at this point a transformation occurs: he 'becomes a biographer'. He begins to reconstruct his subject's life with the help of his imagination. A similar sequence of identification-disillusionment-reconstruction (or 'imagine-dead-imagine' as Samuel Beckett put it) underlies the therapeutic process for both patient and analyst.

The same pattern is to be seen in dreams. The dreamer dreaming is identified with his dream. He wakes, with relief or disappointment: the boundaries of reality and phantasy are re-established and he realises it is 'only a dream'. But the dream-work has been done, the past preserved, the metaphors made. With the help of the therapist, the dream can be made to do further work, should that be needed. The dangers lie either in idealising dreams à la Stewart, or in dismissing them in the name of 'scientific' psychology. In psychiatry dreams are perhaps becoming, as Liam Hudson (1985) suggests, an endangered species. How many psychiatric trainees question their patients about their dreams, or routinely ask, as did the psychoanalyst Henri Rey (1975), 'what do you think about while you are asleep?' Dreams reveal the basic meaning we attribute to the world, the architecture of our thought, before it is clothed with deceit or modified by reality. So they offer not perhaps a Royal Road, but an open window into the machinery of our thinking. The brain needs to dream: REM-deprivation leads to temporary madness. A society deprived of art withers. Both dreaming and art depend on metaphors: as States (1988) puts it 'metaphor is the dream-work of language, and the language of dream-work'. Perhaps both are necessary because they resonate with and reveal a fundamental property of our psychobiology. A psychiatry deprived of psychotherapy, and a psychotherapy which has lost all touch with neurobiology, will be similarly diminished.

Chapter 3

Obsessional phenomena and the development of imaginative competence

Obsessional phenomena are common in children, especially between the ages of eight to twelve. They are usually transient and have been dismissed as being of 'little significance' (Slater and Roth 1969). It is known, however, that some obsessional neuroses begin around this age, only to surface clinically in adult life (Black 1974). My contention in this chapter is that childhood obsessions, so far from being trivial, reflect important underlying developmental themes which in turn throw light on their clinical appearance and disappearance.

Although there are often concomitant physiological features (Beech and Perigault 1974), obsessional thoughts and actions are essentially psychological phenomena – products of the imagination. Classical psychoanalytic theories of obsessionality focus on the *content* of the obsessional phenomena – their meaning in terms of defences against underlying libidinal or aggressive drives, or both combined in anal-sadistic form. The form and timing of the onset of obsessional thinking remains unexplained. Behavioural explanations, on the other hand, tend to emphasise the *form* of obsessions, accounting for their repetitiousness, for example, in terms of 'failure to habituate to noxious stimuli' (e.g. Rachman 1978). This chapter attempts to add a Piagetian perspective (Piaget 1954), viewing obsessionality in developmental terms as a staging-post, but also as a possible cul-de-sac, along the road to full *imaginative competence*. By imaginative competence I mean the ability to imagine – in words, phantasy, dream or daydream – freely, fully and, for the most part, fearlessly; to know the difference between imagination and reality; and to appreciate the ways in which one may enhance the other (cf. Rycroft 1968, 1979).

This capacity is one that develops in the course of childhood. For the younger child (according to Piaget 1951), the boundary between phantasy and reality is indefinite so that, for example, fairy stories and real life, although differentiated, may overlap at times. Then around the age of ten comes a loss of egocentricity and a resultant sharpening of the distinction between real and ideal. Piaget views this loss of egocentrism as the result of the child's increasing mobility – his ability to move away from himself and his family and to see it from many points of view. The imagination is cut loose from its ties and, as adolescence is entered, its powers are enhanced. Simultaneously, through physical and emotional maturation, reality can be more effectively bent to meet ideals. Physical prowess is valued. Romantic love becomes possible. Sandler and Joffe (1965) call these processes 'affective distancing' and 'reinstatement of the id in the ego'. A radical alteration of perspective has occurred – an invagination of the imagination – far-reaching in its consequences, vulnerable to environmental disruption and creating new anxieties for the growing child.

This parallels an earlier and equally decisive development shift, described by Margaret Mahler (1965) as the phase of 'rapprochement' in the toddler and which can also in Bowlby's terms (Bowlby 1988) reflect the balance between the need for a 'secure base' as a bulwark against anxiety and the excitement of exploration. Early in the second year of life the young child is fearlessly excited by everything around him, his 'love affair with the world'. This may then be followed by a period of unexpected anxiety and clinging to the mother. It is as though the child has suddenly realised that his symbiotic union with his mother is a fiction and is appalled at the discovery. Fortunately this moment coincides with an increasing mastery of language which provides a compensatory increase in his connections with the wider world beyond his mother (siblings, father, grandparents) and this in turn is the starting point for further growth.

Similarly, as the pre-adolescent child enounters the wider world, he too can no longer maintain the fictions of familiocentrism and parental omnipotence. In a famous passage, Freud described a moment of disillusion with his father on one of their walks together when he was eleven (Freud 1900). His father was telling him how he had once been struck off the pavement for being a Jew. The boy could not at first grasp how such a thing could happen to his all-powerful father. This incident then became for Freud, in analysing his series of dreams about Rome, the germ of his later ideal of entering that city in triumph – perhaps along the Via Venita, the 'Royal Road'. The omnipotence of the toddler is 'reinstated' in the universality of language; that of the adolescent is reinstated through the autonomous imagination, in the formulation of ambitions and ideals (Table 3.1).

The child in latency, not yet ready for the 'reinstatement', may deal with his anxiety by a kind of phobic avoidance. Thus Gardner and Winner (1979) report a 'retreat from metaphor' at this stage in children who, both earlier in childhood and subsequently in adolescence, will happily play and make up stories. This scorning of make-believe is paralleled by the contemptuous attitude that children of such an age have towards the opposite sex.

Obsessional phenomena at this stage can be seen as another attempt to deal with these anxieties, to allay the danger that the child's phantasies might actually be real, to allay their feelings of powerlessness. The child tries to reassure himself that he *can* influence reality, if only by magic. Sadistic and

Table 3.1 Comparison of developmental issues at ages 1–2 and 10–12

	Age 1–2	*Age 10–12*
Stage 1	'Love affair with the world'	Continuation of carefree play, skill acquisition
Transition	'Rapprochement', clinging	'Retreat from metaphor', obsessionality
Stage 2	Language acquisition	Adolescent creativity, independence

binding phantasies extend this in an attempt to pin the world down, to punish it for not being perfect, to control its unpredictability.

In this chapter I try to apply these ideas to three examples of the disappearance of obsessional symptoms, two clinical and one literary. Throughout I shall be using the term 'obsessional' in its wider, looser, psychodynamic sense, rather than in a more formal phenomenological one. A brief theoretical discussion concludes the paper.

Case One: Mr D

Mr D was sixty-four when he first came to the hospital out-patient department. By occupation he was an accountant, just due to retire from the firm for which he had worked all his life. He had been sent by his GP, to whom he had complained that he had become troubled of late by disturbing sexual phantasies. They had started around the time that his wife, whom he loved, had had a series of incapacitating strokes. These phantasies were of two main types. In the first – which he described as the 'silent movie type' – a young innocent girl was undressed and subjected to rape and 'degrading torture'. This usually involved some sort of anal attack or anal intercourse. The second type was set in the past, the seventeenth century. A girl would be dragged on to the village green, accused of a sexual crime such as adultery and then burned at the stake or tortured. In the phantasy the patient was always a passive bystander, unable to intervene. At times these mental obsessions became so strong that he felt compelled to draw them. He produced a pile of drawings, quite well-executed, showing women being degraded and tortured and sexually assaulted. The drawings were like elaborations of lavatory graffiti, cartoon-style, with bubble-words coming out of the characters' mouths. The men were abusing the women, accusing them of prostitution, adultery, fornication, while they in turn would be pleading for mercy. Mr D said that he desperately tried to control the phantasies but was unable to. He was frightened on two counts: first that his wife would get to know about all this – for example, that he would say something in his sleep – and second that they were sinful and that, therefore, as a devout Catholic, he believed he would go to hell. It was also evident that the phantasies were pleasurable: he became quite animated as he described them, while he remained somewhat depressed and lugubrious as he told his life story.

He was born in the home counties, the only son of a father he had both feared and revered. This father was a self-made man who had risen to be managing director of the firm he had first joined as an office boy. He described his mother, whom he loved greatly, as a petite, charming, nervous housewife, slavishly devoted to her husband and son. He had been a rather sickly, lonely child who was always very good at his books and was awarded several scholarships. When he finally got an award to university his father insisted that he refuse the bursary, stating that he had made quite enough money to pay for his education.

Mr D said that his father had influenced him in three important ways. First, he had inherited from him a violent temper. Because of this he had resolved that he would never become a bully like his father, either to women or to his employees. Second, he had deliberately chosen to remain a private soldier during the Second World War and in the 1930s he had joined a liberal firm whose aim was to provide professional services to the underprivileged. The third effect was that immediately after his father's death – but not a moment before – he became a Catholic convert: as he put it, 'I replaced one absolute father by another'. His father had been a firm atheist.

The most important fact about his sexual life was that he had never had satisfactory intercourse with a woman. He had fallen romantically in love at the age of sixteen with an older woman he admired from a distance. At eighteen he had picked up a prostitute and had derived his pleasure from masturbating her. These two figures in his emotional life, the idealized older woman and the prostitute, had remained with him more or less unaltered ever since. He continued to go with prostitutes from time to time but confined himself to masturbating them.

When he was thirty-eight he met his wife. She was fifty. They married two years later, soon after his father's death. She too had had no previous sexual experience. She had been a singer and then a writer of stories for romantic women's magazines. Mr D described her in ideal terms: a beautiful woman, rich and gifted, slender and elegant, witty and with remarkable psychic powers. He bitterly compared this with her present vegetable-like state. Their sexual life had never been a great success. They had had intercourse on their honeymoon but Mr D felt then, as he always had done, that his erection was inadequate and they had tried only infrequently after that. There had been some mutual masturbation for a while and then finally their relationship settled, brother and sister-like, into one of pure companionship.

After about six years of marriage Mr D formed a crush on one of the secretaries at work. He said she strongly reminded him of his mother and even spoke in the same tone of voice. He had eventually confessed this obsession to his wife, who had immediately accused him of adultery. He wrote to the girl, who had by now married and left the firm, and this put an end to his longing for her.

The dream sequence

Mr D was seen in out-patients for hourly sessions and, because of his great anxiety about leaving his wife, these were arranged at three-weekly intervals. No active therapeutic steps were taken beyond history and encouragement to talk; no tasks were set, no drugs prescribed nor transference interpretations attempted. At the third session Mr D reported that his obsessions had gone. He said that this had coincided with a series of dreams which were remarkable in two ways: first, each was entirely coherent and told a story, and second, they were sequential and extended over a series of nights. He was adamant that these were not daydreams or phantasies or hypnagogic phenomena, but true dreams.

In the first dream he was looking at pictures in an art gallery. They were from the French school of the seventeenth century and were of classical landscapes, rather grand in design. He then 'entered' the landscapes, Alice-through-the-Looking-Glass-style, and found himself in a country at once both strange and familiar. It was an island named Hesperidea Felix, the Happy Western Isle. On this island there was a classical civilisation, harmonious, warm and untroubled. He was 'among' the people, but invisible, able to observe and to understand their language, which was 'dog' Latin. He noticed that the people of the island were divided into four groups. There were the priests, who were teachers and physicians as well as spiritual leaders; the nobility, who were dressed in military garb and carried shields; the common people, the tradespeople; and, last, the satyrs, who lived naturally in the woods in a state of sensual abandon. He then discovered to his dismay that the island was threatened by invasion from present-day Britain.

Mr D returned for his next appointment in a state of high excitement. A psycho-geriatrician had finally visited and his wife had been taken into hospital for rehabilitation. He then went on, almost without pause, to continue to recount the dream sequence.

The invasion had actually happened! The priests, by their special powers, had been able to project a spurt of fire at the invading ships and thus defend the island. The United Nations had then intervened and decreed that the island should henceforth be perpetually neutral, and that a team of medical observers should be sent to study life there. One stipulation was that they should negotiate only with the priests.

The next night a peace celebration was held. The chief priest sent for Mr D and told him 'it is time for you to return to your own country'. 'How will I get back?' 'A boat will be provided, self-steering, with adequate provisions, which will take you to a point off the British coast that you know particularly well.' He was then told that a 'lady' would conduct him to the boat. He was amazed to find that this was the girl from the office whom he had loved, platonically, all those years before. He was told by the priest to go back to England and 'do what you know you ought to do'. At this point the priest disappeared and he was left with the girl. He asked her, 'Shall I see you again?' She replied, 'Don't ask your next question unless or until you return'. This, he explained would have been 'Will you marry me?' They then parted tenderly. He found himself on the east coast of Britain. The bell for the train to take him to London rang; it turned into the alarm bell and he was awake. He then wept as he had never wept before.

Following this, Mr D's mental state improved considerably. He remained free of obsessive-compulsive symptoms. He retired from his job. He continued rather slavishly to look after his wife and went on with his skirmishes with the local authorities, but agreed for her to have a holiday admission to an old people's home. He was able to leave her for short periods to go to board meetings of his old firm and sometimes to the pub. He spoke openly of how he sometimes longed for her to die and of what he would do afterwards. He began reading a little and imagined that he would at some time start to write stories.

Comment

Through the use of obsessional defences Mr D had managed to preserve himself in a pre-adolescent state of emotional development. By idealising women and by the avoidance of genitality he protected himself from sexual feelings, including those towards his mother. By his pacifism and placatory posture he managed never to have a head-on collision with his father. The intellectually precocious twelve-year-old that he must have been, he had thus avoided many of the developmental challenges of adolescence, and had managed to carry this state of frozen development into his sexless, idealising marriage. All this was challenged by his wife's illness, the loss of her 'specialness', her impending death. Death forces development: idealisation cannot be maintained in the face of its finality, developmental tasks can no longer be indefinitely postponed. The anxiety it arouses spills over the floodgates of repression. The content of his obsessions was a desperate attempt to maintain the *status quo*. The drawings reflected his wish to retaliate, to attack the woman who had let him down by being fallible, mortal. He had never imagined that his wife would grow old, ill or could die. He always thought that he would go first. He wanted to go back to the past, to tie her down, to preserve her, to prevent change and decay. In his phantasies he began to experience his sexuality, albeit in a split-off, degraded way. The obsessional creation was thus a partial attempt to jump the development hurdle of early adolescence. He baulked it, sitting on the fence: a facility displayed with great virtuosity by most obsessionals. In the end it began to hurt: he became frightened, guilty and depressed.

In the dream sequence he began to resolve his dilemma. Its form – rather like an adventure yarn – would be just what might appeal to an eleven-year-old. The island community represents his self with its saturnine, priestly and worldly elements. At the start, however, his felt self is invisible: an observer with no power to influence things, a knowing but frightened little boy. The island is threatened by invasion from across the sea. This is the threat of death. He is besieged – the origin of the term obsession – by death. Death is represented by modernity, change, which threatens to destroy his ideal world. He repulses the invasion by the use of a magical device that throws fire across water. This is his potency, ejaculation. A compromise is reached through the use of medical mediators, and he is now able to converse, is made visible, can join in with the adults and speak to a girl whom he desires. With the help of another phallic image, a self-steering boat, he is enabled to leave his fortress and join the real world. He is able to cry, to mourn the loss of his ideal: he is relieved.

Through this sequence Mr D progressed from his obsessional pseudo-solution, the phantasies, to a real acceptance that his wife would die. He was able to do this once he had reinstated the ideal in an autonomous, imaginative form: the dream. To do this he had to recover his imaginative capacity, hitherto safely projected into his wife, the 'creative one'. He could then abandon the 'transitional' vehicle of the obsessional drawings in which he was stuck between childhood and adolescence.

Case Two: Mrs E

Mrs E, a twenty-nine-year-old woman, presented herself as a person with problems of obsessionality only gradually as a family muddle unravelled. Her husband had been first to ask for help, with feelings of irritability and depression. He was then seen with Mrs E and their two-year-old child. The immediate difficulty was to do with the fact that husband and wife, both of whom were professionals, had swapped roles. He looked after the child and she went out to work, However, neither was really happy. She really wanted to be a mother, and he to work. They seemed to have settled for an arrangement in which neither was satisfied. It emerged that this arrangement had evolved because she had always assumed that she would have no maternal feelings and so when she got pregnant she arranged to go back to work as soon as possible. When, soon after the birth, she found an intense upsurge of love for her child, she was surprised and taken aback and did not dare to act on it. Her feelings of depression surfaced when the interpretation was made in the joint sessions that both parents seemed to be putting all their liveliness into their very engaging toddler, but seemed themselves to feel rather depleted and colourless.

Mrs E's feelings of depression took the form of worthlessness and in particular a sense that she was 'bad' for her husband. After four sessions the joint meetings came to an end, partly because one of the co-therapists was leaving, and also because at this point the husband was accepted for an analysis. Mrs E then asked for individual therapy herself, initially to deal with her acute feelings of depression and worthlessness.

She was the only child of her mother's first marriage. Strictly speaking she was illegitimate, as her father, who was from overseas, was a bigamist; soon after he had married her mother this had been discovered and he was deported. Mrs E, however, had borne his name. He left home when she was only a few months old and she remembers nothing of him. Mrs E had then been sent to live with her maternal grandmother and grandfather. She thought of this as being the happiest period of her childhood. She was especially close to her grandmother, whom she described in idealised terms with tears of gratitude. She saw her mother infrequently and said that there was a feeling of awkwardness between them which had persisted. When she was five her grandfather died. Not long afterwards her mother remarried and Mrs E duly went to live with her. A year or so later, when Mrs E was eight, her half-brother was born. It was around this time that she first devised what she later called her 'system'. This was an obsessional device, based on numbers. For example, she was eight years old, so she would count to eight before getting out of bed, put her clothes on in eight movements, eat her toast with eight bites, etc. She continued to use the 'system'. Without it, she said, 'I would not have survived'; she would have been paralysed by indecision, misery and muddle. By using the system she could conduct her everyday life, and especially cope with those 'womanly' functions which otherwise defeated her: which dress to wear, what food to cook, how to keep herself and the house clean. By using the numbers she could get through.

When she was fourteen her mother and stepfather's marriage broke up, and her mother was consequently glad to have her at home as a companion. She was sent to a convent school and did well academically. She had no boyfriends but formed a romantic attachment to one of the masters at the school, who continued to correspond with her after she left. Her first year at university was a great surprise to her: she felt happy and fulfilled almost for the first time since she had lived with her grandmother as a little girl. She made friends. She found she had something to say and that people would listen.

At the end of her first year she met her husband and they married. She trained professionally and was clearly competent at her job, although she disclaimed this.

Treatment

This section describes material from the early months of treatment. Mrs E began, in the first session, to describe her obsessions, of which I had been unaware during the period of family therapy. She said that she lived in a sort of chaos – at least to anyone but herself it appeared so. For example, her clothes: she could never decide what to wear in the morning, so, depending on the day and the month, she would choose, say, the third dress from the left in her cupboard. Without this 'system' she would be totally paralysed and unable to get on with her life. Another example was washing-up: people who came to her house could never understand why the washing-up was never done. In fact it was, but according to the system. She would wash every third cup, fork, plate, etc., and leave the rest until next time, so that gradually it would all get done. Everything she did was arranged by the system: when to go to work, which bus to take, what time to leave and so on.

She also mentioned some more worrying obsessional fears; for example, she thought that she might have had a younger brother whom she had killed and had now completely forgotten about it.

Soon after the beginning of therapy she announced that her system had gone. In the same session she went on to say that she had a guilty secret, something she felt embarrassed to reveal. She had 'looked me up' in the telephone book, the medical directory. She had even thought of using some of her professional knowledge to find out more about me. I reassured her that this was a very common and natural phenomenon in therapy, but why should she feel so guilty about it? What was her fantasy of what she would find?

The things she wanted to know were common enough – was I married, did I have children? This led on to a phantasy that I could not possibly have children because I would have no time left for them after I looked after all my patients. She was then able to link this to recent thoughts she had had about her father. She imagined going abroad to find him where he would be surrounded by a new family, and she would push her way through them to sit on his lap. At this point in the session she looked sad and became tearful. She said she had a 'feeling of wanting to be held'. Finally, she said she felt that there must be something fundamentally damaging or wrong with her, otherwise I would not be so remote and would not object to her 'knowing' about me.

The next theme that appeared was that of her 'special' relationship with her grandmother, their telepathic understanding; for example, she dreamed of her grandmother the night she died. This emerged from a phantasy of the 'perfect silent session' in which she would sit against me on the floor, with her back to me. In the next session she described a dream about the Gestapo taking children and beating them, and linked this with her anger at me for being available only once a week, and not at times when she really needed me. She also mentioned in the same session how she sometimes felt tyrannised by her child, who sits on her lap endlessly and interrupts her reading.

These themes continued as the therapy progressed. Mrs E became terribly sensitive to rejections from me. For example, she confessed that she had again looked me up in the electoral register and felt utterly rebuffed (rightly perhaps) when I rather nervously told her that I had moved since the previous list was made. One day I wore a suit – unusual for me – and this made her very anxious until she noticed I was wearing the usual shoes and thus the continuity was preserved. She found the end of sessions very difficult, comparing this with her son who cries when she leaves *him*, although he goes off quite happily when he is leaving *her* to go out to tea.

At Christmas she brought me a cake. My immediate thought about this was that she was telling me that she was not getting a big enough slice of the cake. Then she confessed on the second session after the break that she had imagined me getting it tested for rat poison. She said that she felt I was rather like a nanny in a nursery, concerned, able to love my children, but also hating them at the same time. She accused me of holding her at a distance, comparing me with her husband's analyst, who was much more open and who saw him at her home, working from home and revealing herself in a way I never did.

Comment

Mrs E had created in her early childhood an ideal world, symbolised by her grandmother: a refuge from the chaos and confusion of her parentage. She was safe in the world from the frightening muddle of her feelings: resentment towards her mother, murderous jealousy towards her imagined half-brother, erotically tinged awkwardness with her stepfather. But already by the age of eight this illusion was cracking. Her grandfather died, her mother had remarried and was pregnant. There was nothing Mrs E could do to stop it. She felt threatened by brute reality and her powerlessness to influence it, the force of her feelings. Then her system came to the rescue: a magical device by which her world, inner and outer, could be controlled. With it, she could protect reality from her anger, preserve her ideal from disillusionment. The method continued to work until motherhood once more tested her capacity to believe in her reality, this time to the limit: she became depressed.

In therapy all this was repeated in reverse order. She could once more recreate an ideal relationship; through the 'perfect session' she could have the ideal father who loved his perfect daughter. Her 'system' was no longer needed as the treatment itself, with its own obsessional periodicity, became a method of survival, a source of good feelings and a repository for bad ones.

The remaining threat to this was her curiosity: would she 'find out' about me, and so be found out and punished by my withdrawal?

Through the dream sequence Mr D transcended his obsessionality. Mrs E, in therapy, also lost her symptoms, but by a backwards movement, regress-ively. Mr D began to see the ideal and the real as separate autonomous categories; he moved, to use Piaget's terminology, from the real to the possible. Mrs E returned to a childhood state in which she maintained the hope that the ideal was possible. She longed for the 'perfect session', and chafed at the intrusions of reality which she felt interfered with this. She regressed therapeutically to a stage at which she could still maintain the illusion of an ideal world, and experience her fury and hatred at its limitations. Her sado-masochistic phantasies were a retaliation against an environment which had let her down – perhaps a wish to achieve through attack the closeness she felt she could never get through love.

Freud (1917) and Abraham (1924) have written of the cannibal – oral – infant's devouring love for his enemies. After the Christmas break Mrs E described how, for the first time for many years, she had had feelings of good and optimism inside her; she wanted to 'get her teeth into reading', had an 'appetite for books'. At this point I made some comment using the word 'creativity'. She corrected me, and I think she was right in this, by saying this feeling was a stage prior to that. Creativity at some level implies the capacity to separate 'reality' from 'fiction'; she had yet to achieve that. One can cook, but not eat, creatively. She was still in need of nourishment; she still wanted someone to bake *her* a cake.

'A LA RECHERCHE DU TEMPS PERDU'

My third and concluding example is from Proust (1941). Towards the end of *Swann's Way*, Part 1, his narrator gives a beautifully clear example of a minor obsession and its resolution. The protagonist is preoccupied by the spires of two churches in his locality. One is double and the other single. Whenever he is out driving with his mother in the coach, she inside and he on the box, he becomes obsessed with the alignment of the steeples and by the need to 'place' the single spire between the twin ones. Then one evening he writes:

I caught sight of them for the last time, far away, and seeming no more now than three flowers painted upon the sky above the low line of fields. They made me think too of three maidens in a legend, abandoned in a solitary place over which night had begun to fall; and while we drew away from them at a gallop, I could see them timidly seeking their way ... drawing close to one another, slipping one behind another, showing nothing more, now, against the still rosy sky than a single dusky form, charming and resigned, and so vanishing into the night.

At the moment I had finished writing it (this passage) I found such a sense of happiness, felt that it had so entirely relieved my mind of the obsession of the steeples and of the mystery which it concealed that, as though I myself were a hen and had just laid an egg, I began to sing at the top of my voice.

The obsession, through its imaginative transformation into the image of the three flowers, the three merged maidens, was relieved. How was this possible? What developmental issue was this boy struggling with? The answer lies in the passage which immediately precedes this one. Here Proust describes in perfect detail the process of the disillusionment of childish ideals, followed by their reinstatement in love, the imaginative separation of reality and illusion, the lack of which, in my view, lies near the heart of obsessionality.

As a boy, the protagonist's ideal female love-object, his 'queen' based on his mother, separation from whom he finds so unbearable, is the local countess, Mme de Guermantes. Painter (1977) recounts that this is an exact account of Proust's 'half-incestuous love for "a lady old enough to be his mother", Countess Laure Chevigne'. He has long imagined her, and one day he sees her in church. To his intense disappointment he discovers that she has a large nose with a spot on it, and red cheeks. He writes:

My disappointment was immense. It arose from my not having borne in mind, when I thought of Mme de Guermantes, that I was picturing her to myself in the colours of a tapestry or a painted window, as living in another century, as being of another substance than the rest of the human race. Never had I taken into account that she might have a red face, a mauve scarf ... and the oval curve of her cheeks reminded me so strongly of people whom I have seen at home that the suspicion brushed against my mind (though it was immediately banished) that this lady in her creative principle, in the molecules of her physical composition, was perhaps not substantially the Duchesse de Guermantes but that her body, in ignorance of the name people had given it, belonged to a certain type of femininity which included, also, the wives of doctors and tradesmen.

He contrasts her reality with his previous mental image of her:

an image ... which was so real that everything, even the fiery little spot at the corner of her nose, gave an assurance of her subjection to the laws of life, as in a transformation scene on the stage, a crease in the dress of a fairy, a quiver of her tiny finger, indicate the material presence of a living actress before our eyes, whereas we were uncertain, till then, whether we were not looking merely at a projection of limelight from a lantern.

But a miraculous transformation has also taken place in Proust's (or rather his protagonist's) mind. He falls in love with Mme de Guermantes:

And now ... whenever I brought my mind to bear upon that face – and especially, perhaps, in my determination, that form of instinct of self-preservation with which we guard everything that is best in ourselves, not to admit that I had been in any way deceived – I found only beauty there.

Proust takes his obsession and, by an imaginative transformation into flowers, maidens, resolves it. He is no longer in the box with his mother but out in a world in which he can dispose his erect spires as he chooses. Before he could do this there had been disillusionment with the fairy-tale (or pantomime) countess, his horror at her reality; then the revival of this illusion through love, her transformation into an object to whose love he can aspire.

Thus has Proust described the three phases to which I have tried to accommodate the symptoms of Mr D and Mrs E: a contrast between fairy-tale ideals and grim reality, disillusionment and defensive obsessionality, re-instatement in adolescent idealism and the beginnings of the acceptance of reality.

DISCUSSION

The central role of anxiety and the defences against it in symptom formation features so prominently in psychoanalytic thinking (e.g. Malan 1979), that it is salutary to recall that it was not until 1926 that Freud first adopted this viewpoint. His earlier formulations of neurosis focused on the nature of the repressed impulses (their 'where' and 'whither', Freud 1915) and saw the anxiety of the neurotic only as a by-product or a result of partially successful attempts at repression, rather than as its cause. In his earlier papers, therefore, including the 'Rat-Man' (1909), obsessional symptoms were thought of according to the rules of symptom formation, a compromise between libidinal drives and the forces of repression. In obsessional neurosis he postulated a regression to the pregenital stage of development of the libido, an anal-sadistic phase, where the primary sources of gratification lie in control and mastery of one's self and one's immediate environment. In Freud's later view anxiety itself becomes the cause of neurosis, while symptom formation represents the ego's only partially successful attempt to control this anxiety. Subsequent writers, especially Anna Freud (1966) and Sandler and Joffe (1965), have detailed obsessional defences against such anxiety, including isolation, undoing, reaction formation, identification with the aggressor, displacement and omnipotence, while Fairbairn and Melanie Klein emphasise the essentially ambivalent object relations of the obsessional (Cawley 1974).

Freud's distinction between 'ego anxiety' (fear of dissolution or abandon-ment) and 'signal anxiety' (fear of attack or castration) provides a link between his earlier formulations and the views of contemporary analysts. The earlier formulations of obsessional neurosis were focused on signal anxiety.

He conceived the obsessional as defending himself against libidinal impulses which would, if openly expressed, lead to retributive attack. Thus, the 'Rat-Man's' obsessional symptoms started with his wish to defy parents who disapproved of his fiancée. Later writers have responded to Freud's call in 1913 for a need to understand 'the development of the ego instincts' and have applied these to obsessional neurosis. Zetzel's review (1966) of the Rat-Man case sees his obsessional symptoms in terms of 'vertical splits' in an otherwise normally functioning personality. This idea has been variously described in terms of 'splits in the ego' (Freud 1927), 'failure of synthetic function' (Kohut 1971), several 'ego nuclei' (Glover 1956) and 'disavowal' (Gedo and Goldberg 1973). In all there is an emphasis on the lack of integration of the ego, of the unsynthesised coexistence of infantile and mature elements in the personality.

In this chapter I have tried to demonstrate how this lack of integration can be related to developmental 'failure' occurring around the ages of eight to twelve although earlier difficulties may of course set the scene for such a failure. Transient obsessional phenomena may then be considered a response to the normal anxieties of latency in which the child has to relinquish his egocentrism and sense of parental omnipotence, but before he has gained in its place an autonomous imaginative capacity which develops alongside his increasing physical capacities.

Enduring obsessional phenomena may arise or persist from childhood when this process fails to occur. This may be for one of at least two reasons. The first is when a child has prematurely to detach him or herself from egocentrism, as in the case of Mrs E, and this is usually the result of some environmental disruption or failure. Obsessional symptoms then act as a kind of sextant in a sea of anxiety the child is not yet a mature enough navigator to negotiate.

In the second case, typified by Mr D, the child is in a sense postmature, or dysmature, 'small for dates', to use an obstetric metaphor. The problem here is the maternal anxiety (often with a narcissistic basis) which prevents detachment at a time when it would be phase-appropriate. The obsessional symptoms reflect attempts to short-cut the path from phantasy to imaginative capacity without the intrusion of reality. The role of the father as a mediator between the softness of illusion and harsh reality may be important in this type.

Mr D was stuck on a developmental hurdle that he had baulked. Mrs E, on the other hand, *prematurely* leaped from childhood in early adolescence and, as her environment had failed to hold her, developed her obsessional system as a rigid grid which would hold her together instead. Her anxiety appeared as ego anxiety, Mr D's as signal anxiety; he fears attack, her fear is of abandonment. However, these must be seen as two layers of a related process. He experiences his fear as an attack, but since it is death that is attacking it will leave him abandoned. Conversely, although her fear is of abandonment, she feels this is punishment for her anger, her curiosity, her demandingness and her poisonousness.

In the three cases I have described there was a rapid remission of obsessional symptoms. In the case of Mrs E, this was when perhaps a regression to a secure therapeutic bond which, with its elements of periodicity and punctuality, contains an intrinsic obsessionality, obviated the necessity for her symptoms. In the case of Mr D a dream sequence enabled him to progress towards a more mature separation of phantasy and reality. For Proust it was 'falling in love'. These kinds of changes are common enough in normal maturation as well as in psychotherapeutic settings. The success of behaviour therapy in helping the more severe forms of obsessional neurosis may have to do with a therapeutic approach which forces a real wedge into imagined dangers. This may then accelerate the differentiation of reality and phantasy: the confusion of which is, in my view, a central developmental element in obsessionality.

Chapter 4

Adolescent loneliness, solitude and psychotherapy

INTRODUCTION

Feelings of loneliness are common, if not universal, among those seeking psychotherapeutic help. The aim of this chapter is to suggest a developmental framework within which these feelings can be understood. It focuses on *adolescence* as a crucial stage in which separation from the family – the central issue in loneliness – has to be negotiated.

The discussion is based on a distinction between three separate but related states: loneliness, isolation and solitude. *Loneliness* implies an emptiness, a lack, a longing for company and closeness. It has a time-dimension: there is a sense of something lost and a wish to replace it. The lonely person is in a state of tension. *Isolation* is akin to loneliness but involves a cutting-off from feeling: it is the lack without the longing. The emptiness of isolation is a void, an absence of desire; that of loneliness is a hunger to fill a space. *Solitude*, by contrast, is a tension-free state in which an individual can be, temporarily at least, self-sufficiently alone and untroubled by time. It is a mature state in which recuperation, productive work or creativity can occur.

My main argument is as follows. Loneliness is an inevitable part of the separation from parents and family that occurs in adolescence. The capacity to tolerate loneliness leads on, if development is successful, to the ability to form close relationships on the one hand, and to experience and make use of solitude on the other. Adolescent difficulties or even breakdown can often be seen in terms of defence against loneliness. This can happen through denial, i.e. by isolation; or by avoidance, when the young person clings to family and peers in such a way that separation and the feeling of loneliness are never really experienced.

Parkes (1972), Bowlby (1980) and Weiss (1974) have described the loneliness of the bereaved and two important points of relevance to adolescence can be adapted from their work. First, loneliness is the inevitable result of the *loss of an object*. Leaving home (Haley 1980) can be seen as a major family event in which both parents and adolescents 'lose' one another and so are in a sense bereaved. Second, these authors distinguish between social and psychological loneliness, showing how psychological feelings of loneliness persist even in 'well-supported' widows. Only when the necessary work of grieving is done may new attachments be formed, and it is at this point that social isolation may reinforce psychological loneliness. Adolescent loneliness is rarely simply due to lack of opportunity for company: but discos or halls of residence can be lonely places for a young person still emotionally tied to the family. Similarly the adolescent Indian girl who on marriage leaves her family to join her husband and his female relatives may feel deeply lonely even though she is surrounded by people.

I shall approach my subject via Winnicott's well-known paper 'The Capacity to be Alone' (1965). In it he describes the ability to be alone as 'one of the most important signs of maturity in emotional development'. His central insight is that the childhood origins of this capacity are based on a paradox: a child learns to enjoy solitude through the experience of 'being alone in the presence of the mother'. Small children normally have periods in which they play quietly, absorbed in their own world of phantasy. This, according to Winnicott, can only happen when the mother is able to adopt a particular role, watchful but non-intrusive, rather like a guardian angel. If she is preoccupied or neglectful on the one hand, or interfering on the other, the child will be unable to enter this state of solitude. Winnicott sees the mother as 'lending' her 'ego functions' to the child, thus acting as a temporary 'auxiliary ego'. When things go well the child internalises this process and will be able to enjoy and make use of solitude in adult life. As an analyst and not a mother, Winnicott's main interest was in the relevance of these ideas to therapy. He saw a similar need for non-intrusive holding by therapists, and part of the polemic of his paper is to argue for the holding as well as the interpretive function of the therapist.

WINNICOTT AND THE POETS

I want now to look at some of Winnicott's ideas in more detail, comparing them with some poetic accounts of solitude. Solitude is a subject that appears to be of particular interest to poets. This is not, I suspect, because poets are necessarily by nature solitary types, which may well be a romantic illusion, but because poetry is a form of art based on solitude. Unlike painting, poetry-making requires no 'life model' or mechanical skills; unlike music there are no 'instruments' of poetry other than the poet's inner ear; and unlike novel-writing the modern 'lyric' poet often has no characters to depict or narrative to tell. The poet is mostly alone with his own self which he has to be able to enter and render into words. It might also be said that the 'contents' or thoughts of a poem are 'held' by its form – rhythm, metre, rhyme structure – in just the way that, according to Winnicott, the mother holds the child in play, and later the ego 'holds' the self in solitude. This form is an invisible structure, strong and unintrusive, which both links the poem with past tradition and gives it its unique character. Similar considerations, such as the reliability of the therapist and the measured time of the sessions, apply to the apparently formless activity of psychotherapy (cf. Chapter 11).

Solitude requires the presence of another person

We know that when Wordsworth wandered 'lonely as a cloud' he was in fact with his sister, Dorothy, who had taken over as caretaker and companion to her brother when their mother had died when William was eight. The phrase 'auxiliary ego' seems appropriate when we consider Dorothy's diary entry of 15 April 1802:

> I never saw daffodils so beautiful they ... tossed and reeled and danced and seemed as if they verily laughed with the wind that blew upon them over the lake, they looked so gay ever glancing ever changing.
>
> (Davies 1980)

Two years later this is what her brother wrote:

> Beside the lake, beneath the trees,
> Fluttering and dancing in the breeze.

The whole movement of *Daffodils* can be seen as an illustration of Winnicott's theory: a shared experience – alone in the presence of another – is internalised and then drawn on in moments of solitude:

> when on my couch I lie
> In vacant or in pensive mood,
> They flash upon that inward eye
> Which is the bliss of solitude.

The external play-space, held by the mother, becomes an internalised part of the self, a safe retreat in moments of reverie.

William Cowper also grasped the same paradox of solitude-in-the-presence-of-another when, half a century before *Daffodils*, he wrote:

> How sweet, how passing sweet is solitude
> But grant me still a friend in my retreat
> Whom I may whisper – solitude is sweet.

The nurturing, maternal aspect of solitude

The rhythm of infancy and childhood involves an alternation of activity, exploration and social interaction followed by periods of comfort and quiet in which the child wants to be close, to 'snuggle up', without being over-stimulated by the parent. In adult life this sequence may be replicated with a spouse or partner, and is also to be found in the need for 'peace and quiet' or solitude.

This maternal aspect of aloneness is well captured by Milton in *Comus:*

> Wisdom's self
> Oft seeks to sweet retired solitude
> Where with her best *nurse* contemplation
> She plumes her feathers and lets grow her wings
> That in the various bustle of resort
> Were all too ruffled and sometimes impaired. (*my italics*)

The inability to find a secure inner place in which recuperation can take place is particularly common during adolescence. The adolescent's anxiety is often an indication that they cannot find such a place; the parental link has been severed but has not been replaced by an internal comforting parent. The depressed or self-destructive adolescent is confronted by an internal world which seems alien: a body which feels 'wrong', and a pull towards relationships which appear frightening or perverse.

Solitude and regression

The word alone, from which my theme is derived, comes from the Middle English *al one*, i.e. 'all one'. There is in solitude a notion of prelapsarian unity or, as we would now secularily formulate it, a return to a state of primitive unity with the mother. A beautiful account of this regressive aspect of solitude is to be found in Andrew Marvell's poem *The Garden*.

The poem starts with the poet deriding the vanity of ambition:

> How vainly men themselves amaze
> To win the palm, the oak or bays

and contrasts these single fruits with the 'delicious solitude' and plenitude of the Garden itself (the Garden of Eden). He compares its delights to those of sexual love:

> No white nor red was ever seen
> So amorous as this lovely green.

Marvell was a powerfully ambitious and (as evidenced by *To His Coy Mistress*) sexual man. The movement of the poem turns on the tension between this ambition and sexuality, and the attempt to quiet and master both by contemplation of the Garden. The young, like Marvell, have to enter a world of both academic and sexual competition; to survive, an inner garden is required which permits retreat from time to time.

Marvell then goes on to show that he has a clear grasp of the difference between retreating from the relationship on the one hand and bearing the pain of the loss on the other.

> Fond lovers, cruel as their flame,

> Cut in these trees their mistress' name ...
> Fair trees! wheresoe'er your barks I wound
> No name shall but your own be found.

Relationships can be painful and cutting; they involve necessary separations and differences. In the Garden (regressed states) this does not apply. Distinctions are abolished; absorbed into the Garden the poet can merge into himself:

> The mind, that Ocean where each kind
> Does straight its own resemblance find;
> Yet it creates, transcending these,
> Far other worlds and other seas;
> Annihilating all that's made
> To a green thought in a green shade.

The state of primitive unity seeks escape from the physical body:

> Casting the body's vest aside,
> My soul into the boughs does glide.

This wish to escape from the body, the need to come to terms with the new body image which is one of the central and hardest tasks of adolescence, and the need to commune with nature are central themes in young people.

By the end of the poem Marvell imagines a state of purity and peace:

> Such was that happy Garden-state
> While man walked these without a mate ...
> But 'twas beyond a mortal's share
> To wander solitary there:
> Two paradises 'twere in one,
> To live in Paradise alone.

The last two lines are more than just a simple 'two-in-one' sum (i.e. Paradise plus solitude). They are also a reference to the Bible-myth of the origin of woman, according to which Adam had Eve within him. There is an important sequence here. The poet deals with the tension of loneliness and wanting by retreat into the maternal Garden (planted by the Father). He is made unhappy by the pain and tensions created by individual differences and wants to be 'annihilated': he wants to trust this mother Garden, put himself not just in her hands but actually be inside her.

This, however, provides a frightening reminder of one's vulnerability. The 'two paradises' are a defence against this fear: the 'male fear of the maternal imago' (Chasseguet-Smirgel 1985) is more acceptable if a man imagines his mother as coming from *him*, rather than vice versa.

Solitude and intercourse

Winnicott pointed out another paradox: maturity requires the capacity to be alone after intercourse. Separation from the family and the inevitable resulting loneliness create an inner space in the young person. Here the adolescent needs to encounter his own body and its sexual urges which can be expressed in what the Laufers (Laufer and Laufer 1984) call the 'central masturbation phantasy'. If this feels unrealisable or perverse the individual may reject or attack his body. The sudden emergence of homosexual phantasies, for example, may lead to an apparently unheralded suicide attempt in a young person who has just left home.

The aloneness of adolescence also creates a space in which phantasies of intercourse can emerge. The 'primal scene' phantasies contain the residues of imagined parental intercourse. The child's inevitably ambivalent attitude towards his parents' bodies and their relationship will colour his own attitude towards his sexuality. I will produce clinical evidence on this point later but now wish to quote two well-known poems in support of the view that solitude creates a potential space into which phantasies of intercourse can erupt.

The first is Hardy's *Convergence of the Twain*, lines written on the sinking of the *Titanic*. The poem starts by creating the setting:

In a solitude of the sea

then describes how the great ship and the iceberg approached one another, how different they seemed:

Alien they seemed to be:
No mortal eye could see
The intimate welding of their later history.

until the collison came:

Til the Spinner of the Years
Said 'Now' and each one hears.
And consummation comes, and jars two hemispheres.

The second poem is Matthew Arnold's *Dover Beach*. The poem starts by describing the waning of faith, which he compares to the receding tide. This, like the loss of childhood and family in adolescence, he describes as a

melancholy, long, withdrawing roar.

He then turns for consolation to his love, begging her to be true, in contrast to the uncertain world of adulthood, and where (even in intercourse perhaps)

ignorant armies clash by night.

The pain of solitude

I turn now to pathologies associated with loneliness and as an introduction to this I will end with a final poetic account, again from Cowper, a gifted poet who almost certainly suffered from manic-depression. His mania is probably revealed in his best known poem *John Gilpin*, a humorous account of a horse that goes out of control. The other side of his nature is shown in his lines:

> Monarch of all I survey
> Oh solitude where are the charms
> That sages have seen in thy face
> Better dwell in the midst of chaos
> Than dwell in this horrible place.

This also points to two commonly used defences against loneliness found in adolescence: 'dwelling in chaos' (avoidance) or the attempt to be a 'monarch' of a solitary kingdom (isolation).

LONELINESS AND ADOLESCENT BREAKDOWN

Bertrand Russell, who was brought up deprived of contact with his peers by grandparents, nannies and private tutors (he never went to school), movingly describes in his autobiography (Russell 1972) the intense loneliness of his adolescence and how it lead on to the three great themes of his life:

> three passions, simple but overwhelmingly strong, have governed my life: the longing for love, the search for knowledge and unbearable pity for the suffering of mankind. These passions, like great winds, have blown me hither and thither in a wayward course, over a deep ocean of anguish, reaching to the very verge of despair.
>
> I have sought love first because it brings ecstasy – ecstasy so great that I would often have sacrificed all the rest of my life for a few hours of this joy. I have sought it, next, because it relieves loneliness – that terrible loneliness in which one's shivering consciousness looks over the rim of the world into the cold unfathomable lifeless abyss. I have sought it finally because I have seen, in a mystic miniature, the prefiguring vision of the heavens that the saints and poets have imagined. This is what I have sought, and though it might seem too good for human life this is what – at last – I have found.

Russell, perhaps a perpetual adolescent, describes three themes – love, truth and compassion – that are central proccupations for adolescents of whatever intellect, privilege and romanticism. All three involve the exploratory capacity to experience separateness from family and parents and an ability to tolerate the resulting loneliness (Bowlby 1980).

Margaret Mahler (1963) has described what she calls the *rapprochement* phase in the process of separation-individuation during the course of the second year of life (cf. Chapter 1). Here the germs of independence begin to show themselves, but emotional object constancy is not yet fully established: so periods of exploration alternate with moments of anxiety in which the child clings to the mother. A similar pattern is common when adolescents first leave home. One girl rang her mother three times a day for the first few weeks of starting college; it was only when she moved out of rather gloomy digs and set up with friends that the phone calls began to taper off. Parents have to tread a thin line between availability and over-concern during this phase. One patient, looking back on an undiagnosed breakdown in which he dropped out of university and returned home to his parents where he spent nearly six months lying in bed, remembers his father (who was a regimental sergeant major) shouting at him as he lay there: 'What on earth is the matter? There must be something wrong with you.' Ten years later the patient commented: 'If only I could have told him that there *was* something wrong I might not be seeing you now.' Another young man whose parents had separated and who was living with his father recalled how his depression had started when he returned from a holiday to find that their flat was sold and his father had moved in with a girlfriend.

In J. M. Barrie's *Peter Pan* (1904), after the children disappeared to Never-never land, Mr Darling made two mistakes: he shut the sitting-room shutters and then abandoned his wife's bed and retired to the dog-house. For secure exploration adolescents have to feel that they can return home if necessary, and that the parental relationship will survive their absence. A family crisis may brew up just as the young person is leaving: one parent may fall ill or threaten separation. Here the parents or family system cannot tolerate the adolescent leaving; there is often a shared family phantasy that the parents will break up when the children leave home.

It is a common experience in psychotherapy with adult patients to find that there has been some degree of breakdown in adolescence that passed by undiagnosed or untreated. The concept of covert or postponed breakdown is captured in another of Winnicott's paradoxes when he says of adult breakdown: 'the breakdown has already occurred'. It is important to acknowledge the importance of these silent adolescent breakdowns and to work with them psychotherapeutically rather than to leap over them, making straight for an early childhood constellation. The patient at first is far more likely to be in contact with adolescence than with early memories and sensations. With this in mind we may classify adolescent breakdown under three headings:

Overt breakdown

Here the young person becomes clearly symptomatic with psychotic features, anorexia nervosa, opiate addiction, suicide attempt, obsessional behaviour, etc.

Covert breakdown

Here the manifestations of disturbance are milder, kept secret, or go unnoticed. They include excessive drinking or drug abuse, bulimia, depressive withdrawal, seclusion and avoidance of peers.

Breakdown postponed

This overlaps with covert breakdown. There are three main patterns, each of which can be seen as an avoidance of the pain and loneliness of separation:

1 Clinging

Here the young person continues to behave as though they were still in the early phases of adolescence. Within the family they are happy and bright, but they become anxious when issues of separation arise, for example when involved in peer activities, especially if it involves the opposite sex. This is not an uncommon pattern in anorexia nervosa. The battle for independence is fought out over food.

2 Isolation

Here the young person appears independent. They deny the need for others and lead an apparently normal but in fact isolated life. Loneliness is avoided by denial of feeling.

3 Pseudo-independence

A common pattern is to be found in the young person who clings compulsively to peers and is terrified of solitude. Premature pregnancy may occur, or parents may be shunned as the young person makes a wholesale transference of dependency to a peer-group or partner. A young man had asked to be sent away to boarding school at the age of ten because he got on so badly with his parents, especially his father. He became a detached but not unhappy adolescent, with a love of sport. At eighteen he went to a polytechnic and met a girl on his first day with whom he was inseparable for his three years as a student. It was only when they left college and the relationship broke up that he became seriously depressed, discovering for the first time the loneliness he had been avoiding since his childhood.

LONELINESS IN PSYCHOTHERAPY

When these defences against loneliness break down, the patient may then experience panic, anxiety and depression and seek psychotherapeutic help.

The hope is that, through therapy, loneliness may lessen. This may indeed happen initially, but inevitably as the patient becomes aware of the circumscribed hour, of breaks, of the therapist's separateness, the unpleasant feelings return. The patient will attempt to avoid them by his habitual defence. The isolate will remain detached and aloof in therapy; the clinger will attempt to ingratiate himself, to lessen the distance between patient and therapist by all possible means. The task of the therapist is two-fold. First, to understand the pain, anger or emptiness and interpret the patient's defensive manoeuvres. Second, to provide a setting in which loneliness can be experienced and not avoided; to hold the patient (metaphorically) in such a way that they can be alone-in-the-presence-of-another and so lay the foundations of the capacity for solitude. If this process goes well, the patient will gradually begin to use the therapy as a setting for self-exploration or 'play' in which the therapist is a non-intrusive collaborator. The patient's attempts to coerce the therapist into colluding with defences against loneliness (for example, by developing a more 'real' relationship, or by avoidance of change) will diminish.

I shall now describe in some detail the once-weekly therapy of two cases which illustrate these processes. The first case is one in which loneliness was avoided by clinging and pseudo-independence; the second by isolation.

Miss F: 'Dwelling in chaos'

Miss F asked for psychotherapeutic help with a fairly common problem: she and the boyfriend with whom she lived got on well in most spheres but they never made love. They had already had sex therapy which according to her had not 'worked' because her boyfriend would not cooperate with treatment. Now she was seeking help in her own right. It soon emerged that the problem with sex was one of several difficulties. She felt depressed and pessimistic most of the time but was determined not to let anyone see this. She drank quite heavily. Her referral had been precipitated by an incident where she had become drunk and aggressive at a party and felt very bad about this afterwards. She was also rather promiscuous; she was involved in several secret affairs with different men.

Miss F was a lively, attractive, intelligent woman who had a demanding, 'glamorous' job. Two themes emerged very early in the course of the therapy. She was terrified of being alone, even for an evening. Her boyfriend was often away on trips and it was then that she desperately sought out and saw other men. Second, despite her appearance and lively manner, she felt deeply unsure of herself as a woman. She had virtually no women friends; she needed to compete with them for men's attention, and viewed her fellow women too much as rivals to be able to get close to them. Although she slept with many men she found it hard to enjoy sex and had to drink before she could go to bed with them. She saw herself as no good at 'feminine' activities: she was a hopeless cook. This, she said, was an advantage because it meant that her boyfriend took care of her, bringing her breakfast in bed and treating her like a queen. She could never imagine having children: she could not visualise remaining consistent and 'faithful' to a child year after year.

Miss F was the youngest child of an unhappy marriage. Her mother had made it quite clear to her that she was an unwanted 'accident'. She had two much older sisters, neither of whom was married, one of whom had had a serious breakdown in her teens. Most of her childhood (as she recalled it) was spent alone with an unhappy, unresponsive mother. When, in the course of therapy, she spoke about her childhood to her sisters they reminded her that as their younger sister they had adored and spoiled her. The main excitement and happiness of her childhood centred around her father. He had an interesting job, which often took him away from home; but when he returned he treated her like a mistress, showering her with presents, kisses and attention, and neglecting her mother. He had several real mistresses: she remembered on one occasion being introduced to a strange woman and being asked how would she like to have her for a new mummy.

Miss F did well at school. She started at college but dropped out at the end of her first year and went to live with her boyfriend. Her parents disapproved of him and at this point she severed all relations with them. She seemed to have 'ablated' (Rycroft 1985) them and, when she came into therapy several years later, still had virtually no contact. She had, however, never been alone: she had always lived with a boyfriend and had never left one until she had lined up his successor. She was terrified of being left and would ruthlessly end relationships whenever she detected the slightest signs of cooling ardour on the part of her lover. 'Always leave, never be left,' was her guiding principle. This had the effect of creating a crowd of ex-lovers who continued to hover around her and who would be reinstated, albeit temporarily, whenever loneliness threatened.

Therapy initially went well. Her feelings of depression lifted. She became interested and involved in therapy but found my silence and apparent unresponsiveness very difficult. She mocked me and accused me of being a diehard 'Freudian' but at the same time she made considerable efforts to be honest and to understand herself. Then came the first 'break'. She ridiculed my suggestion that she might find it hard, accusing me of typical therapist's self-aggrandisement. She missed the first session after the break, and then came drunk to the next. She reacted with fury when I remarked that she may have felt lonely in my absence and have wished to punish me for exposing her to these feelings. She was even more contemptuous of my attempt to link this sequence with feelings she may have had towards her father while he was away.

The treatment continued: she became more and more dissatisfied with her boyfriend. She longed to leave him but felt too terrified to do so. Initially she had attributed all their sexual difficulties to him; now she began to own that she was not really attracted to him and to see that she had made him into a sort of mother on whom she depended for security but with whom she suppressed all overt feelings of excitement or anger.

The next break appeared to go smoothly but she announced on resumption that she was in love. She had found the most marvellous man with whom she could make love successfully without having to be drunk and who, unlike me, actually told her how wonderful she was rather than making her feel bad. This was the first time in her life that she had really felt good about herself as a woman. The fact that he was married with small children was no impediment. The only problem was that the good feelings he gave her did not endure in his absence, and she had to be sure to see him at least twice a day for it to be sustained. She continued for several weeks to feel happy. Therapy became quite static: I was a spoiler pointing out flaws in what for her was a perfect arrangement with two men, one of whom looked after her, one of whom made her feel good.

The crisis came after a holiday with her regular boyfriend. She had felt utterly miserable: they had been unable to make love and she felt jealous of all the other couples in the hotel. It became clear that if she chose either of the men in her life she would have to face feelings of loneliness. She had to have them both and yet this was an inherently unstable arrangement. Coming to therapy merely reminded her of this conflict. If only she could live entirely in the present everything would be perfect; but I kept pointing her to the past and the future, neither of which she could face. At this point she began to miss sessions saying that she had to choose between seeing her lover – who resented her coming for therapy – and me. Reluctantly, and knowing that she had baulked in some way, she decided to stop treatment rather than risk experiencing my supposed abandonment of her. With hindsight I can see that I failed to interpret the transferential implications of the love-affair soon enough. She was triumphant; I felt helpless. She was, through 'projective identification', exposing me to the experiences she had had as a child when, in different ways, she felt excluded and abandoned by her parents.

This woman's life was organised around the need to avoid being alone. Being by herself made her feel depressed and inadequate. The idea of a satisfying solitude was as alien to her as the possibility of forming a lasting relationship with a man. She had experienced aloneness with her mother as flat, boring and empty. To be alone was to be reminded of how *like* her mother she felt she was. She was physically similar and would begin to hate her body and what she perceived as its fatness. Although she could enjoy and be excited by her father's presence she was always aware that it was short-lived and that he would soon be off again. By dividing her relationships into one that held her and gave her security and one that gave her excitement, she ensured that she never felt abandoned. The price she had to pay for this was that she was never wholly *with* either of her men.

In summary:

1 Miss F had not acquired the capacity to be alone in childhood; alone with her mother she felt anxious and abandoned (as perhaps her mother herself felt). Being by herself meant being 'by' a body which was equated with her mother by whom she had not felt accepted and whom she in turn had rejected.
2 Unable to be alone, she could not tolerate loneliness in adolescence. She dealt with this by 'ablating' her parents. By pretending to herself that they did not exist, she did not feel their loss. At the same time she created multiple relationships so that she would never be fully alone.
3 She did initially feel 'held' in therapy and was able to be 'alone' enough with the therapist – whom she constantly tried to prod into responsiveness – to experience some sadness.
4 However, she found the therapeutic breaks in the once-weekly therapy intolerable. Through her affair she found a rival 'therapist' who did not abandon her. Despite its problems there were some positive features in this relationship that were new. She felt feminine for the first time. She was able to talk with her lover about her fear that she would be compelled to leave him, as she had left all her other attachments, including therapy, rather than act on it.

Mr G: Isolation as avoidance of breakdown

Miss F broke down when threatened by loneliness; Mr G became ill when his isolation was no longer impregnable. He had broken down while at university and had been hospitalised. Now, three years later, he was referred to me.

He spent his time lying in bed at his parents' house crying and wailing and berating his 'friends': 'The bastards, they just don't care. No one cares about me. Will no one help me or tell me what to do?' The immediate precipitant of this state was his inability to decide whether or not to accept a job which he had been offered. The psychiatric diagnosis was best seen as that of a depressive state with hysterical features.

At twenty-four Mr G was the third of four children. His older brother had been killed in a car crash six years before. His mother suffered from manic-depression and had had several mental hospital admissions during his childhood. He saw his father as weak, nervous and ineffectual – everything he feared he was becoming.

He described himself as a bored, difficult and angry child. His mother was 'useless' – 'I just ignored her'. He would reject his food, say 'this is shit' and then rush up to his room for hours and refuse to be coaxed out. He remembered her throwing a sweet to him from a balcony while she was in hospital. He was standing beside his father who offered his hand but the patient pushed it away.

Mr G saw himself as totally isolated: isolated from his mother as a child by her illness; from his father by his 'emotional incompetence'; from his siblings because he was bright and so 'different'; from his peers at school because of his delayed adolescence (he remained pre-pubescent until he was seventeen). The effects of the latter had been disastrous for him: he experienced himself as inferior and was obsessed by the appearance of other men whom he saw as hairy and muscular, with fully developed genitals, in contrast to his own hairless, thin, inadequate body.

A feature of our early sessions was a crescendo of shouting and crying and banging the chair in which he would repeat over and over again how desperate he felt. I felt a great pressure to intervene either by reassurance, or by telling him what to do, or by telling him to shut up (I was wondering what on earth my colleagues next door were thinking). I managed more or less to resist all these, although I did contact the referring social worker and suggest that it might be an idea for him to move out of home into an after-care hostel. But I stuck, as best I could, to my interpretive last. I suggested that the problem as I saw it was *not that he felt bad but that he felt nothing at all*; or rather that he did not know what it was that he *did* feel, and that his weeping and wailing was an attempt to get himself and me to believe that at least he felt *something*. The immediate and subsequent effects of this intervention were quite dramatic. He came out of his reverie of self-absorbed fury and started to talk in a normal voice and to allow the beginning of a dialogue. In the next session he asked if he could lie on the couch. Once settled there he started to share his feelings rather than wailing or talking about himself in a completely detached way. Soon afterwards he moved out of his parents' home, found a shared flat and accepted the job he had been offered.

It was not, and is still not, entirely clear to me what it was about this intervention that had 'worked', while all previous attempts at interpreting this behaviour – for example, as an attempt to get in touch with an ill mother by identifying with her – had failed. It was certainly important because he referred back to it several times in the following months. By sitting it out and *not* allowing myself to be coerced or intimidated but pointing to his inner loneliness I had perhaps 'held' him so that, 'alone in the presence of another', an inner space was created in which he could tolerate his feelings.

What then emerged was a torrent of passion about a young man with whom he had been in love while at university. Mr G had been thrown into a confusion of relief and despair by his response to this man. The relief was that he could have desires; the despair came from knowing they could never be realised. At this point his anxiety became unbearable; he had broken down and been admitted to hospital.

We were then able to reconstruct his phantasy which was of merging with this man, so absorbing his potency; how he had identified his own body as being, like his mother, 'useless'; and how painful it was to have desires when he experienced himself as so unlovable. Further progress emerged in a dream of a cycling race in which he 'nearly came off', overtook most of the field and finally 'came second'. This was important because it revealed his hidden adolescent feelings of bodily prowess. Nearly 'coming off' related to orgasm – his fear of what he called the 'vulnerability' of orgasm, and the difficulty he had in imagining trusting anyone with himself at that moment. 'Coming second' related to his passivity (he 'let' the winner 'come first'). Underlying the latter was an important piece of progress: he could now *choose* passivity and so imagine, through 'trial action', not merely merging but some possibility of intercourse between his body and another's. This was symbolised by a masturbation phantasy in which he allowed himself to take his pyjamas off as he went to bed, and thus, symbolically, to lie for the first time 'by' himself.

This patient, dependent yet isolated as a child, had avoided the loneliness of adolescence by aloofness and detachment. When this defence was swept aside by feelings of love, he broke down. The desire that was revealed to him seemed impossible and frightening. Therapy, in so far as it was effective, was not so because of clever interpretations which tended merely to reinforce his intellectual defences. What seemed to help was an effort at holding and allowing him to experience his loneliness and, at the same time resisting the temptation to relieve it. This then enabled us to examine his phantasies within a safe place.

CONCLUSIONS

Adolescence is the orphan of psychoanalysis. It is neither childhood, where the origins of neurotic disorder are laid down; nor adulthood, where the failure to resolve conflicts is made manifest in symptoms. The distinction between normal and abnormal is hard to make in adolescence: periods of depression and rebellion are common and have to be distinguished from real breakdown. Standard psychoanalytic technique is hard to maintain in a patient who may be acting self-destructively and feel intensely threatened by an opaque and silent therapist. Freud himself could be said to have had difficulties with adolescents: of his five major case-histories only one, Dora, was adolescent and her treatment, though fascinating, was a failure. One might even see Freud's great schism with Jung, his chosen successor, as a failure to understand the dynamics of adolescent rebellion.

My thinking in this chapter has been influenced by three main groups of writers, all of whom, in their different ways, have been making up for this lacuna in psychoanalytic thought. The first is Winnicott (1979) and his followers, who emphasise the holding and space-creating role of the therapist as opposed to the interpretive function. The second are the Laufers (1984) who, while remaining in the mainstream of psychoanalysis, have fought to establish adolescence as a psychological 'stage' in its own right, stating: 'The period of adolescence has a specific and essential contribution to make to psychological life and the psychic disruptions of this period need to be understood differently from those of childhood and adulthood.' I have drawn particularly on their ideas about the central role of the body in adolescence, and how gradual separation from the parents, and especially the mother, is fought out in the arena of the adolescent's relationship to their body.

The third influence has been family therapy, especially the work of Haley (1977) who emphasises the fact that leaving home is a family rather than an individual matter. Family therapists show how the family can be helped to 'hold' the detaching adolescent (and holding implies firmness as well as concern) rather than have a therapist take over this function. The converse of this is equally important: the importance of the recognition of adolescent breakdown and of insisting that the adolescent receives treatment when it is required.

These three groups of authors have lead me to make four main points:

1 Adolescent loneliness is an inevitable accompaniment of the process of separation from the family, which is part of the developmental task of adolescence.
2 Where adolescents and their parents can tolerate this separation they can then move on to a more mature state in which intimate adult relationships can be formed and being alone is felt as pleasant solitude rather than painful loneliness.
3 Adolescent breakdown is associated with a failure to separate from the parents, i.e. an avoidance of loneliness; or as failure to move on from loneliness and form new intimate attachments. In both cases there is an incapacity to tolerate solitude.
4 Part of the therapist's role is, paradoxically perhaps, to provide a setting in which the young person can be held and so profit from, rather than be defeated by, the pain of loneliness.

Chapter 5

Supportive analytic therapy

Psychotherapists tend to feel uneasy about supportive psychotherapy. It has a dull ring to it, with overtones of buttressing and trussing rather than revelation or radical restructuring. This leads to the rather patronising view that it is a treatment espoused by the uninitiated who believe that psychotherapy is all about being nice to people.

Those who practise supportive psychotherapy have done little to challenge this view. The literature directly concerned with supportive psychotherapy is sparse (Bloch 1987). At the same time there is growing research evidence for the importance of 'non-specific factors' in psychotherapy. The cuttingroom floor of psychotherapy research is littered with examples of the effectiveness of 'placebo' psychotherapy (Garfield and Bergin 1986) which often contains a significant supportive component. This has lead critics of psychotherapy to dub its practitioners 'placebologists' (Shepherd 1984) and its supporters to rebut this by claiming that 'the placebo *is* psychotherapy' (Frank 1983).

This chapter comes to two contradictory conclusions. First, that there is no such unique thing as supportive psychotherapy: what this account attempts to describe is just psychotherapy practised with difficult patients in a low-key way. Second, that there is no such thing as *un*supportive therapy: all therapy is, or should be, supportive. Psychotherapy *is*, among other things, about being nice to people – not in the sense of pandering, but by attending to them and taking them seriously.

There are two aspects to supportive psychotherapy. The first concerns a group of patients who are so vulnerable or damaged that they are unlikely to survive the rigours of intensive analytic therapy and who therefore need more than the usual amount of the supportive component that exists in all therapies. The second is about the modification of technique – in which the 'pure gold' of psychoanalytic psychotherapy is alloyed (cf. Freud 1919) with more than the usual amount of suggestion, advice, reassurance, empathy, guidance and encouragement. Its practitioners may be those who are so experienced they can afford to break the rules of therapy (for example, never give advice) or so lacking in experience that they do not know they are breaking them. In this chapter I shall consider both aspects, describing a particular form of attenuated analytic psychotherapy that is suitable for patients who are so 'difficult' that they would not normally be considered for analytic therapy within the NHS but who can, with the right approach, be helped.

I shall first comment on why such a method needs to be defined. I shall give an account of the model and then describe two illustrative cases.

WHY SUPPORTIVE THERAPY?

There is a group of potential psychotherapy patients who are casualties of what Tudor Hart (1971) has called the 'inverse care law'. This holds that those most in need of good medical care are, through disadvantage and disability, least likely to receive it. The psychotherapeutic version of this means that the more psychologically disturbed a patient is, however deserving, the less likely they are to be considered suitable for psychotherapy.

From the viewpoint of cost-effectiveness, this may make sense. It might be argued that the uncertain outcome with 'difficult' patients does not in the NHS justify the cost of the intensive, prolonged treatment they require (Wilkinson 1986). But it is inherent in the nature of their disadvantage that they are unlikely to be able to afford private psychotherapy. There is a need to find a form of therapy for these patients that is both effective and expedient.

The second group for whom a definition of supportive psychotherapy is needed is psychotherapists themselves. Analytic psychotherapy with damaged patients has many pitfalls. The inexperienced dynamic therapist may get engulfed in a regressive transference that leads to abrupt termination; the more experienced therapist will take cover behind the Utopian conclusion that 'what this patient *really* needs is five-times-a-week analysis'; while behavioural treatment may produce a brief improvement followed by an inevitable relapse.

The third group for whom supportive psychotherapy needs to be defined are those most likely to be delivering it: GPs, psychiatrists, community psychiatric nurses, psychologists and psychiatric social workers. It is the 'multidisciplinary team' rather than the specialist psychotherapy service that carries these patients, often without support or supervision.

My aim in this chapter is to show that supportive psychotherapy with difficult patients can be rewarding, 'dynamic' and survivable without being all-consuming of time or inner resources. Supportive psychotherapy is about survival. The three essentials of any treatment are the survival of the patient, the survival of the therapist and the survival of the therapy. Supportive analytic therapy tries to steer a course between an over-intensive or even persecutory psychotherapy leading to regression and uncontrollable dependency, and a too-timid psychiatric approach that medicalises the patient's experience or concentrates on 'management' rather than meaning. One produces psychotherapy without support, the other support without psychotherapy.

SUPPORTIVE ANALYTIC THERAPY: SUPPORTIVE FEATURES

Treatment is prolonged but non-intensive. The patient is seen for regular sessions of defined length, at non-frequent intervals. The usual length of session is half-an-hour. Intervals between sessions vary. The two cases I shall present were each seen monthly. There need be no holiday breaks. When there is a major crisis, for example, psychotic episode or suicidal feelings, the patient may need to be seen more frequently for a limited period. The therapist must 'titrate' the interval between sessions so that it is frequent enough to keep the therapy alive but not so frequent as to arouse unmanageable feelings in the patient. A good rapport, often based on a prolonged assessment interview or an admission to hospital, is essential from the start.

The therapist relies predominantly on 'non-specific factors' (Stiles *et al.* 1986) to produce change. He must be caring, consistent, reliable, professional and positive in his behaviour. Above all he must offer *containment* to the patient who can come to feel that the illness, however painful and incomprehensible, is held by the therapist in and between the sessions. All this combines to produce in the patient what Frank (1973) calls remoralisation. The therapist is sparing in his use of any interpretations of behavioural directives which may threaten the security of the containment.

The therapist sees himself as part of, and helps to create if necessary, a containing and supportive network for the patient: he must be prepared to collaborate with the patient's GPs, social worker, priests or friends if necessary. The patient must be aware of this collaboration and inter-communication. This provides support for the therapist as well as the patient who may unconsciously wish to seduce the therapist into thinking that only he or she can help. The symbolic message to the patient that he is supported by a 'combined parent' (psychiatrist *and* GP or social worker) is important as a defence against destructive and splitting tendencies and also because the patient may often have lacked united parental support in childhood.

When therapy is effective the patient will usually find another therapeutic focus which sustains him between sessions. This may be a night-class, a creative activity like writing or painting, or a sport or craft. The therapist will often sense that the patient is dependent on them in more than a recreational way. These 'extra-curricular' activities which sustain the patient between sessions are encouraged; they are only interpreted with extreme caution.

The Italian Marxist writer Gramsci (Joll 1979), who spent many years as a political prisoner, described the correct attitude of the revolutionary as 'pessimism of the intellect, optimism of the will'. In other words: 'hope for the best, expect the worse'. This would be good advice for the therapist attempting supportive psychotherapy. It is often said that a defining feature of supportive psychotherapy is that the patient's defences should be shored up rather than challenged (Bloch 1987). An example might be the patient (second case-history, below) who longed for a relationship with a man and finally managed a tête-à-tête with a male colleague. She felt the meeting had been a 'disaster'. Rather than exploring what was disastrous, or the transferential implications, the supportive therapist emphasised (as might a cognitive therapist) the positive fact that she *had* met a man, even if it did not turn out as she would have wished. She could then laugh at her schoolgirl hopes and fears. Shafer (1976) has divided the components of psychotherapy into the comic, the romantic, the tragic and the ironic. Supportive psychotherapy always emphasises the comic and the ironic at the expense of the romantic and tragic.

The expectations of the supportive therapist must always be limited. A positive outcome will lead to the patient becoming more autonomous, less miserable and more creative, but he may not succeed at 'lieben und arbeiten' in the way that the therapist might wish. The therapist, if he can empathise with his patients, will almost certainly learn from them what it is like to stand alone, to feel 'different', yet survive.

PSYCHOTHERAPEUTIC FEATURES

In defining psychotherapeutic aspects of supportive psychotherapy it is necessary to consider other models of care for difficult patients. These include *management* where the vehicle of treatment is change in the patient's circumstances, for example, entering a rehabilitation hostel; *medical* treatment, where the mutative element is a drug or ECT; and a *pure dependency* model where the patient comes to rely exclusively on professional care.

Supportive psychotherapy contains elements of all three, but differs from them in two subtle but vital respects. In non-analytic supportive therapy, the relationship between patient and therapist is seen as a *vehicle* for drug prescription or management and is usually not examined. It is ground, not figure. In supportive analytic therapy this is reversed. The *relationship* with the patient and the *content* of the sessions are central.

The success of any supportive psychotherapy greatly depends on positive transference. There is probably an element of mutual self-selection in supportive analytic therapy. The therapist catches a glimpse of hope despite the difficulties the patient presents. The patient senses this appreciation of his specialness and responds positively. These positive feelings of the patient for the therapist must not be mistaken for reality, but should be interpreted only with extreme caution. It is often a relief when negative transference finally surfaces. This can be interpreted more freely, especially when there are management or medical issues that are understandable in terms of trans-ference. For example, in one patient a problem arose about the refusal of depot phenothiazine injections. The therapist became more and more insistent; the patient became more and more frightened and resistant. The deadlock was broken when the parallel between this situation and the patient's experience of rape by her father was interpreted.

In a similar way the inevitable dependency of supportive psychotherapy is both accepted but, where appropriate, interpreted and challenged. A request for antidepressants by another patient was agreed to, but at the same time interpreted as (a) a wish to remain in symbolic contact with the therapist between sessions; (b) a reproach to the therapist that he had failed to understand the patient's mental pain; and (c) a self-pitying plea for charity from an orphan who was seeing the therapist with the same dependency, gratitude, envy and resentment with which she had viewed her caretakers in the Barnardo's Home where she had been brought up.

A second difference from both the medical and management model involves the structure and content of the sessions. Lewis (Adams 1986) coined the term 'distributive psychotherapy' to describe sessions in which the therapist distributes his attention and questioning over different aspects of the patient's life: his job, his home, his symptoms. This is all right as far as it goes, but at a certain point in the session the history-taking has to stop. At this point the therapist must attend to the emotional, unconscious, unexpressed aspects of the patient's story and how he tells it. Here the therapist moves from a supportive to a psychotherapeutic mode. The therapist now is *not* trying to fit the patient's experience into a psychopathological symptom-pattern, nor attempting to find a practical solution to his problem. He is just listening, trying to understand and, with the patient, trying to put that understanding into words. One patient dreamed of his therapist as a 'watch repairer' because 'you watch and repair'. At this point the therapist, as Enid Balint (1963) puts it, is neither present, nor absent, but 'just there'.

Patients are always, in a sense, trying to get their carers to be 'bad' therapists, too involved or too detached. In supportive psychotherapy the therapist has to avoid too much involvement which will freeze the relationship into one of pure dependency or destroy it via demands for more and more attention, physical holding and friendship. At the same time he must resist becoming so detached that he is no longer 'just there', and out of touch with the patient's lived experience.

Ms H: the need for silent support

This case illustrates two key features of supportive therapy in patients who have a severe psychiatric illness. First, a multimodal approach is needed in which physical and psychotherapeutic methods of treatment complement each other, and in which individual and family therapies can usefully be practised together. Second, the rhythm of regular supportive sessions, even if little appears to be happening dynamically, can provide a basis of trust which in time the patient can come to value and use.

Ms H was a twenty-year-old who left home for the first time to work as a nanny in a distant town. There she met a young man of whom she became very fond. Their relationship was platonic; she spent a lot of time 'mothering' him – washing his clothes, cooking for him, and helping him with his career. Her profound depression was precipitated by the discovery that he already had a girlfriend. She felt deeply ashamed of her 'mistake' and returned home to her parents, unable to continue with her job. She became more and more miserable, mute and retarded while her parents – especially her mother who had herself been depressed when Ms H was a baby – became frantic with worry. She was treated with antidepressants, lithium and anti-psychotic drugs, but there was little improvement. Admission to hospital for a course of ECT was considered, since the suicide risk seemed very high. Her parents, especially her mother, were opposed to hospital admission and felt that the staff could never provide the level of vigilance and concern which they could offer at home. The mother decided to give up her job to be with her daughter full time. Any suggestion that separation from home might be beneficial was met with intense anxiety and anger in the mother who felt she was being criticised and judged. Meanwhile the therapist, who was seeing the patient for weekly half-hour supportive therapy sessions, felt increasingly worried, helpless and sidelined. The patient was nearly silent throughout the sessions and appeared to resent having to come to see him. He felt that his interpretations were irrelevant and ineffective, and (perhaps like the patient's father) that all important communications were between the patient and her mother, and not with him.

Eventually it was felt, in view of the suicide risk, that ECT was the only option, and the patient was admitted to hospital for a few days, and then started attending as a day patient. There was a perceptible but slight improvement, but the situation remained stuck and worrying. With the help of a family therapist a new formulation and management plan was made. Ms H's depression was seen in terms of separation–individuation. Separation from her family had activated separation anxiety, linked to her low self-esteem. This in turn may have been related to her mother's depression when she was young: anxious attachment meant that she lacked a secure base of good feelings inside herself, the confidence that her needs would be responded to. She had dealt with this by caring for others, rather than expose her own needs and the possibility of rejection. Her awakening sexuality and the actual rejection by the boyfriend confirmed these feelings, and reproduced the family constellation of a preoccupied and anxious mother and a hard-working but emotionally detached father (described by his wife as absolutely brilliant at every-thing – except psychotherapy!).

Under the regressive influence of the depressive illness Ms H had returned to a symbiotic state of fusion with her mother, the ultimate expression of which was her wish to die ('in their death they were not divided'). In addition to the individual supportive analytic therapy the family were offered family therapy in which, rather than trying unsuccessfully to separate mother and daughter, their intense mutual involvement was encouraged, hoping to create a secure base for Ms H through her mother's responsiveness (cf. Chapter 1) which would ultimately enable her to move away with more confidence.

Supportive therapy was mediated through the mother, and the sessions were framed as 'supervision' for her in the vital work of keeping her daughter alive. At the same time the importance of the parental relation-ship was emphasised by asking them about their life when they were courting and before they became parents. Any evidence of differences of opinion between family members were highlighted, in the hope of helping them to see that they could be separate and yet remain united as a family.

The patient began steadily to improve and, after months of sticky and mostly silent therapy sessions, changes began to emerge. Desperate for unconscious material, the therapist asked her if there were any fairy stories she had liked as a child. She immediately recalled Anderson's *Little Mermaid*, in which a mermaid falls in love with an earthly prince and is allowed by the sea witch to leave her watery home and join him. She pays a terrible price for this: each step she takes is agony and she looses the power of speech. Eventually, he tires of her silence and falls in love with someone else. Overcoming her murderous jealousy, the little mermaid returns to the sea. But she has lived on earth so long she is no longer able to swim. Neither fish nor flesh, her only hope is death: she becomes part of the sea, a happy bubble of foam.

The fairy tale seemed to encapsulate Ms H's experience of falling in love. The perilous transition from water to land which went so wrong symbolised all her fears and inhibitions about emerging from childhood into womanhood, about making the move from attachment to her mother to finding a man. The sessions began to come alive. She was able to confess that she felt angry towards her therapist for being so smug and silent and not holding out a hand to help her more (at the height of her suicidal depression she had imagined herself falling into a hole, vainly holding up her hands for someone to pull her back to safety). She brought a dream in which an older man tried to provoke her and her family into anger, while a depressed girl watched from a hole in the ceiling. Her associations to the dream were that her father was sometimes obstinate, and her relief that her depression was almost out of sight. Following this dream she said that a most unusual family row had broken out at the dinner table, in which to her surprise she had joined in. The row came to an end when someone wondered what the neighbours would think about this normally sedate family shouting at each other, and they all dissolved into helpless laughter.

As she gradually improved so the frequency of the supportive sessions was reduced, although she continued to come for several more years. The transferential aspects of the treatment were often transparently clear, but the therapist deliberately did not focus on them in his comments, except in a half-joking way. The sessions were often light and inconsequential-seeming. She described an incident which had coincided with the start of her illness in which she was driving home with her mother from her job. It was dark. The car suddenly seized up on the motor-way with huge lorries rushing past, The fault appeared to be due to her mother's carelessness, failing to look after the car properly. Her father was called out and rescued them, but 'it took him a long time to get the engine clear and working again', she said, wiping away a tear.

Miss I: dependency without destruction

Miss I was a very different case. Thirty-eight years old, she was not psychotic but had severe personality difficulties. At the first consultation she collapsed on the floor of the interview room, having first vomited over the medical student who was doing a preliminary clerking. I sent her home in a taxi, told her to arrive sober next time and arranged to see her on my own. Rather to my surprise she complied and never to my knowledge came drunk to any of the monthly half-hour sessions that took place over the next nine years.

Miss I was a single woman who had been referred by her female GP with whom she had developed a very intense relationship and who was feeling worried and overwhelmed by her. Her notes contained voluminous correspondence with this GP and also an account of a year-long mental-hospital admission when she was eighteen in which she had formed a very close relationship with a female psychiatrist. More recently she had been admitted to a special unit for patients with personality disorders. She had had a tragic life. Born in Wales, both her parents, who were publicans, had died of alcoholism before she was ten. She was brought up in a Children's Home, was academically bright, had trained as a teacher but had never worked in a school. She supported herself by clerical work. She had never had a sexual relationship with a man or a woman. She was friendly with a professional family, for whom she baby-sat occasionally and with whom she spent Christmas. She was affectionate but envious of them and delighted in their family discords and muddles. She was a large woman who dressed like a neglected eleven-year-old. She carried her belongings around in a Scandinavian rucksack. She saw herself as miserable and desperately in need of help. Her few positive feelings were associated with Sweden. She identified strongly with the playwright August Strindberg, on whose life and work she was an expert. She spoke good Swedish and lived in a hostel where young Swedish girls stayed in England for short visits. How she managed to get a place there was a mystery, but it was a tribute to her persistence and instinct for survival. She was fascinated and threatened by the girls and their confident sexuality.

In her early sessions Miss I was tearful and self-pitying. She demanded to be 'looked after' and 'seen as often as possible'. Together with a social-worker colleague – a mature and very experienced woman – it was arranged to see her regularly.

Thanks mainly to the work of the social worker over a period of a decade, there was a remarkable transformation in her life. Miss I developed a successful career as a writer and journalist. She left the hostel, moved into a small council flat and formed a small circle of friends. She began to look and dress in an adult and more feminine way. Although her sexual life remained barren she was able to relate to men and women in a more confident, straightforward manner.

Perhaps the most important aspect of this treatment, and one which applies to many patients in supportive psychotherapy where progress is so slow and faltering and where the pace of change is, glacier-like, imperceptibly slow, concerned the assumption of a victim-role. Miss I saw herself as a miserable creature, unwanted and rejected by society, one of 'the wretched of the earth'. She hated and envied normal people who, in her eyes, did not know what it was like to suffer. Behind her self-degradation she could be devious, greedy and demanding towards the therapist and others. She justified this on the grounds that it was the basis of her survival and that I would certainly stop seeing her unless she made it impossible for me to do so. She feared that every session would be her last and that she would be replaced by a more deserving case. I began to dread the sessions and indeed did long to discharge her. I tried to link her fear of discharge with her parents' death – but she dismissed this angrily, saying that of course she knew that, but how did it help? I began to feel more and more trapped and helpless and guilty about my wish to reject this unhappy woman. Symington (1986) has written of the 'X-factor' in psychotherapy which represents the inner freedom of the therapist to do or say what he feels, without which therapy becomes frozen and a subtle, mocking form of dependency can take over. As this began to happen with Miss I a way had to be found both to acknowledge her real deprivation *and* to challenge it. She had to be confronted with the view that she was not as helpless as she insisted, to show her how terrified she was of normality. Seeing herself as a freak, an outcast, made her feel safe. Her destructive dependency was very powerful. There was a comfort and familiarity about failure. Envy was so much easier than hope.

Her conviction that I was angry with her and would dismiss her was turned round in a transference interpretation. I suggested it was in fact *she* who was angry with *me*, and that it was her wish to dismiss *me*. My inaccessibility and our infrequent meetings maddened her. She responded to this by saying that it was the fact that I was a *man* she found so difficult and disturbing and she went on from this to discuss the hitherto taboo subject of her sexuality.

In parallel with challenge she was offered real help: a course of antidepressants, a letter to the council about a flat, support for her grant application. At times she resisted progress, insisting that on her salary she could not possibly afford to be normal. Each step forward was a milestone: moving to a flat, buying a dress, acquiring a telephone, taking a holiday, getting a job, buying a word-processor. Progress terrified her: it brought her closer and closer to her real self, further and further from Strindberg. As she became more of a person, she had to face the pain of her real loss: her difficulty in being a woman (it was much easier to persuade herself that she had no gender), her loneliness, her knowledge that she would probably never have children. She found comfort in an article showing that single women had lower mental-illness rates than those who were married and which discussed discrimination against the unmarried in society.

In working with such a patient a balance always has to be struck between the supportive and the psychotherapeutic. Real deprivation has to be acknowledged; self-pity challenged. Sublimatory activity like writing, painting, sending letters to the therapist has to be accepted and encouraged; at the same time the underlying transferential longings at some point have to be brought into the open. Intense dependency will inevitably occur; sufficient distance must be maintained for it not to become destructive of the therapist, the patient or the therapy.

CONCLUSION

Why is supportive psychotherapy such an unsung craft and rarely well taught if at all to young psychiatrists? There are several reasons. First, it is by its very nature prolonged. Outcome studies of patients seen for five years or more are unlikely to be promising research topics for young doctors. Sadly, termination in supportive therapy is more often a result of the therapist leaving or retiring. Second, it can seem superficial, unadventurous, unspectacular work, propping up patients rather than getting to the root of their problems. Third, if it is to be successful, it almost always involves a powerful positive transference with occasional outbursts of rage, both of which, as Kohut (1971) has shown in his work with borderline patients, have initially to be accepted rather than challenged or interpreted. All this places a powerful burden on the therapist's narcissism: he will see little change and may have to accept violent anger and disappointment. Fourth, supportive psychotherapy is about acceptance. The therapist has to learn to accept the patient as he is; to help patients to accept themselves and their reality. Change in supportive psychotherapy is seachange, not instant enlightenment. For all these reasons, supportive psychotherapy is no country for young men. But there can be great rewards from this prolonged contact with severely ill and disadvantaged patients. Psychotherapists are sometimes guilty of creating patients after their own image. Supportive psychotherapy forces an encounter with the differentness, individuality and bravery of the human spirit. The therapeutic task is sometimes to cure, often to relieve, always to comfort. Supportive psychotherapy has to find a middle ground between the attempted cure of analytic psychotherapy and the comfort of pure dependency. Its aim is neither pure cure, nor cosy comfort, but the relief that comes from acknowledgement and acceptance.

Psychotherapists have shied away from supportive psychotherapy, although I suspect it is an important element in what many of them do: they feel it refers to the generality of helping relationships and not to the refinement of them that constitutes their special skill. It has been left, by default, to psychiatrists. I have tried to describe a model of supportive psychotherapy that is applicable in psychiatric settings and yet is dynamic in content: a meeting place for psychodynamic psychiatry and medical psychotherapy.

Chapter 6

The sibling in psychotherapy

THE PSYCHOANALYTIC VIEW: THE SIBLING AS RIVAL OR PARENT SUBSTITUTE

For Freud the central human drama, the 'kernel of the neuroses', was the Oedipal situation (Freud 1916–17). He was aware of the part played by the siblings, but in his writings they are given few lines. When they do appear it is usually as an understudy for one of the parental roles: as a substitute for the longed-for parent, or as another rival for their love.

Freud seemed to view the primary sibling relationship as hostile, only to be 'overlaid' later with affection. He visualised far-reaching effects of this on the personality.

> A child who has been put into second place by the birth of a brother or sister and who is for the first time now almost isolated from his mother does not easily forgive her this loss of place; feelings which in an adult would be described as greatly embittered arise in him and are often the basis of a permanent estrangement.
>
> (Freud 1916)

> The boy may take his sister as a love object by way of substitute for his faithless mother. When there are several brothers all of them courting a younger sister, situations of hostile rivalry, which are so important for later life, arise already in the nursery. A little girl may find in her elder brother a substitute for her father who no longer takes an interest in her as he did in her earliest years. Or she may take a younger sister as a substitute for the baby she vainly wished for from her father.
>
> (Freud 1921)

Subsequent psychoanalysts have generally followed Freud's emphasis on the negative aspects of the sibling relationship, seeing in it a reflection of the child's relationship with his parents. Anna Freud (1969) cites her experience with the Bulldog Bank orphans as the exception which proves the rule. She claims these children showed little evidence of normal sibling rivalry and attributes this to the lack of intimate parental relationships about which to feel rivalrous. Bettleheim (1969) has also maintained that sibling rivalry is inconspicuous in communally raised children.

Anna Freud on the other hand pointed out that hostile and erotic feelings towards siblings are often less repressed than those towards parents, and thus siblings may be 'used for the discharge of libidinal trends deflected from the parents'. She also saw an influence on future character development: 'since contemporaries outside the family are treated like the siblings, these first relationships to the brothers and sisters become important factors in determining the individual's social attitudes' (A. Freud 1969). Fleugel (1921) quotes mythology from Cain to Chronos revealing the unconscious significance of the sibling relationship. He saw the displacement of libido from parents to siblings not as a defensive manoeuvre but as an important part of normal maturation.

Adler: Personality and birth order

Freud remained, to the last, his mother's first son – although he did have two much older half-brothers by his father. Among the early psychoanalytic writers it was Adler, a fourth-born who emphasised the importance of sibling relationships as one of the primary determinants of personality (Ansbacher and Ansbacher 1958). For him, the sibling relationship was an issue in its own right, not merely a screen where the elemental Oedipal triangle could be projected. Adler claimed that personality types could be derived from birth position. According to him, the eldest is the one who has been 'dethroned' by the arrival of the next child: he is the conservative, interested in the past, longing for the good old days, hoping to win parental approval by being a good organiser and protector of the weak; the second-born, never special, always has to contend with feelings of envy and slight; while the youngest, never to be dethroned, is the favoured one, the youngest son of fairy stories who, against all the odds 'gets the fame and the money all at one sitting' (Larkin 1955).

There have been many attempts to put Adler's ideas to the test, mostly based on studies of 'normal' US college students (Warren 1966). The results have generally been equivocal, or contradictory, or both. For example, McArthur (1956) found first-borns were more serious, sensitive and parent-oriented than their placid, easy-going, peer-oriented second-born fellow students; Greenberg et al. (1963), however, found no significant correlation between birth order and personality variables; and there is no correlation between neuroticism score and birth order (Althus 1966). It is noteworthy that the majority of these studies are both male-oriented and success-oriented.

Birth order *per se* is probably not a simple determinant of personality any more than it is of psychiatric illness (Hare and Price 1969). In studies of life events and depression Brown *et al.* (1975) have shown that it is not necessarily the life event itself which leads to breakdown, but its 'contextual meaning' in the microsocial environment of the individual. Similarly, although sibling position is clearly a significant part of the individual's self-experience, it is the *context*, social, familial and psychological, which must determine the effect of such position of his personality or proneness to psychiatric illness.

Child observation studies

Child observation studies are such an attempt to study the microsocial environment: they suggest that there are indeed birth-order related differences in parental handling and child behaviour, and that many of these differences persist over time (Sutton-Smith and Rosenberg 1971); it is not known whether they persist into adult life. According to Waldrop (1965) differences may start even in the neonatal period when, she claims, high 'sibling density' infants (i.e. from close-spaced families) cry and suck less vigorously than others. Mothers interact about twice as much with their first-born at the toddler stage as they do with second-borns. Although at a given age they *expect* first-borns to be more independent, the first child is actually *more* distressed by a short absence of mother from the room than are his younger siblings (Cushna 1966; Gewirtz and Gewirtz 1965).

Lasko (1954) showed how first-borns experience a greater *change* in parental handling than subsequent children: around the time of birth of the second sibling there is a sudden decrease in intensity of interaction, with a changeover from warm positive reinforcement to the use of punishment and prohibition. Second and subsequent children tend to get more consistently warm handling, albeit at a lower intensity. Interpreting these findings, Sutton-Smith and Rosenberg (1971) suggest the first-born is treated as a kind of 'mini-adult' by the beginner mother, who has unrealistic developmental and emotional expectations for her first child, which she then readjusts for her later offspring.

Koch (1955, 1956), in an ambitious study, set out to relate the behaviour of pre-adolescent children in home and school to their sibling position. She found that the intensity of sibling rivalry depends on the age- and sex-gap between siblings: where the age-gap is more than four years, the older child is most jealous of a same-sex sibling; where the gap is less than four years then opposite-sex siblings excite greatest rivalry.

Koch's interpretations of her complex results have been criticised (Brim 1958); they are certainly open to a number of different explanations. A psychoanalytic view of the above might be as follows: if a same-sex baby is born when the older child is in the Oedipal phase – between the ages of three and five – this will be felt by them as a threat to their relationship to the opposite-sex parent and rivalry will be intense. When the gap is narrow and the older child is still in the oral phase, they may then be most threatened by an opposite-sex sibling and come to feel they are the 'wrong' sex, or that they have the 'wrong organ' to get maternal attention. As one of Koch's little interviewees said in reply to the question 'Would you like to be like your new baby brother or sister?', 'Yes, I would; then I could yell my head off and my mamma would take care of nobody but me.'

Looking at personality, Koch found definite sex/positional effects. For example, girls with older brothers tended to be more tomboyish than those with older sisters. Boys with older sisters tended to be more self-confident, less attention-seeking, less aggressive, than those with older brothers. This would follow if parents tend to favour their first boys, who are then able to build their identity as they like, or 'personally', to use Slater's (1961) personal/positional classification. Girls, or second-born boys, on this view, would be tempted to build their identity 'positionally' rather than 'personally', via envy of the favoured sibling's position, or 'identification with the aggressor' (A. Freud 1936).

Child analysis: the sibling as a trigger for regression or maturation

The influence of the sibling relationship on identity formation and its pathology has been noted by many child analysts. Rollman-Branch (1966) suggests that when a new sibling arrives, the older child faces a developmental challenge to which he may react in one of two ways: he may identify with the parent, moving in the direction of greater autonomy and ego-development; or he may identify with the newborn child, leading to regression and loss of independence (Dunn and Kendrick 1982).

Since presumably all non-only children have to face such a challenge, the question remains whether, and under what circumstances, the sibling relationship becomes a significant determinant of psychopathology.

David Levy (1935), a child analyst particularly interested in the subject, maintained that sibling rivalry becomes important only when there is also a disturbed relationship with the mother. He postulates a 'mother, ignorant and emotionally immature who over-indulges her infant, creating excessive dependency on her, and when as a result the child becomes difficult, discards it'. The 'discarded' child may then become excessively rivalrous towards the new arrival who, in his turn, begins to feel guilty about this, and may himself later feel discarded if a further sibling is born. Klein (1969) said of such youngest children:

> Youngest and only children often have a strong sense of guilt because they feel their jealous and aggressive feelings have prevented their mother from giving birth to any more children. I have frequently found that fear and suspicion of schoolmates or of other children were linked with phantasies that the unborn brothers and sisters had after all come alive, and were

represented by any children who appeared hostile. The longing for friendly brothers and sisters is strongly influenced by such anxieties.

THE SIBLING RELATIONSHIP IN CLINICAL PRACTICE

Psychoanalytic observation and child-observation studies have suggested that the sibling relationship may influence the adult personality in a number of different ways: the birth of a sibling may become a 'fixation point'; there may be effects on character formation and sexual identity; and the sibling relationship may be intricately linked with the Oedipal situation. I shall now try to exemplify these points with cases taken from once- or twice-weekly out-patient NHS psychotherapy practice (cf. Kahn and Lewis 1988).

The birth of a sibling as a fixation point

Feelings aroused at the time of birth of a sibling may become a focus around which neurosis is organized in adult life. The birth of a child or an abortion may reactivate emotions from this period.

Case 1 was a young woman whose symptoms of recurrent depression, and her inability to sustain relationships with men, dated from an illegal abortion some years before, in which she had become ill with a uterine infection and had to go into hospital. At the time she thought that she was dying. She had never felt fully herself since. She was the older of two sisters: the younger was her mother's favourite. The patient had turned to father, but when she was eight, he had died. She described her guilt and depression about the abortion; she then linked this to the wish that her mother had never had her sister and her envious anger at her sister for taking her mother away from her. She made a link between her abortion and her childhood wish that her sister would die. Illness and depression were her punishment.

Comment

The pregnancy and abortion acted as a seed around which her sibling jealousy crystallised. In this were condensed her murderous feelings towards the younger sister; her guilt about this; self-punishment in an attempt at expiation; the reparative implication of pregnancy; envy of her mother's capacity to have intercourse with her father and produce children; and sadness at the loss of her father. Sibling jealousy was the thread on which she could hang these many feelings.

Abraham (1924) claims that one of the precursors of adult depression is 'a severe injury to infantile narcissism brought about by disappointments in love', and cites the birth of a sibling as one such possible disappointment. The next case exemplifies this.

Case 2 was a markedly depressed young man. He felt that life had never been fair to him: he had always got the worst of things, the worst jobs, the worst girls. Everyone was better off than he. In the course of treatment he recalled that these feelings had started with the birth of his sister when he was three. After she was born everything was different. All the attention went to her, father loved her, no one put pressure on *her* to do well at school and made her life a misery as his was.

After the session in which he had recalled these feelings, he dreamed that he stabbed his sister with a long knife pushed through a letter box, and was then arrested for killing some 'old folks'.

Comment

In the dream, sexual and aggressive impulses towards the sibling are explicit (cf. Chapter 2), while the parents are only dimly present as 'old folks'. The sibling relationship may be accessible to consciousness, while the underlying Oedipal structure is still buried.

The sibling relationship in identity formation

Patients with character disorders form an increasing proportion of psychotherapeutic practice, and the influence of the sibling relationship on the psychopathology of such patients will now be discussed.

Lewin (1951) described the 'oral triad' of mother, baby-at-the-breast, and watching older sibling. The older sibling may feel excluded, and enjoys the excitement vicariously by identifying with one or other pole of the mother–child dyad. Where the envied sibling is of the opposite sex there may be an envious cross-sex identification. This paradigm is exemplified by the next two cases.

Case 3 was a man who became depressed when his divorced wife refused him access to their daughter on the grounds that he was homosexual. He was the oldest child, with two younger sisters, one only a year younger than he.

He described the family scenario: his mother preferred his sisters; his parents did not get on; his father rejected him; the only person he felt close to was his sister; the only way to get love in the home was to be a girl; even now, he and his sister are so close that when he feels suicidal he imagines she must too. Being homosexual was being 'like a girl' and so being liked like a girl, as his sister was.

Case 4 was a young woman who presented with depression. She was the only girl among three boys. Her parents did not get on; her father was a drunkard; her mother preferred the boys; at the age of five she said to herself 'I don't belong to this family', imagining that she was adopted, and disowning her mother. She started to rock herself to sleep every night, thus 'becoming' her own mother. The only happy memories of childhood were when she was out in the woods with her father, climbing trees, when she performed more daring exploits than her brothers. Her depression started at puberty, when perforce she had to give up her phantasy of being a boy.

Comment

In the oral triad the watcher is estranged from his true identity, identifying instead with the envied sibling, or mother, or both at different times. In Case 4, the patient tried first to 'be' her brothers (climbing trees) then at puberty switched to 'being' the mother she felt angry with for preferring the brothers, i.e. a useless mother. Both patients became depressed when they could no longer maintain a phantasy identification with the opposite sex which flew too blatantly in the face of reality. In Case 3 the patient was confronted at his divorce with the fact that he was not really a 'mother' to his daughter. In both cases it seemed that the father was not available as an alternative reliable source of love for the child who felt their mother was preoccupied with the other siblings. Thus the role of the father may be crucial in facilitating adjustment to sibship. Progress in therapy seemed to depend on the therapist providing a safe base from which the patient could deal with their feelings of sibling rivalry.

The Argentinian peasant mother says to the whiny displaced older child 'Go suck your father's testicles' (Levy 1939). If a father, or grandparent, is not available at this time the older child may remain psychologically trapped in the oral triad long after the younger sibling has been weaned from it.

The sibling relationship as a key to the Oedipal situation

In the next case I shall try to show how understanding the sibling relationship provided the key which unlocked some of the core psychopathology as treatment progressed.

Case 5 was a young man in his early thirties. He was severely obsessional; he had great difficulty in separating from his parents; he had never had sexual intercourse; he had powerful sado-masochistic phantasies in which he was alternately tied up and beaten by, and tied up and beat, an older man. He had one sister, three years older than he.

He described himself as a complete 'failure': he had gone into the same profession as his father, but could never hope to rival his eminence in it; he was a failure with girls. His father had married a former beauty-queen, how could he hope ever to marry someone like that? He denied any rivalrous feelings towards his father, who he said was a kind man who helped him in every possible way, even though he was such a disappointment to him. In the transference he reproduced his relationship with his father, making constant efforts to please the therapist by applying for new jobs, taking girls out, but the end was always the same: a failure. At this point he would turn triumphantly to the therapist and say 'What did I tell you? I'm a failure. Why don't you get rid of me and take on a patient who will be a success?'

When asked his phantasies about this hypothetical patient, she turned out to be a woman, a little older than himself, rather like ... his sister.

This phantasy unlocked a flood of material about his sister: she was their father's favourite, she always sat next to him at table, she could do no wrong. As a child he used to get into her bed when he felt frightened and at the start of his depression he had felt intense sexual desire for her.

In the next session he brought a dream, the first in the therapy: he was taking a girl home to meet his parents; the four of them sat round the dinner table, mother and father, he and the girl; he looked at her and suddenly saw she was so ugly she would never be acceptable to them. He said the dream showed how he wanted to be close to his father, but his 'sister' (the girl) was there sitting next to him, how envious he felt of her, and how this made her ugly in his eyes.

He suddenly saw that the girl was like every girl he had been attracted to: they all had qualities which he envied. Then he revealed how he then had compulsively to find something wrong with them. At this point he started to feel angry at his father for making him feel that his sister was better than he. He finally accepted the often-repeated interpretation that his self-punishing 'failure' was a reproach to his father for this as well as a punishment for having these ungrateful angry feelings.

Comment

The movement here was from 'I am unsuccessful with girls' through 'I am only attracted to girls whom I envy' to 'I envy my sister's position *vis-à-vis* my father'. At this point the underlying father-sister-self triangle was uncovered. He was unable to make this movement until he could face his sibling rivalry. This fits with Beiber *et al*.'s (1962) finding, in a study of the psychotherapy of homosexuality, that a good prognosis was associated with an ability to acknowledge sibling rivalry.

The sibling relationship in therapy

In the last example I want to show how sibling rivalry reached near-psychotic intensity in the treatment of a depressed patient with a severe schizoid personality disorder (who later developed a frank schizophrenic illness), and how understanding this helped in the minute-by-minute maze of her sessions.

Case 6 was a woman in her middle thirties who presented with depression. She dressed and behaved for the most part like a small child. She had lived alone for most of her adult life. The only beings she loved were her two cats. If only cats could talk, she said, she would be perfectly happy.

Her sister was two years younger. Soon after she was born their mother left home and they were brought up together in institutions and with relatives. She stated that she had 'no' childhood and had been 'given away' by her mother.

I shall now describe two consecutive sessions.

In the first she started by talking about cats. How was my cat? Did it miss me while I was at work? Her cats got jealous of one another: the older one pushed the younger one off her bed where they slept.

Then she drew a picture. It showed a house, divided down the middle. In each half there was a female figure, and a clock. The figure on the left was young and pretty, the clock showed three o'clock; the figure on the right was old and untidy, the clock showed four o'clock. Her comment was 'This shows how you can grow old in an hour.'

Then she became quiet and lethargic. She tried to draw again, but couldn't. 'What do other people draw?' she asked. Then she showed me her bag. It had been given to her by a friend, a fellow-student from college days. This girl had invited her to her art exhibition but the patient couldn't go. 'I just couldn't bear it, it wasn't like ordinary jealousy.'

Now it was time to stop. Do the 'others' mind if she comes again next time? (She asks this often.) She rang later in the day and asked: 'Could I come and sit in your room, not to disturb you?'

Comment

This session is saturated with the feeling of sibling jealousy. The older cat is jealous of the younger one. She is worried about my cats: are they jealous of her? When her sister was born she had to 'grow old in an hour'. Her anger made her grow ugly. She felt unwanted. The only hope was to find what 'other' people drew, to imitate them; but it is impossible, her jealousy is so strong she can't bear to look at her friend's pictures. Leaving me means being replaced by 'others'; she rings later to check if a rival is with me.

The next session starts with her apologising for ringing me. She felt so alone: she has been alone all her life. 'My mother didn't like children.' She draws a picture: a large voluptuous reclining female figure; below is a smaller, frightened-looking female.

Then comes an early memory. She had to have her photograph taken. She was frightened of going into the dark room; a man gave her a doll to comfort her. After the picture was taken she had to give it back. This made her cry. She commented: when her sister was born she was 'given away' like that by her mother.

She remembers how her mouth used to hurt when her teeth came in: how she used to bite the other children at school. 'You wouldn't believe it now, but I was a real terror at school.' Once she tried to kill another child.

It is near the end of the session. Do I really want to see her next week? It is such a long time to wait. Nothing happens in between.

Comment

In this session she shows her feeling that her mother betrayed her by bringing a rival into the world. She had to give her mother 'back' like the doll in the memory. She felt murderous towards the rival: she could bite and scratch – like a cat perhaps. She can get mother back by being mother to her little cats. Sometimes she can imagine me as her mother, but the illusion is shattered by the end of the session when I 'give her away'. 'Nothing' happened between sessions, just as she had 'no' childhood. She has built her life around this denial of the painful reality of being a sibling.

DISCUSSION

At the core of the sibling relationship is an ambivalence: the paradox of rivalrous allegiance of two children to the same parents. As Hopkins (1953) put it: 'Abel is Cain's brother and breasts they have sucked the same'; or, in Freud's formulation: 'each of us wants to be the favourite; the older child would like to eliminate his successor, to rob it of his privileges. At the same time he recognises that his rival is equally loved by his parents; he cannot destroy him without destroying himself' (Freud 1921).

This rather grim view of the sibling relationship runs through the psycho-analytic canon. But there is a positive side: if the 'belly of the mother is the universe of the infant' (Klein 1969) then to be a sibling is to find one is not alone in the universe. Acceptance of siblings seems to be associated with health, and coming to this acceptance an important ingredient in treatment. A preliminary to this, however, may be the acknowledgement of feelings of sibling rivalry.

Thus, the arrival of a sibling, whether in reality for the first-born, or psychologically, in the developing consciousness of the later-born, presents the child with a developmental challenge. The child has to accept that he or she is not the sole object of parental love, but that love has to be shared with others. The child's earliest emotions centre on the parents. When siblings arrive the situation changes: he is now for the first time faced with an equal towards whom he has mixed feelings.

The child may deal with hostile impulses towards his equal in a number of different ways. There may be open hostility, with remarks such as 'Why don't they send the baby back to the shop?'; the hostility may be directed towards himself, when he becomes whiny and miserable or withdrawn; or the child may deny the reality of the newcomer altogether, ignoring him or pretending that he doesn't exist.

Other children may want to play with their new sibling at once and feel furious at their unresponsiveness. The child may cope with hostile feelings by regressive identification: with temporary bedwetting, for example. Finally, the child may deal with his rivalry by becoming a 'little mother' to the baby, helping with nappy-changing and feeding.

These reactions are probably seen transiently in all children (Sturge 1977). Which of them predominates and whether or not they remain in the child's character, may depend on the family context in which they occur (Dunn 1985).

How can we characterise this context? Parsons and Bales (1955) have pointed out that entry into the Oedipal phase involves moving from a two- to a four-body system, not to a three-body system as it is usually construed. As the child becomes aware of his parents as separate entities, and of the differing roles of his father and his mother, simultaneously he becomes aware of the fact of sexual differentiation among children: his gender is his destiny and he or she is a little boy or a little girl and cannot be both. As Freud (1916) puts it 'When other children appear on the scene the Oedipus complex is enlarged into a family complex.'

The world at this stage can be divided 'vertically' into males and females, and 'horizontally' into parents and children. This gives a four-way matrix with which the child can categorise himself and his family. This matrix contains the Oedipal triangle of mother-father-child, but also two more triangles: mother-sib-child and father-sib-child. Each of these can be 'positive' or 'negative' (Freud 1923), loving or hating, and each interlocks with the others (cf. Malan 1979).

The predominant mode of the sibling relationship depends on this four-way matrix and its vicissitudes. A range of environmental constellations can be imagined. A crucial factor may be the availability of the father. Thus he may be physically absent, or angry at his wife's preoccupation with the new baby, or he may vent his feelings on the other child who has turned to him. Conversely he may mediate between the displaced child and his newly preoccupied wife – after all they are both in the same boat. The mother may be able to relate easily to only one child at a time, thus fostering feelings of exclusion in the others. She may sexualise her relationship with the infant, encouraging an envious cross-sex identification in the older child. She may favour older children, which may lead to self-denigratory or depressive feelings in the younger ones, especially if they are of the opposite sex. On the other hand she may have the happy knack both of being able to respond to her children's individual needs and of maintaining a balance in the whole family so that those needs can best be met.

Where one child is handicapped or exceptional, there are important reverberations throughout their sibship. Their brothers and sisters frequently feel neglected and may experience intense guilt at their own hostile reactions to their disadvantaged sibs – they may imagine themselves responsible for the handicap. Excessive guilt, or even hysterical reactions modelled on the sibling illness, may follow in later life.

Finally grandparents, like fathers, may play a vital role in helping families to adjust to a new member. The older children may be handed over to their grandparents and so for a while enjoy the advantages and disadvantages of the grandparental relationship. This is often a unique blend of indulgence and conflict-free love, together with a lack of the normal intensity of parent-child feelings.

The grandparent is often a focal point in the family network and the child may feel – through contact with other family members via his grandparent – an enrichment that more than compensates for his lost sense of specialness. But if the 'handing over' is felt to be irreversible and the child feels he has lost his parent for ever, however loving the grandparent, there may be an enduring sense of loss.

Family growth links through the sibling relationship with the growth of the individual. Here the family matrix offers the growing child a chance to develop a sense of equality and an ability to share; it is also at this critical point that family difficulties may be internalised as individual pathology.

Part II

Individuals and families

Individuals and families
An introduction

Anyone trying to practise psychotherapeutic psychiatry will find that no one model or method of therapy is sufficient to meet the needs of the variety of patients and their problems which are presented to him. Family and marital therapy are in my view an essential part of the repertoire of any psychiatrist. The three essays in this section are attempts to understand how systemic and analytic therapy overlap and diverge, both in practice and theory. The first is a theoretical overview of the problem. The second takes one of Freud's classic cases – Dora – and looks at it from a family-therapy perspective. The third takes the common psychiatric disorder of agoraphobia. It tries to show how the analytic and systemic viewpoints can be combined into a unified theory, and how in such cases brief marital therapy sessions can have positive results.

Chapter 7

Family and individual therapy
Comparisons and contrasts

It is one of the paradoxes of psychotherapy that although most practitioners are fierce champions of their own particular approach or school, there is no firm evidence that any one method is more effective overall than any other. It seems, rather, that psychotherapy is a Caucus race in which as Luborsky and Singer (1975) have put it, quoting Frank quoting Carroll, 'everyone has won and all must have prizes'.

This alerts us to four important themes. First, the notion of winning or losing has to be radically revised in the face of psychotherapeutic values – the substitution of 'ordinary human misery' for neurosis recommended by Freud (1916–17) is a long way from 'winning' in the Olympic sense. Second, it emphasises the importance of 'unconditional positive regard' ('all shall have prizes') as an essential element in any psychotherapeutic endeavour. Third, it points to the centrality of paradox in psychotherapy – a theme which runs throughout this book. Finally, it should not be forgotten that it was the Dodo which gave out the prizes at the Caucus race; it is still uncertain whether NHS psychotherapy will, like the Dodo, become extinct, as some of its critics apparently wish (Shepherd 1984; Medawar 1984); or whether (as seems more likely) it will, like hysteria, outlive its obituarists (cf. Chapter 15).

The aim of this chapter is to compare two very different modes of psychotherapy – individual analytical and family therapy. Although I see them as separate and autonomous disciplines, each with its own interests and therapeutic power, I shall try to show how their differences are often more apparent than real and to look for areas of overlap and similarity. A central objective is to find a theory of change that applies to both. A secondary aim is to find a framework within which to consider their indications and contraindications.

Some discussion of definitions is necessary. The terms 'individual' and 'family' therapy refer simultaneously to a practical arrangement and to a theoretical approach. By individual *psychotherapy* I mean primarily dynamic or analytically-orientated therapy – derived from psychoanalysis, with a central focus on the unconscious as the arena of therapy and transference as the vehicle of change. *Family therapy* is harder to define. Madanes and Haley (1977) have differentiated at least seven approaches, ranging from behavioural to psychodynamic, through 'systemic' and 'strategic' techniques that are more unique to family therapy. It is perhaps best seen as an overall approach in which the family itself is the object of interest, a movement away from the atomic individual to molecular patterns of interaction in the family as a whole.

The family is a 'system', a term borrowed from cybernetics, and one that is also hard to define in a way that is both useful and succinct. Hall and Fagan (1956) define a system as a 'set of objects together with the relationships between the objects and their attributes'. This, as it stands, may not seem very illuminating, but its emphasis on relationships and its focus on 'objects' (i.e. family members) as a set, rather than individuals, are the key issues for family therapy. The great advantage of seeing the family as a 'system' is that a number of known properties and functions of systems – boundaries, subsystems, hierarchy, openness or closedness, homeostasis, and non-summativity (i.e. the sum being greater than the parts) – can then be applied to family patterns and pathology. It is worth noting that almost anything, including an individual or the 'unconscious mind' could be seen as a system. Finally, 'paradox' is defined by the OED as a 'seemingly absurd but perhaps well-founded statement'. This chapter could be seen as an exploration of absurdity and its foundations in relationship to two forms of therapy.

CHANGE

Despite a considerable literature, it is still not known how psychotherapy brings about change. Although it is likely that the helpful elements in any therapy are much less specific than its practitioners like to believe, both analytical and family therapists have tried to isolate out the 'mutative' elements in their work, and I shall now consider these.

Within family therapy, the most influential force has undoubtedly been Gregory Bateson and his followers – the Palo Alto group (Bateson 1973; Watzlawick *et al.* 1967). In their view, the aim of psychological methods of treatment is a change of frame or context within which the symptom is viewed. They follow Epictetus: 'Men are disturbed not by things, but by the view which they take of them' (Barker 1983). This approach is inherently paradoxical. It suggests that if you say to someone that reality cannot be altered, but your way of looking at it can, then change will follow. Although the Batesonian view of change is cognitive rather than affective, this fits well with Freud's archaeological metaphor (1916–17); in this, he compared psychoanalysis to the disinterring of buried remains, which in the unconscious appear huge and terrifying, but seen in the light of day shrink down to mere remnants of a past era.

Simply saying to a patient or family that they should look at their problems in a different light is unlikely to produce change. Both psychoanalysis and family therapy postulate built-in mechanisms which maintain the status quo: resistance or homeostasis. The techniques of therapy are designed to overcome these mechanisms, which Watzlawick called 'therapeutic double binds' – the patient is put in a situation in which they cannot *not* change. The most extreme example of this is the technique of 'prescribing the symptom', in which the patient is instructed to maintain his/her symptom – depression or anorexic behaviour, for instance – often with the accompanying explanation that by doing so, he will bring benefit through his own suffering and self-sacrifice to other members of the family (Palazzoli *et al.* 1978). According to the theory, this will lead to change whatever happens. Either the patient follows the instruction, in which case he will have (a) shown that he has some control over his symptom and (b) implicitly accepted the authority of the therapist rather than that of the illness, *or* he will disobey the instruction, and so will have (a) demonstrated some presumable desirable autonomy and (b) been relieved of the symptoms which led him to seek help.

An important element in the double-bind hypothesis is the condition that the subject is 'held' in the situation, or as Bateson put it (1973): 'cannot leave the field'. Jackson and Haley (1963) have tried to apply the therapeutic double-bind theory to psychoanalysis; they see therapy as a situation where the patient is 'held' and subjected to the 'be spontaneous paradox'. An example of this would be the patient who in his first psychoanalytical session, when told of Freud's 'basic rule' (i.e. say everything that comes into your mind however embarrassing or irrelevant), replied 'If I could do that, I would not need to be here in the first place.' When the patient *is* able to achieve the basic rule, he would therefore no longer need therapy. As Hans Sachs said (Watzlawick *et al.* 1967): 'Therapy comes to an end when the patient realises that it could go on for ever.' This approach can be extended by seeing the analyst as a kind of Zen Master (Watts 1961) who sets his patient impossible tasks, such as 'Find the sound of one hand clapping,' which lead eventually to cure, or enlightenment, when the patient realises that there is no 'answer' and that he can be responsible for his own life, not needing to depend on a parental analyst or guru.

Although such anti-analytical analysis is witty and not without a grain of truth, this approach does not really take us to the heart of analytical therapy. Here, Strachey's classical formulation (1934) of the 'mutative interpretation' still holds sway after half a century (Sandler *et al.* 1973; Malan 1979); he saw the key change-producing interpretation as one that brings together the present relationship with the therapist, the patient's external 'problem' or situation, and the early childhood relationship, usually with the parents. The analyst's imaginative capacity to link together these three apparently heterogeneous elements into one coherent pattern is the core of his work. The analyst has simultaneously to enable a living, affectively-charged relationship with the patient to develop, and be detached enough to interpret it.

There are two steps involved in this process. First, the symptom – the 'external' problem – has to be seen in a new context; this is the context of the unconscious – the childhood conflict of which the patient is unaware, which nevertheless invisibly shapes his destiny. Second, this unconscious context is made manifest in the transference, which conjures up the past in a metaphorical and so controllable way. Transference makes the reality of unconscious determination an inescapable fact for the patient.

This more profound view of how change comes about in analytical therapy is still compatible with the Watzlawick model. Analytical change does involve a 'change of frame'; the patient learns in therapy to differentiate past and present, phantasy and reality, unconscious and conscious, body and thought, and to render unto each that which is appropriate to each. Change does come about through paradox, in that it involves a 'real' relationship with a therapist that is laden with the unconscious 'fictions' or transference. To these, psychoanalysis adds two further elements: the need for an active transferential therapeutic experience, if change is to take place, intellectual insight alone not being enough (neither necessary nor sufficient); and the view that the central arena of change is in the unconscious – in those parts of himself of which the patient is mostly unaware and where primary processes predominate. These two elements are also to be found, albeit translated into systems language, in family therapy.

Family therapists would agree with the analytical emphasis on the importance of a living therapeutic experience, which Minuchin (1974) has called 'enactment'. The family do not merely describe their problem – they demonstrate it, as the family interactions unfold themselves before the therapist. A warring couple will row in the session, if necessary, before their differences can be resolved. A seductive and husband-undermining woman will exchange glances of exasperation with her son every time her husband speaks. In these living minutiae can be found, holographically (Cooklin 1982), a microcosm of the total family pattern of relationships.

The concept of the unconscious is the hallmark of analytical therapy and one that family therapists, especially those with behaviourist leanings, have done their best to expunge. There are, however, important parallels between the concepts of the 'system' and the unconscious, both in the part they play in the theoretical structure of the two therapies and in their formal properties.

Both system and unconscious are of a higher 'logical type' than the symptom, i.e. each provides a wider context within which the apparently incomprehensible symptom makes sense. An unconscious fear of paternal disapproval ('castration anxiety') might be seen analytically to account for repeated self-sabotage ('fear of success') in adult life, while 'a systemic need' for 'distance regulation' (Byng-Hall 1980) which simultaneously keeps parents apart and holds them together may explain disturbed behaviour in a child.

In both, system and unconscious provide an explanatory concept to which the illness is referred; each represents a reservoir of past experiences and present influence which mould the patient and of which he is unaware. Power is seen to reside not in the individual, but in the impersonal force of the system or the unconscious: the sick individual is trapped in illness by forces over which he has no control. Both theories hypothesise that a direct attempt at influencing the unconscious or system may be futile. Cure will involve a rearrangement of the relationship so that the individual and unconscious or system are working harmoniously. As Freud saw it, the unconscious is a horse which the conscious rider has to control sometimes by giving it its head.

The paradoxical prescriptions of the Milan group, in which an anorexic or psychotic child is told to continue to sacrifice himself in order, say, to remind the family of a dead grandfather who is in danger of being forgotten (Palazzoli *et al.* 1978) also contain the idea that change is more likely to occur by recognising the strength of the opposing forces than by direct confrontation. By referring symptoms to the impersonal 'not-I' of system or unconscious, both family and individual therapy eliminate the guilt which so often accompanies psychiatric disturbance: or rather they redirect it from the destructive self-referential guilt of neurosis to a reparative guilt, at having inauthentically avoided one's biological destiny and human responsibility.

The impersonality of system and unconscious allow the coexistence of opposites; as Freud put it, the unconscious knows no negatives: in it love and hate can coexist. The system, too, contains apparent incompatibles. Silverstein and Papp (Papp 1976) have developed a technique of therapy in which finely poised alternative interpretations are offered by each therapist, leaving the family free to choose which they accept. Just as analytical therapy opens up to the patient the range of forces within him of which he had been unaware and against which he is defended, so this technique reveals to the family members a wider spectrum of possibilities and roles than had seemed possible in their dysfunction. Both system and unconscious widen the range of choices, but neither therapy will choose for the patient; widened choice means more autonomy – an escape from the traps (Ryle 1982) with which the patient and family presented themselves.

The Batesonian attempt to 'go one meta-' over psychoanalysis by translating analytical procedures into therapeutic double binds can be accepted as possibly true; the notion of the system also owes much to and is in many ways similar to that of the unconscious – the system might even be seen as an 'inside out' unconscious.

DIRECTION AND REFLECTION: CLINICAL EXAMPLES

Although there are some clear similarities between the formal theoretical properties of the unconscious and the system, as therapies they appear very different. Family-therapy techniques are designed to act on the system, in a directive way, while psychoanalysis appears rather to reflect on the un-conscious. This polarity in treatment approaches is well established and has been described many times, for example as a dichotomy between 'directive' and 'exploratory' theory (Shapiro 1981) or between 'doing to' and 'being with' the patient (Wolff 1972). It may also be related to Piaget's (1954) accommodation/assimilation dichotomy, which he sees as fundamental to all developmental processes. Action, like accommodation, involves visible modelling and moulding between environment and organism; reflection, like assimilation, has to do with an invisible change of internal structures. Both are required for change. The interplay between the two therapeutic modes may be illustrated by the following clinical example.

A divorced woman with three small children asked her GP for a psychiatric appointment for her boyfriend (this 'A asks for an appointment on B's behalf' constitutes an indication for conjoint rather than individual therapy). They were seen together. Their problem was that they were fond of each other; they got on well in almost every respect, and had been on the point of marriage several times. But whenever the wedding day ap-proached, he became beset with doubts and depression and insisted that they call it off: they had cancelled the wedding three times. What was surprising to them was that in every other area of his life, he was strong and decisive.

An initial intervention was in the interpretive, reflective mood. It was suggested that his depression had to do not with his intended marriage, but with the death of his mother which had occurred two years before and which had been followed in a very short time by his father's remarriage to a young widow who herself had, like his fiancée, three sons still at home. His difficulty in deciding whether or not to marry, it was suggested, reflected his grief at his mother's death, his unconscious guilt at wishing to find a substitute for his dead mother in his present girlfriend (whose oldest son had the same name as his own), and his Oedipal rivalry with his too-rapidly-remarrying father.

These comments were linked with and derived from tiny transferential elements of rivalry with the therapist, including openly expressed scep-ticism about the value of therapy, to which he had been dragged somewhat reluctantly by his girlfriend. This linked too with his evident pleasure but ambivalence about his outstanding academic gifts, his difficulty in deciding on a stable career, and his recurrent disappointment in tutors and bosses whom he sought as gods but found as mortals.

The impact of these comments was hard to determine. The doubts continued and the pressure on the therapist to suggest some course of action other than reflection intensified. At this point, a different tack was tried, linking his doubts with the girlfriend's problems. It was suggested that his difficulties must be important in some way to their relationship:

she had had a very hard time, with a broken marriage and bringing up three children on her own. It was important for her to feel decisive and competent and not to doubt her own capacity to make a stable relationship with a man. By 'carrying' all the indecision and depression, it was suggested, he was helping her to feel strong and continuing to do so was probably as an expression of his love for her.

Rapid change followed. He changed his job for a better one, they married – to their apparent mutual satisfaction – and decided they no longer needed therapy. There was, however, an interesting sequel. Some eighteen months later, they again made contact and asked for help. They said that their marriage was basically strong; they had had a baby, now four months old, but the wife – who had originally asked for help – had now become badly depressed. This was leading to escalating rows between them, which they both found very upsetting. She complained that he had become just like his father, expecting her to be a subservient wife and to suppress her autonomy. He complained of her irrational angry outbursts.

On this occasion, the therapy centred on the wife – who had originally asked for help for her husband. The rebellious, depressed part of her that had been suppressed in a rigid religious upbringing as an (unwanted) late last child finally surfaced within this marriage, which gave her the security to express her needs but lacked the flexibility to meet them. It was decided to refer her for individual therapy, but, once again, active directive intervention was needed to defuse the escalating rows and to help the couple to find common ground where they could be together without the demands of the children. When they presented originally, the wife had appeared the stronger and the therapist had sided with the husband by suggesting to him that his depression was his way of helping his wife; the wife was now 'down'.

In an attempt directively to reverse this, it was suggested that she had an 'unfair advantage' over her husband, whose first marriage and first experience of parenthood it was. She must expect him to find it difficult to adjust and make it her task to help him to live in a family and to survive.

This is an example of how family-therapy techniques can deal often rapidly and effectively with crises in relationships, but how underlying and long-standing difficulties may remain untouched. The initial period of therapy might have been seen as success, had the self-chosen 'follow-up' not happened. The distinction between active and reflective techniques illustrated here suggests that family therapy does not necessarily promote the understanding and hence the change of internal mental structures that is required to sustain long-term benefit. Watzlawick *et al.* (1967) has called these two models 'first-order' and 'second-order' change. The first might be likened to Freud's concept of transference neurosis. Here the patient loses his symptoms in the early phase of therapy, only to replace them with a pathological dependence on the therapist which, if threatened, will lead to the re-emergence of the illness.

I have implied that family therapy can be equated with action, crisis, and first-order change; analytical therapy with reflection, second-order change and long-term development. Although there may be some rather obvious truth in this, the distinction is far from simple. The 'directives' of paradoxical therapy often prohibit change, with the aim of promoting it. The paradoxical message often contains quasi-analytical understanding of the problem (the case described above could easily be seen in terms of mutual projective identification), but phrased in action-language. Similarly, the reflections of analytical therapy are implicitly designed to promote change; the structural arrangements of therapy – a commitment to regular and prolonged treatment – constitute active direction of the patient's life. Khan (1983) gives some interesting examples of the structural arrangements that he insists on before working analytically with his group of privileged but disturbed young people: for example, making regular attendance at school a precondition of undertaking analytical therapy and giving the parent the task of enforcing this.

In general, one can say that the active and reflective elements are present in both (probably all) psychotherapeutic techniques, but that the proportion and sequence with which they are applied varies with different therapies. Three other brief examples may illustrate this.

Active techniques are often an essential preliminary to reflection. In family therapy, for instance, it is inappropriate to try to explore family dynamics while a disturbed teenager is tearing the house apart: some degree of parental control has first to be established.

> In a joint referral, a depressed mother and a delinquent fifteen-year-old girl were presented. The family's main complaint was about this girl, who was often out all night, got into violent rows with her mother and fights with her father, used the telephone all day long, and played loud music in her bedroom while her parents were trying to rest. A paradoxical suggestion that her behaviour was an attempt to help her mother by showing her that she was not going to be depressed and was determined to have a good time produced just enough reduction in chaos for it to be established that both parents had been so confused in their adolescence – the mother by strict, puritanical, elderly parents, the father by a liberal *laissez-faire* regime – that both felt too guilty to impose discipline on their children or to allow themselves some enjoyment.

A fundamental tenet of analytical therapy is the translation of feelings and actions into words: understanding has to substitute for action. This, as Freud saw it, was the great trade-off required by civilisation – instinctual satis-faction (action) is renounced, to be replaced by thought. The child defers satisfaction, but gains an inner world of imagination, plan, structure; the *word* is the prize the child acquires in this struggle for development. In the Kleinian view, 'the depressive position' characterises this heroic renunciation that admits us to humanity; in exchange for a split and persecutory world of instinctive and immediate gratification, we may achieve wholeness and concern. In one sense, neurosis may be seen as a reversal or protest against this process. In therapy, the patient has to be led away from action to reflection, but, ultimately, the need for action returns. Psychoanalysis assumes that a change in internal structure will lead to effective action, just as directive therapies assume that a change in behaviour will produce internal (and so lasting) change.

After two years of weekly analytical psychotherapy, a thirty-five-year-old man – who had presented with a cardiac neurosis apparently precipitated by a severe illness in his mother – became engaged. As the wedding-day approached, he became more and more preoccupied by his inability to tell his fiancée that he was in therapy, having concealed this fact from everyone – almost from himself. The action of entering therapy and the need to tell his fiancée were structural facts, which lacked internal representation. Both were linked with a fear of being thought abnormal and with his intense jealousy of her previous boyfriends. This led to a retaliatory concealment of his secret relationship with the therapist. All this connected with his intense jealousy of his one-year-older sister and guilt about his collusive and father-excluding secret attachment to his mother. Only when he understood these connections would he be able to act on them by telling his fiancée that he was in therapy.

Paradoxically, directive approaches are by no means confined to family therapy, but are also to be found, often unobtrusively, within the analytical literature.

Freud's Dora (1905), whose case will be discussed in more detail in the next chapter, was an adolescent who found great difficulty in leaving home. This was partly because of her great love for her father and for her father's mistress's husband, Herr K. Freud 'cured' her after only three months in therapy, when he suggested that she should marry Herr K, who would have to divorce his wife to do so, thus leaving her father free to marry Frau K; in Freud's words, 'this would be the best solution for all the parties concerned'. This paradoxical direction seemed to have done the trick. Within a year, Dora had left home and was married to a suitable young man. The fact that this directive phase of therapy – this 'fragment' – was not followed by a reflective one, may account for the sad fact that at 'follow up' twenty years later (Deutsch 1957), Dora was as neurotic as before and as deeply, and unplayfully, involved with her teenage son as she had been with her father.

PLAY

Both family therapy – in so far as it is not exclusively behavioural – and individual analytical therapy approach symptoms indirectly. Both assume that as therapy proceeds, symptoms will disappear from prominence, to be replaced by unconscious or systemic issues. When this does not happen, it is usually a sign that the treatment is not going well.

In both forms of treatment, the client (patient or family) approaches the therapist expecting a solution to his/its problem, but what they are offered instead is a new problem – that of therapy. In individual therapy it is the therapist who becomes the object of interest, rather than the symptom; in family therapy it is the family itself. It is only when the patient begins to take an interest in the therapist – to wonder why they are always seen at such-and-such a time, what the therapist's other patients are like, whether he/she is married, to wish they could meet for a drink, – that mutative therapy in the Stracheyan sense can really begin. In family therapy the process is reversed, but the effect is the same. It is when the family forget about the therapist and begin to interact among themselves, when the children begin to play and the parents to argue, rather than woodenly sitting and waiting for questions from the therapist, that the symptom slips away and the therapist can begin to reintroduce himself as an agent of change. This replacement of the problem by the 'non-problem', which in group therapy gradually takes over as a patient becomes assimilated, more interested in the life of the group itself and less in his own particular difficulties, has been described by Garland (1982). To take an analogy from the 'gate' theory of pain, the heat of the group, of family life, of the transference, like 'cupping', by raising the threshold for psychic pain, reduces it.

But how do we understand this new process that takes over from the symptom, this interest in the therapist who is not a 'real' person, in the group that is not a 'real' group, this family life that is so intense and yet (unlike the symptom which cries out to be removed) has no clear object? The common thread which runs through them all, I would argue, is that of *play*.

As will be discussed in Part III, there is a deep seam in British psychoanalysis that centres around the notion of imagination and creativity: its exponents include Sharpe (1937), Milner (1971), Winnicott (1965), Khan (1983), Rycroft (1968), Wolff (1972) and Pedder (1979). The creative imagination is inherently playful: it must be in touch with the primary process, but not be overwhelmed by it. Winnicott defined the essence of psychoanalytical therapy as learning to play, referring to play in its widest sense, including 'cultural' forms of play such as the arts and sport. Play is inherently paradoxical – both deeply serious and at the same time un-'real'; a still-life is a picture of a bowl of fruit; its calorific value is nil. Play involves what Humphrey (1983) calls 'rhyme', in which 'cat' rhymes with 'mat', but not with 'cat', it can be related to metaphor, finding likeness in difference. As Pedder (1979) has pointed out, transference is etymologically equivalent to metaphor; one is Latin, the other is Greek, but they mean the same: 'carrying across'. In therapy the patient experiences metaphorically with the therapist the relationships, feelings and phantasies derived from the past and dominating the present; played with, they lose their power.

If play is seen as a paradoxical conjunction of 'serious-unserious', we can ask how this state of mode is signalled. How does play stay play, remain outside the realm of the real? The esential mechanism is the uncoupling of action from consequence (Segraves 1982). In a pre-match interview, a tennis player threatens to 'murder' his opponent: at the end of the game, they shake hands (just). Romeo is passionately 'in love' with Juliet, but they do not 'make' love on the stage (it is precisely this lack of uncoupling that separates pornography from art). The rules of analytical therapy, the regularity of time and place, the neutral stance of the therapist create just such an uncoupling. How many therapists have had to face the bitter complaints of their patients that they do not 'really' care for them, that they are just doing a job? Winnicott (1965) stated that the end of the session is the analyst's expression of 'hate in the counter-transference'; it is also his way of saying that he does not 'really' hate the patient – it is just that the game is over for today. When this understanding of the metaphorical nature of therapy breaks down, as in a psychotic transference on the one hand, or in alexithymia (Lesser and Lesser 1983) on the other, therapy cannot proceed.

Where do we just learn to play? It is of course in the family, at our mother's knee. The functions of play remain a subject for research and debate, but there is no doubt that as well as being a rehearsal for 'real' tasks, play contributes to making humans into 'natural psychologists' (Humphrey 1983). It is through play that we achieve the knowledge of our own and others' feelings that is essential for survival of a social species. In individual therapy, both therapist and patient are participants in play which may resemble the intense involvement of a rebellious adolescent with a parent, or the sometimes gentle and sometimes violent play of a baby at the breast. As discussed in Chapter 4, Winnicott (1965) describes the self-absorbed play of the small child in the presence of a watchful but unintrusive mother as a prototype of one mood state that may be achieved in analysis and which may then generalise to the capacity to form intimate non-dependent relationships. The 'understanding' which the patient seeks in analytical psychotherapy is more akin to this state – one in which the patient feels secure and attended-to enough to begin through phantasy or 'thought-play' to understand himself – than it is dependent on any intellectual formulations or diagnosis.

The aim of the family therapist, too, is to rekindle the family's already existing capacity to play, not just in the sense of 'playing' cards, but in the sense of teasing, joking, chatting, fighting, sulking, singing, hating, living, making up, without being overwhelmed by any of them, that is the essence of family life. In individual therapy, the therapist is an active participant; with a family, he is more like a referee who gets the game going and who throws back the ball into play when it goes out of touch. Here, too, uncoupling is central: the therapist tries to break up the repetitive and well-worn patterns of argument that lead nowhere (the 'gramophone record' that most families play at the start of therapy), and to generate playful inter-action that, like speech itself, is an open system, an infinite source of variety and change woven from simple and repeated elements. Paradoxical techniques like 'prescribing the symptom' and Kelly's fixed role therapy (Kelly 1955) are uncoupling devices, designed to signify and generate play.

INDICATIONS AND CONTRAINDICATIONS

Analytical and family therapies are both non-specific or broad-spectrum treatments, which include a mixture of different techniques and strategies. It is not possible to isolate a single active principle in them which would lead to cure, however much practitioners (and critics) would wish this were so. The consequence is, as several reviews have shown (Skynner 1976; Martin 1977; Clarkin *et al.* 1979), that there are few clear-cut indications which would lead to choosing a particular therapy, but only trends and tendencies.

This article would suggest that the two main issues affecting choice of treatment are *change* and *context*. Change in family therapy involves helping the family to find healthy patterns from within an existing repertoire, which will then lead through the family's own growth to new structures. In individual therapy, the therapist, rather than being a referee, is often a regression-inducing participant; new patterns will be generated within the treatment itself. It follows that family therapy is indicated when either the family is in a state of crisis or transition, which generates its own change, or when family members are changing rapidly themselves, as with the very young or very old. Individual therapy, on the other hand, is indicated when there is no great biological drive towards change (i.e. adults) and when the pathology of the patient is too great for spontaneous improvement, but not so great that no change is possible (e.g. psychosis, severe personality disorder – but cf. Chapter 5).

The second main factor determining choice of therapy is the *context* of the referral. When one member of a family asks for help on another's behalf an initial family interview is usually desirable. When an individual patient is regularly accompanied by a spouse, or parent, or child who waits patiently outside while the official patient has their session, joint therapy is often indicated ('waiting-room syndrome'). Where there is multiple pathology in the family, joint interviews should be strongly considered. 'Secondary gain' from illness often involves collusion between the family and the patient who has adopted a sick role; in this situation, family therapy can sometimes 'unstick' a chronically intractable case (Chase and Holmes 1990). Family therapy also often has something to offer when the more stringent requirements of individual analytical therapy would exclude the patient.

Considerations of IQ, age, psychological-mindedness, and psychosis are less important in family therapy than in individual therapy, but patients with severe paranoid anxiety do badly in any group situation, including family sessions. Motivation, commitment to change, and a positive view of therapy are important preconditions of any successful therapy, probably even more so in family therapy than in individual.

CONCLUSION

There are many points of contact and overlap betwen the two disciplines; no clear-cut guidelines indicate one or other therapy in any given diagnosis and each case has to be considered on its merits. Psychotherapists should not despair of this, however, since therapy is always concerned with the individual case. We constantly confront the false alternatives ('dilemmas', Ryle 1982) with which patients torment themselves: 'Either I am un-married (which I do not want to be) and strong, or married and weak (which I do not want to be).' The art of treatment is to unhook the patient from his dilemma and help him to see that his weaknesses may be strengths, and vice versa. The same is true for therapy itself. It is not a question of either family therapy *or* individual therapy. For example, in adolescence, family therapy can be immensely helpful in making a teenager feel less stigmatised and trapped, and free him to leave home and make his own life. Equally, individual therapy may provide – may be the only way of providing – the intimacy and privacy that a disturbed young person needs to face fears of madness, perversity and death that prevent him from embarking on adult life. Therapists can offer no certainties in the face of the unpredictability of illness and neurosis.

Phlegmatic rationality starts and shakes its head at those unaccountable prepossessions [passions] but they exist as undeniably as the wind and the waves, determining here a wreck and there a triumphant voyage.

(Eliot 1876)

Family therapy may be a beacon, psychoanalysis a sea chart. The wise sailor needs both.

Chapter 8

Psychoanalysis and family therapy
Freud's Dora reconsidered

Freud's case-histories are a new form of literature – they are creative narratives that include their own analysis and interpretation. Nevertheless, like the living works of literature they are, the material they contain is always richer than the original analysis and interpretation that accompany it; and this means that future generations will return to these works and will find in them a language they are seeking and a story they need to be told.

(Marcus 1974)

INTRODUCTION

A *Fragment of an analysis of a case of hysteria* (Freud 1905) was written in 1900. Freud had just published *The Interpretation of Dreams* (1900) and turned to neurotic symptoms with the same *élan* and virtuosity that he had used to unravel dreams. His aim was similar in both works. True to the tradition of nineteenth-century science, he was looking for the fundamental laws that determine human psychology. Thus the essence of each work can be summarised in a single formula: dreams are hallucinatory wish-fulfilments; neurotic symptoms are unconscious expressions of the patient's sexual life.

The preoccupations of family therapy can also be set in context. This is the centrality in the contemporary science of information, language and control (Bateson 1973). Freud sought the formulae of the psyche; family therapy is looking for the rules, patterns and grammar of family life.

In my view these two approaches should be seen not as alternative theories, one of which will eventually be proven 'truer' than the other; nor as competing 'paradigms' in the Kuhnian sense of rival scientific ideologies (Kuhn 1962). To paraphrase Auden, psychoanalysis and family therapy are no more theories now but whole climates of opinion. The clash of paradigms often produces a false polarisation. Family therapists make sweeping, ill-informed attacks on psychoanalysis (e.g. Haley 1977; Hoffman 1981), while psychoanalysts turn a wary or even blind eye in response.

By taking one of Freud's major case-histories, I hope to clarify some of the real differences and similarities between the two approaches. I have chosen 'Dora' because, although it has provoked extensive commentary, this has not, to my knowledge, been from a family-therapy perspective. Several of the other cases have been looked at in this way, notably Schreber (Schatzman 1975), Little Hans (Haley 1976) and an early case of hysteria (Sander 1974).

I have used the portmanteau phrase 'family-therapy perspective' throughout, rather than adopting one of family therapy's sub-paradigms, for example structural, strategic or systemic. Like psychoanalysis, family therapy is far from being a unified body of theory or practice, but nevertheless it does represent a very distinct therapeutic ideology. It is the broad perspective that I want to contrast with that of psychoanalysis.

DORA'S STORY

Dora was brought by her father for help when, at the age of sixteen, she began to suffer from a nervous cough together with periods of aphonia, dyspnoea and headaches. Although Dora was the patient, it soon emerged that she was surrounded by a network of unhappy people whose antics read like an opera plot or dream-novel (Thomas 1982).

Her parents were estranged. The father complained that he 'got nothing' from his wife. She in turn suffered from a 'housewife's psychosis' – compulsively concerned about her home and children. Dora's father had first consulted Freud several years earlier, when he began suffering from bouts of mental confusion and paralysis. Freud – who had been one of Europe's leading neurologists – diagnosed syphilis.

Dora's father had been taken to see Freud by Herr K who headed the second family with which Dora's was inextricably linked. His wife – Frau K – and Dora's father were lovers. Their affair seems to have started when Dora's father was convalescing with TB at a health resort in southern Austria. Dora was then about six. Frau K had first nursed him – and then become his mistress. As the years went by, Dora, like her father, became very fond of Frau K and of her two children. Meanwhile Herr K, the cuckolded husband, who, like Dora's father, 'got nothing' from his wife, began to have designs on Dora. On two occasions he tried to kiss her. On the second – by the lake – he was rebuffed; Dora then told her mother about the incident. Dora immediately fell ill. Her father was by now away at the resort with Frau K. Herr K sent bunches of flowers every day to hasten Dora's recovery. Later, all three adults tried to deny that anything had happened and rushed Dora off to Freud to be 'cured'.

Thus Dora was deeply involved with the two older men in the network: her adored father and Herr K. To begin with she was very fond of the latter; later, when he made advances to her, she appears to have become furious with him.

There were two minor but important characters in the drama. The first was

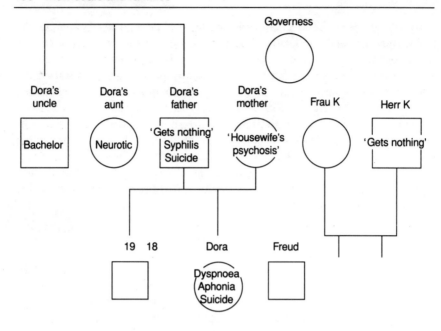

Figure 8.1 Dora's genogram

the K's governess, a young woman to whom Herr K had also made love but whom he later dropped, possibly when he became interested in Dora. Then there was Dora's brother, of whom little is revealed in Freud's account, but who we suspect was very close to his mother, and who later became a leading Austrian socialist (Rogow 1978).

We may agree with Rieff (1971) that 'the sick daughter has a sick father, who has a sick mistress, who has a sick husband, who proposes himself to the sick daughter as her lover'. Rieff is critical of Freud for focusing on Dora alone and ignoring the sick milieu in which she lived. Erikson (1962), has also argued that Dora's illness and her suicide attempt must be seen as a legitimate adolescent protest against the hypocrisy of her parents and their generation. The family therapy paradigm demands that we now understand her illness in terms of the workings of the whole system – the network consisting of the two interlinked families of which Dora was just a part.

THEMES

I will pick out several of the themes that characterise the system. The first is that – as Freud presents it – there are not really two separate families, nor even a group of separate individuals, but rather a collection of several intimate pairs and triangles (see Figure 8.1). Each of these potentially involves the transgression of a conventional boundary. Sub-systems are intermingled, so that parent and child, family and family, doctor and patient, employer and employee are intimately and often sexually linked.

The corollary of this is that in neither family are the parents united, either as husband and wife, *or* as parents. The strongest adult sexual bond is that between Dora's father and Frau K and the main focus of the story is the tension between this relationship and that between Dora and her father. Dora is in effect asking her father: 'Who do you love most? Frau K or me?' Even the relationship between Dora's father and Frau K is problematic since Dora's father is impotent: according to Freud, the couple are therefore confined to oral sex for their love making. Nevertheless, one gets the impression that there is a loving relationship between this couple that is not apparent elsewhere in the system.

Dora's father's impotence is an example of another important theme, that of illness and rescue. It is the role of the K family to rescue Dora. Herr K takes Dora's father to see Freud. Frau K starts her affair with Dora's father after she has nursed him through TB; later she saves him from suicide. Herr K is enabled, by Dora's illness, to send her flowers every day. Dora, however, maintains that only her father can save her. As we shall see later, the theme of rescue is also strongly present in both of Dora's dreams.

The pattern of illness and rescue leads on to another motif that permeates the system – hypocrisy. The desire to help is rarely disinterested or altruistic. Each of the saviours has his own ulterior motive and each victim has something to gain from their affliction. This is most explicit with Frau K and Dora's father: in one sense their hypocrisy, being transparent, is the more healthy. Her need to 'nurse' him is more of a conscious cover for their affair than anything. For instance, she decides to change her room in the hotel to the one next to his, so as to be near him should anything 'happen' in the night. The other members of the families – with the eventual exception of Dora – appear to collude with this. Other examples of hypocrisy include Herr K's wish to 'help' Dora when he really wants to flirt with her; most blatant is the way in which Dora's father used his 'concern' for Dora's health as an excuse to go to the health resort where he can meet up with Frau K.

Freud's own position as both a legitimiser and potential exposer of this hypocrisy is interesting. Herr K may well have brought Dora's father to Freud in the first place as an attempt to draw attention to his wife's lover's syphilis and put her off him. Freud was certainly being asked, as Erikson (1962) has pointed out, to 'rescue' both families by curing Dora of her 'delusion' that Herr K had made advances towards her by the lake. Here the father, Herr K and Frau K are united as in nothing else. Such invalidation is only possible when there is transgenerational transgression. The children are seduced into 'marriages' with the parental generation: they remain pawns to be sacrificed whenever the game demands it.

As Freud (1916–17) put it elsewhere:

> No one who has any experience of the rifts which so often divide a family will, if he is an analyst, be surprised to find that the patient's closest relatives sometimes betray less interest in his recovery than in his remaining as he is. When, as so often, neurosis is related to conflicts between members of a family, the healthy party will not hesitate long in choosing between his own interest and the sick party's recovery.

However, as Freud makes so clear, Dora was no passive victim of a conspiracy, but played as active and vigorous a part in creating the seduction as did the adults.

This adolescent vigour which, all being well, might have led to Dora's leaving home to make her own life, is hindered by one final theme that haunts the system: the fear of death. Dora's father suffers from TB – then a fatal illness whose psychic reverberations were similar to those evoked in our times by cancer (Sontag 1979). This fear permeates the families and paralyses them. Underlying it is an equation between separation and death: to leave the family is equivalent to dying or causing death; equally, the only possible escape is through death. Both Dora and her father's suicide attempts can be seen in this light. This theme was continued into Dora's own marriage, which was deeply unhappy. Her husband submitted to her neurotic manipulations until his premature death. As Deutsch (1957) put it, he 'had preferred to die ... rather than to divorce her'.

DORA'S SYMPTOMS

Freud's project was to trace the sexual origins of Dora's physical symptoms. He found a way to understand her bodily symptoms as communications about her sexuality. He does this by linking symptoms with specific incidents from the past and relating these to Dora's stage of sexual and emotional development. The key to this is the Oedipus complex and its derivatives which informs and explains Dora's actions and emotions. Freud sees a symptom as a compromise; just as the dream is the 'guardian of sleep' so the symptom enables the individual to adapt to stress – both internal and external – without disintegration. Thus a symptom is adaptive and homeostatic.

For the family therapist the organism is not the individual but the family or system as a whole. The aim is to find the meaning and function of the symptoms within the system: their appearance must make sense within the specific context of the family and this is be determined by the stage of the family lifecycle. The framework for this is the dimensions of family functioning: the maintenance of parental and children's sub-systems, privacy, communication, authority, nurturance and the capacity for evolution and change.

By being ill Dora served the needs of the whole system. With the help of her symptoms both families could continue to function in their pathological ways without disintegrating. Initially, Frau K and her father had a 'common love affair'. Dora was locked into this as her father's accomplice, as a surrogate partner for Herr K, and by her own unconscious need for her father and her wish to protect him. At this stage Dora was relatively well, and it was her father who was ill. Then two important developments occurred. First, the affair deepened. Frau K abandoned her bedroom and her children so as to be near Dora's father, while he spent more and more time with her at the resort away from his family. As Freud suggests, at this point there was a real possibility that the couple might leave their spouses – so disrupting the entire system. Second, Dora began to enter adolescence – the little girl was turning into a beautiful and intelligent young woman. Her 'affair' with Herr K and indeed with her father could no longer remain innocent. Dora – the hub of the whole system with links to every member in it – was nearing an age when she could leave home and lead her own life; and even, as Freud suggested, go off with Herr K.

The function of Dora's illness was to preserve the *status quo*. A sick adolescent is still an ill child. Her parents could be united in their common concern about her health. There would be no question of her father going off with Frau K and so abandoning his daughter when she needed him most. At the same time she could, through her illness, maintain Herr K's interest while punishing him with her rejection of his advances. These are the negative aspects. There was a positive side as well. With the illness Freud was brought in and with him the hope of cure. Also, her illness was a desperate attempt to activate her mother who until this moment had been conspicuous by her absence throughout the whole story. It was to her mother that Dora first turned, after Herr K had made advances to her by the lake.

As Lewin (1973) has suggested, the kaleidoscope shifts again at this point from a story of father-and-daughter love to one of maternal failure. Many of Dora's activities can be seen in this light: her sexualised relationship with her father; her attempt to replace her own absent mother by becoming a little mother to the K's children; her intense, possibly homosexual, feeling for Frau K and the governess. This leads us on to the two dreams on which Freud bases his paper, in both of which Dora's mother is a central character.

DORA'S DREAMS

The first dream is brief (although Freud's analysis of it takes thirty-five pages) and I shall quote it in full:

> A house was on fire. My father was standing beside my bed and woke me up. I dressed myself quickly. Mother wanted to stop and save her jewel-case; but father said: 'I refuse to let myself and my two children be burnt for the sake of your jewel-case.' We hurried downstairs, and as soon as I was outside I woke up.

Taking the manifest content, and using a family perspective, the dream states the dilemma faced by Dora and her family. Their house, i.e. the family, is on fire, i.e. endangered by sexuality. Dora's father comes to her bed, rather than to her mother's where he should be. Dora is caught in an incest-trap. Her only hope of escape is for her parents to be reunited sexually: her mother must yield her 'jewel-box' (i.e. her genitals) to her father, and he must insist on this. As soon as Dora is 'outside', i.e. away from home, she can 'wake up', i.e. become sexually awake, also 'wake up' to what is happening in her family.

The dream also refers to the relationship between Dora's brother and their mother. Dora's association to the dream was to a dispute between her parents because her mother insisted on locking the door of her brother's room at night to protect him from burglars. In the dream Dora protests that her mother's priorities are wrong: she locks the door to protect her son (her favourite, her 'jewel-case') but forgets the greater danger of fire. Unless Dora's mother stops thinking only of herself and her son the whole house will go up in flames. Rather than being excluded from the parents' bedroom the children are 'locked in' their family.

The dream now reads as an attempt by Dora to awaken her mother to the family's imminent danger of disintegration. The dream raises the question of why her mother kept her 'jewel-case' locked. It may well have been the mother's knowledge that her husband had syphilis that made her unwilling to 'give' him anything. Freud links Dora's knowledge of her father's illness to her mother's leukorrhoea which she imagined had come from his VD, and from this goes to Dora's own leukorrhoea, which he then links with her masturbation. At this point Freud stops. For him infantile sexuality is the bedrock: he need look no further. He says of Dora:

> she was well on the way to finding an answer to her question of why it was precisely *she* that had fallen ill – by confessing that she had masturbated, probably in childhood.

But what were the determinants of her masturbation (cf. Laufer 1982)? Here again we must point to Dora's lack of maternal love: deprived of her mother's nurturance and an opportunity of feminine identification, Dora turns to masturbation for comfort, omnipotently becoming in phantasy the comforting mother she lacked in reality.

Freud's virtuoso interpretations of the second dream – too long to be quoted here in full – leave one, like Dora, breathless.

> Dora is living in a strange town. She receives a letter from her mother asking her to come home as her father is dead. In the letter her mother tells Dora that as she had left without her parent's knowledge she decided not to inform her that her father was ill. Dora tries to travel home, but becomes stuck in a thick wood in which she cannot 'move forward'.

Freud ingeniously shows how behind this dream there is a phantasy of defloration and pregnancy and links this with the incident by the lake. He explains her slapping of Herr K and subsequent accusation of him as no more than the fury of a woman scorned, jealous of his previous advances to the governess.

So excited is Freud by his explication of the latent content that he virtually ignores the manifest content of the dream (cf. Chapter 2). In it, Dora's guilt at wanting to leave home is painfully evident. Dora reminds herself (via her mother) that if she tries to get away from the family, she will be punished by her father's death. No wonder she experiences herself as being unable to move. The 'wood' in which she is stuck may not just be her genitals (as Freud sees it) but her own coffin.

FREUD'S ROLE

Several authors have been critical of Freud's technique in this case and of his behaviour towards Dora (Muslin and Gill 1978). Marcus (1974) suggests that Freud disliked Dora and that negative countertransference accounts for some of the curious aspects of the case, including his failure to interpret transference and the four-year delay between writing up and publication. I want to comment on the systemic implications of two of his interventions.

The first concerns Freud's analysis of Dora's childhood symptom of nervous coughing. He manages to trace this to Dora's knowledge of her father's impotence, and to the thought that he and Frau K would then have to resort to oral intercourse.

> She knew very well, she said, that there was more than one way of obtaining sexual gratification ... I questioned her further, whether she referred to the use of organs other than the genitals for the purpose of sexual intercourse, and she replied in the affirmative ... I could then go on to say that in that case she must be thinking of precisely those parts of the body which in her case were in a state of irritation – the throat and the oral cavity. To be sure she would not hear of going so far as this in recognising her own thoughts ... But the conclusion was inevitable that with her spasmodic cough, which as is usual was referred for its exciting cause to a tickling in her throat, she pictured to herself a scene of sexual gratification per os between the two people whose love-affair occupied her mind so incessantly. A very short time after she had tacitly accepted this explanation her cough vanished.

Freud follows this passage with a lengthy justification of speaking frankly to young girls about sexual matters, during which, as Kohon (1986) points out, in his appeal to plain speaking, he disappears twice into French when he says 'j'appelle un chat' and 'pour faire un omelette, il faut casser des oeufs'. One cannot escape the thought that in Freud's hectoring tone and insistence that his point is accepted he is forcing Dora to swallow his interpretations. It is almost as if Freud and Dora are having oral sex. One might ascribe this to 'countertransference', but this term in this context conceals as much as it explains. Are we really to understand Freud's behaviour in terms of *his* infantile sexuality? Surely, rather, we should see that Freud, just as much as Dora, is playing out a script written into the system, in which older men force themselves on Dora, ostensibly in order to help her. This then results in a spiralling symmetrical battle in which they force and she resists until a pseudo-complementary 'solution' is reached when she appears to submit (cf. Bateson 1973). Whatever the origins of this pattern, Freud is caught up in it, whether one views it as a 'dance' (Minuchin 1974) whose steps he is forced to follow, or a systemic transference. Freud has unwittingly become part of a power struggle between the men and women in the system whose effect is most visible in Dora. His crescendo of forceful interpretations is a desperate attempt to assert some authority and to re-establish hierarchy in a system where Dora, the adolescent, appears to hold all the power: power that has been abrogated to her by the four adults with whom she is involved. Her childish symptoms, so powerful in themselves, also express her need to divest herself of this power that she cannot handle and to become a child again.

A second interpretation that has outraged some commentators was Freud's suggestion to Dora that she was really excited by Herr K when he made advances to her and wanted him to divorce Frau K and marry her: that she wanted her father and mother to divorce, and her father to marry Frau K; and that '*this would have been the only possible solution for all the parties concerned*'. Does this mean, as Marcus (1974) puts it, that Freud was really a 'swinger'? I think not. Rather, this must be taken as an ironic challenge to Dora, rather in the style of Carl Whittaker or Milton Erikson (Haley 1977), designed to highlight the difficulties faced by Dora and her family. His comment illustrated for Dora the hurdle which every adolescent has to surmount in order to leave home: a conflict between the wish to be free and the wish to remain safely within the family (cf. Chapter 4). Equally he showed her the parents' conflict between wanting to hold on to their children and the need to let them grow up. By this paradoxical prescription he suggests how Dora and her family could, by his quasi-incestuous solution, both eat their cake and have it. The aim of this was, by a *reductio ad absurdum*, to free her.

Freud reveals Dora's 'internal' conflict, her 'hysteria', as an inability to renounce her father. Her 'external' conflict – the difficulty in 'leaving home' (Haley 1980) is also made visible in Freud's paradox.

THERAPY

We must turn now to Dora's subsequent history. Twenty years or so after her consultation with Freud she was referred to another analyst by a medical colleague, to whom she had presented with Menière's disease. She revealed herself as Dora (Deutsch 1957). She was a miserable and disturbed woman. Her marriage was deeply unhappy and she was entirely preoccupied with her son, a promising musician. She was tormented by *his* wish to become independent and leave home. She lay awake at night listening for his return whenever he went out. Her basic psychopathology seemed unaltered – hysterical conversion symptoms, depression, difficulties with men. She had reproduced with her husband and son the self-same difficulties that she had experienced with her father and family.

This evidence seems to support the view that the problem was not just in Dora's network but also in her psyche. What started as a 'soft spot' in the system had hardened into an individual compulsion to repeat. Could this have been avoided had Freud been able to keep Dora in treatment and so complete her analysis? Would the outcome have been different if we could have entered a psychotherapeutic time machine and treated Dora and her family (and the Ks) with family therapy? Which would have been more likely to succeed?

In discussing this we may use a distinction proposed by Horowitz (1979). He differentiates between 'changes of state' on the one hand, in which an individual may shift from one psychological mode out of his repertoire to another, and internal development on the other hand, in which the repertoire itself is expanded. This distinction between state-shift and development reflects the respective goals of family therapy and psychoanalysis. Family therapy aims to change the state of the system so that the symptom bearer is relieved of his symptoms and can get on with the normal process of development and change. In psychoanalysis the analytic relationship is the vehicle of change; in family therapy it is 'real life'.

In psychoanalysis the aim is to rearrange the patient's mental furniture so that growth and adaptation can occur. In family therapy the therapist has to enter the family system as fearlessly as the analyst faces the unconscious. The simple moves that are made – moving a symptomatic adolescent so that she is no longer sitting between her parents, but is next to her brother, as might have happened with Dora's family – also rearrange the family furniture so that development can continue.

We might speculate that had Dora stayed in analytic treatment with Freud she would have received a 'corrective emotional experience' that might have compensated for her deficient parenting. Family therapy on the other hand might have altered the parental relationship – either by a reconciliation or by divorce followed by a marriage between Dora's father and Frau K. This might then have brought Dora closer to her mother and at the same time provided a 'good-enough' model of a heterosexual relationship. A shift of state may allow healthy development to take off. Perhaps it was this that Freud – anticipating perhaps the notion of 'crisis precipitation' (Minuchin 1974) – sensed when he wrote in the Dora case:

The barrier erected by repression can fall before the onslaught of a violent emotional excitement produced by a real cause; it is possible for a neurosis to be overcome by reality.

The result of Freud's therapeutically engendered crisis was termination and the 'failure' of the analysis. However, from a system's point of view the treatment can be seen as a success. Dora broke off relations with the Ks completely, and within a year or two had left home to get married. Freud, by challenging the myth of Dora's 'illness' and by suggesting that she was an active participant in the behaviour of which she appeared to be a victim, became the scapegoat. This enabled Dora to give up her role as patient. Her symptoms were no longer necessary. Whether she, her family, or the network as a whole were 'cured' is a different question.

DISCUSSION

Whatever their theoretical differences psychoanalysis and family therapy have one thing in common: they are both primarily *therapies* rather than *theories*. Their aim is to produce healing change. It is as theories of change that I want to compare them. As Watzlawick has shown (Watzlawick *et al.* 1974) a psychological approach to producing change essentially involves a *change of frame* or context. This method is inherently paradoxical: if you say to someone who wants to change, 'reality cannot be altered, but your way of looking at it can', then change often follows.

The therapist's craft is based on the particular frame to which he adheres. His skill lies in bringing it to bear on clinical reality. The way in which that reality is defined also derives from the frame he is using. As discussed in the previous chapter, there are some obvious parallels between the way in which family therapy and psychoanalysis define the problems they expect to encounter.

First, both acknowledge the importance of inertia when human beings are faced with a new idea. Both assume that the therapist will be met with some resistance. In psychoanalysis this resistance is ultimately explained by the 'principle of constancy' – the tendency of the organism to maintain equilibrium and to reduce environmental stimulation. In system's terminology this becomes *homeostasis*. One only has to work with a highly enmeshed family to see the principle of constancy at work within the family system.

A second vital parallel is between the pre-eminence in analytic thinking of the Oedipal situation and the emphasis in family therapy on intergenerational boundaries. Both are concerned with what Chasseguet-Smirgel (1983) calls the 'double difference', the difference between the sexes and the difference between the generations. Psychoanalysis tends to emphasise the former; family therapy the latter. The aim of establishing functioning intergenerational boundaries is to create a 'normal' Oedipal relationship: that is, one in which the boundary is not so permeable that the children are seduced and the adults swamped, nor so rigid that the children cannot get the access they need to their parents in order to learn to love and to hate.

A third point of similarity centres on the notion of development. In family therapy the patient's problem is linked to the stage in the lifecycle of the family (Dare 1979); in psychoanalysis personality difficulty is seen in terms of developmental arrest. Both treatments aim to remove blocks so that development can proceed: Dora to abandon her hysterical regression and achieve genitality; her family to allow its adolescents to leave home without precipitating depression in the 'empty nest'.

The psychoanalytic concept that is most compatible with family therapy is that of secondary gain. Freud contrasted the direct advantages that the patient derived from their illness – freedom from anxiety or indirect instinctual satisfaction – with the secondary gains – the advantages conferred by the ill-role that enables the patient to control and manipulate family members and caregivers. The Palo Alto group explicitly state their philosophy of therapy as follows:

> Our fundamental premise is that regardless of their basic origins and etiology – if indeed these can ever be reliably determined – the kinds of problems people bring to psychotherapists *persist* only if they are main-tained by the ongoing current behaviour of the patient and others with whom he interacts. Correspondingly, if such problem-maintaining behaviour is appropriately changed or eliminated, the problem will be resolved or vanish, regardless of its nature, origin or duration.
>
> (Weakland *et al.* 1974)

In short, family therapy aims to remove the symptom by eliminating the secondary gain which it confers.

Against this we can set the gauntlet which Freud throws down in his discussion of the Dora case:

> The symptoms of the disease are nothing else than the patient's sexual activity ... sexuality is the key to the problem of the psychoneuroses ... I still await news of the investigations which are to make it possible to contradict this theorum or limit its scope.

Freud is concerned here with the *causes* of the symptoms; family therapy with its *effects*. Whether or not Freud was correct in his assertion, or, to take a Popperian view, whether he could ever be proved wrong: these are two quite distinct levels. Change may occur at the level of the patient's sexual and phantasy life; it may also occur at the level of the interaction with the immediate environment. If therapy works – analytic or family – change in one may lead to change in the other. Equally, change may occur at one level while the other remains unaltered. This, in my view, is what happened with

Dora. The distinction may be further clarified by a final quotation from Bateson (1973):

> In general in communicational systems, we deal with sequences which resemble stimulus-and-response, rather than cause-and-effect. When one billiard ball strikes another, there is an energy transfer such that the motion of the second ball is energised by the impact of the first. In communicational systems, on the other hand, the energy of the response is usually provided by the respondent. If I kick a dog, his immediate sequential behaviour is energised by his metabolism, not by my kick.

Dog and foot are likely to meet again: the patterning of behaviour is what makes psychology possible. Psychoanalysis is concerned with the 'metabolism' of foot and dog and how this leads them to seek each other out; family therapy with the consequences of their contact. At this stage in the evolution of the psychotherapies it is not clear whether family therapy is the dog and psychoanalysis the foot, or vice versa, and in what ways their relationship is likely to change.

Chapter 9

Phobia and counterphobia
Family aspects of agoraphobia

INTRODUCTION

Family therapists tend to see disturbance in children in terms of parental difficulty. The aim in treatment is to 'return the repressed' (Cooklin 1979) to the parental relationship where it belongs, and so free the symptomatic child from the role of marital 'distance regulator' (Byng-Hall 1980). Those family therapists whose work is primarily with disturbed adults find that the presenting *symptom* or illness often acts in a similar way to that of the disturbed child, being both a concentrate of and a diversion from marital and family difficulty (e.g. Haley 1977). This chapter looks at some phobic and agoraphobic patients and their families from this perspective.

Bowlby (1973) has used the phrase 'the suppression of family context' to describe the commonly unacknowledged fact that the majority of agoraphobic patients have had severely disturbed childhoods. This leads, he claims, to 'anxious attachment' between the pre-phobic patient and her mother, inhibition of exploratory behaviour and ultimately to the development of symptoms.

Others have looked at the contemporary relationships of agoraphobic patients, whose spouses are described by Fry (1962) as 'negativistic', subtly disinvolved men with a tendency to be over-compliant to their wives' demands, thus covertly encouraging dependency and thereby making themselves both indispensable and distant. Haffner's study (1977) confirmed this impression systematically, finding that 'denial of problems and disability and vulnerability was a central feature of the psychological make-up of these men'. These findings have implications for treatment. Family and marital difficulties can reduce the effectiveness of behavioural treatment in social phobias. (Falloon *et al.* 1977) and Haffner (1977) found that agoraphobic patients whose spouses could not cope with their own internal feelings of aggression improved less than those with more self-tolerant husbands.

This chapter attempts to delineate a recurring sequential family pattern seen in some phobic and agoraphobic patients. Two paradigmatic cases are first described in an attempt to establish the pattern. A family model for the development of the agoraphobic syndrome is then put forward. Then, using the model, family methods in the treatment of phobic syndromes are discussed.

CLINICAL EXAMPLES

The steeplejack's wife

A young woman developed phobic symptoms soon after the birth of her first child. Initially her fears were of harming the baby; later she became afraid to go out alone and took to telephoning her mother frequently for reassurance. She insisted on moving house so as to be near her mother. Her mother 'helped' her by looking after the child, and would ring several times a day to see if the boy was 'all right'. When the patient told her mother of a dream in which her son had fallen under a lorry, her mother (who was not likely to have read Freud) told her that this meant she wanted to kill her son. The patient had felt neglected as a child since her mother devoted all her attention to her two younger sisters, one of whom had been chronically ill with kidney disease while the other was epileptic.

In the initial individual session she was able to link her fears of harming the baby with aggressive feelings towards her sisters, but her symptoms persisted. At a joint session she announced proudly that her husband – unlike herself – was afraid of nothing. He accepted this compliment somewhat hesitantly and confirmed that he had indeed been self-reliant since the age of ten, which was when his parents divorced and he and his younger brother had more or less been left to fend for themselves. He worked as a scaffolder on high buildings. When asked if it was true, as his wife suggested, that he was frightened of nothing, he confessed that he had slipped on a rope that morning and had been very scared. His wife seemed surprised at this revelation but visibly relaxed and perked up. He then said that he could never tell his wife about his fears or worries because of her illness. For example, the one thing of which he was petrified was confronting his mother-in-law. This emerged when he was given the task of protecting his wife by answering the telephone, so that when her mother rang to check on the baby, *he* would tell her that she was busy and could not speak. He insisted that this would be impossible: his mother-in-law would not take no for an answer.

The would-be travellers

This young couple's problems also began after the birth of a child: their second. Mrs J, a plump, chatty, attractive woman, became terrified to leave the house. Her first child had just started school and shamed his mother into seeking help when he asked her why their family never went away for weekends or holidays like the other children's. Mrs J was an only child whose mother had gone out to work when she was a baby, leaving her with her grandmother. She became very attached to her parents, had few friends and had often missed school through illness. The very first time she spent a night away from home was when she was sixteen. Her husband, also an only child, was an irritable, withdrawn-seeming man who – in striking contrast to his wife – had developed a remarkable premature independence. From the age of nine he was fascinated by railways and became a railway 'boffin'. His parents had encouraged him to travel on his own from an early age. His wife worried about everything. He had a nerveless, *laissez-faire* approach: he was sure that everything would be all right in the end. He was unmoved by her needless rehearsal of possible disasters. One of her fears of travelling was that the car would break down; he would reassure her that there was nothing to worry about and thus persuade her occasionally to come out with him: but then the car *did* break down. It was the same with money: he would suggest they go away. She – who ran the family's finances – insisted they could not possibly afford to. He would then back down and so the pattern continued: he was frightened of nothing except standing up to his wife; she was frightened of everything except her ever-so-tolerant husband.

ELEMENTS IN THE EVOLUTION OF THE PHOBIA

According to the 'family phobic syndrome' I am putting forward, these cases have a common underlying structure. The phobic patient has or has had a relationship with her mother in which there have been strong elements of dependency and often unconscious aggression. Her father is frequently conspicuous by his absence, either physically or emotionally. She is married to a 'counterphobic', apparently intrepid husband, who himself turns out to be covertly fearful and dependent on his wife and who felt neglected by his parents as a child. The illness is usually precipitated by a life event such as the arrival or departure of children. There are five main elements in this structure which I shall now consider in turn.

1 Anxious ambivalent attachment

According to Bowlby (1973) the key issue in the childhood origins of agoraphobia is 'anxious attachment' to the mother – caused by disturbed family relationships. In the present series there were certainly frequent feelings of disappointment and of having been neglected by parents. The steeplejack's wife, for example, felt that her mother had lavished all her love on her epileptic younger sister. However, such feelings of neglect are not uncommon and some degree of ambivalence is normal between children and parents. The central issue may not be the fact of disturbance in itself, nor the demandingness and resentment that feelings of neglect may evoke in the child, but rather how such demandingness and hostility is handled. As Bowlby (1969) suggests in his discussion of the evolution of bonding, the normal biological response on the part of the primate parent to hostility or demandingness by the infant is an *increase in proximity* between parent and child. Under certain circumstances, however, there may be a paradoxical *decrease* in proximity when the child is demanding or angry – and it is this that can lead to pathology.

There are at least three situations in which this may happen. First, the parent may be physically absent as a result of illness, death or divorce at a time when ambivalent feelings are at their height. An example of this would be the *fifteen-year-old schoolgirl* who came home from school one day after quarrelling with her mother in the morning to find that her depressed mother was in a coma after taking an overdose. When the phantasy is confirmed by reality in this way, the damage may be greatest. Second, there may be emotional distancing by the parent who fails to register or 'accept' hostile responses from the child. This may follow from the mother's guilt about her own hostile impulses towards her child. These are the idealised mother-daughter relationships, so often seen in agoraphobic systems, where daughters are for ever 'good' and mothers are always 'wonderful'. Third, the physically or emotionally absent father may fail to provide an alternative parental figure who can provide compensatory proximity when the mother is withdrawn, or withdrawn from.

The result of any or all of these circumstances, especially if repeated, may be that demandingness and hostility come to be linked in the child's mind with separation and loneliness. The anxiety and pain that this arouses must be reduced. This can happen in one of two possible ways.

(a) Detachment, distancing and denial of hostility. By remaining detached and distant the threatened separation is forestalled, pre-empted, since it has already happened. Denial of hostile impulses further reduces the possibility of the feared separation.

(b) Clinging, cautiousness and compliance. In (a) the hope is that by remaining distant, hostility and demandingness may be avoided altogether. Clinging behaviour assumes that hostility is unavoidable and the defence concentrates on the feared consequence: i.e. the separation, and aims to minimise it by meeting it with an equal and opposite attachment. Defence (b) is that of the phobic patient, defence (a) that of her counterphobic spouse. They correspond roughly with the two main types of anxious attachment described by Bowlby (1973): avoidant and ambivalent attachment.

2 The 'solution': the phobic/counterphobic marriage

The pair, as yet unknown to each other, have in common a central fear of their own demandingness and hostility. They have reacted with contrary strategies to their childhood feelings of loss and disappointment (cf. Dicks 1967; Cooklin 1979). With the unerring antennae of the unconscious they seek each other out. Courtship and early marriage provide them with the ideal escape vehicle from their childhood difficulties (Freud 1916–17; Dare 1979). She has found in him the perfect partner from whom she need never be separate and with whom no feelings of hostility need ever arise. In her, he has found someone whom he can protect and from whom at the same time he can remain detached. So long as she is in need of protection he need fear no separation. Her anxiety about exploration is matched by his fear of being explored. In their 'Jack-Spratt' marriage her capacity to socialise (masking a fear of being alone) is balanced by his self-reliance and independence (masking a fear of closeness). Another common ingredient in such a marriage involves incomplete separation from the phobic partner's mother. The wife, with her inhibition of hostile drives, marries a man who is 'acceptable' to her parents. Her husband, frightened of true intimacy, is happy to settle for an interfering mother-in-law as a buffer between himself and his wife.

3 The precipitant: alone with change

Transient agoraphobic reactions are not uncommon in response to stress. Mothers frequently feel uneasy about going out after the birth of a baby; the bereaved find it difficult to be on their own in the early days after their loss; patients may be frightened to go out alone immediately after leaving hospital. For the potential agoraphobic these experiences are especially frightening since they threaten the illusion of invulnerability she has built up with her husband. The newborn child is a wedge that may split their unity; when grown-up children leave home the middle-aged mothers are reminded of their separateness. Both partners' earlier feelings of being abandoned are reactivated. *Where the spouse is not counterphobic* these anxieties may be accepted and shared and both may grow to feel that it is possible to be separate yet related. Alternatively the non-counterphobic husband may be straightforwardly intolerant of his wife's anxieties and the marriage may break up with the wife perhaps going back to her mother. In neither case is an agoraphobic syndrome a likely outcome. Where the husband is counterphobic he dare not show his weakness and so share it, nor can he be aggressive enough to precipitate a marital crisis. What he does offer his wife is the appearance of increasing invulnerability and apparent concern. The stage is now set for the development of a true phobic illness.

4 The failure of reassurance: escalation

A brief digression on the phenomenon of reassurance is necessary at this point. Reassurance occurs typically between parents and children, doctors and patients, and also from time to time between husbands and wives. The 'weaker' partner expresses an anxiety which is then 'contained' by the more powerful member of the dyad. A number of rules appear to govern the interchange. For example, the reassurer's certainty and power is often exaggerated and any anxieties that he may have are discounted, thus introducing an element of falsehood into the interchange. However, this is strictly limited in scope and there is a ban on 'false reassurance'. There is a similar constraint on the person to be reassured who must be 'genuinely' frightened and not using fear as a covert demand for something else. Repeated requests for reassurance are liable to be treated with suspicion. The normal function of reassurance is the reduction of anxiety caused by an external factor by means of an unequal relationship, but occasionally the inequality of the relationship is tested by means of an anxiety. The child who wakes his or her parents in the night for reassurance may have had a nightmare and want reassurance that the dream was not real; or the nightmare may *be* that his or her parents are not really all-powerful and reassurance is needed that they are. Reassurance involves a subtle, mutually agreed blend of the genuine and the illusional, aiming to place anxiety in its real perspective – somewhere between the foreground of boundless fear and the distance of absolute security.

In the threatened phobic-counterphobic system this comforting complementarity, which has been an integral part of the marriage so far, goes wrong. Rather than assuaging her fears, his reassurances serve only to augment them. She becomes more and more anxious, rings him continually, insisting that she cannot cope, that she needs him. No sooner has she rung off than her doubts redouble, she must contact him again. He becomes more and more of a 'superman', hiding his worries, helping his wife, protecting her from stress, distancing himself from her all the while. He rings her from work, 'just to see how she is'. The more he tries to reassure her, the more desperate she becomes. The stronger he seems, the more helpless she feels.

A good example of this process occurred with *the couple who wanted to emigrate*.

They were a happily married couple in their early forties, with three teenage children. She was renowned in the family as a 'coper' who had looked after her two sisters as a child when her mother had suffered from 'nerves'. Her husband was a 'wonderful' man, laconic, Irish, self-sufficient, who worked every night at an adventure playground as well as his lorry-driving job so as to give his children a better childhood than he had had. Their secure complementarity – in which he coped with 'outside' worries and she looked after the 'inside' of the family – was upset when he decided they should emigrate to Canada where his sister lived. She then developed agoraphobia and he had to take over running the house and shopping, as well as his two other jobs. He accepted this role without complaint. She became more and more 'nervy'. Eventually they heard from the Canadian Embassy that their application had been rejected. The husband opened the letter but did not tell his wife for fear of 'upsetting' her. When he did tell her in a family-therapy session two days later, she was angry at first but then greatly relieved; then *she* was able to help her husband with his denied feelings of upset. Their normally complementary system of reassurance had changed catastrophically into a symmetrical escalation of anxiety and unsuccessful reassurance. The husband's secretive protectiveness acted as a positive feedback to his wife's anxiety, creating a 'runaway'.

(cf. Bateson 1973; Hoffman 1971; Byng-Hall 1980)

5 The new solution: the stabilising role of the illness

Finally the runaway levels off with the emergence of the illness: the phobia. The spouse now knows that reassurance is useless and that professional help must be sought. Through the illness the anxiety is legitimised and so, partially, relieved. It is no longer the couple's relationship that is in question, their mode of communication and interaction, but the illness that is the problem. The illness becomes a 'distance-regulator' (Byng-Hall 1980) that maintains the marriage by saving the wife from her fear of separation and the husband from his fear of intimacy.

The relationship has now become a 'compulsory marriage' (Fry 1962). The wife is tied to a husband whom she needs to help her cope with a world from which she is excluded by her illness. He is tied to her by her need for him. Through the illness they are kept together – and safely apart – she in her sick role, he in his care-giving role. Thus they can, as a unit, 'avoid and control' their inner demandingness and angry feelings of deprivation that have pursued them from childhood. They have achieved – albeit at the price of sacrificing freedom and intimacy – the very relationship they felt they lacked as children: *un*anxious *un*ambivalent attachment.

TREATMENT

A number of different theories have been used in building this model of the evolution of agoraphobia. These include (a) a life-events approach, with its emphasis on the 'contextual threat' of a life-event (Brown and Harris 1978); (b) attachment theory; (c) psychoanalytic ideas, especially projective identification; and (d) systems theory, especially the symmetrical/complementary dichotomy. I would not view these models as essentially incompatible; indeed elements of each are required if the richness of the clinical phenomena is to be encompassed. However, such an eclectic approach does pose problems when treatment is to be considered. Here there are two main questions. First, what method is most appropriate – systemic, strategic or psychoanalytic? Second, what is the best focus for intervention? The model suggests five possible levels at which treatment may be directed. In a given case it may be necessary to focus on any one or more of these levels. Each represents a different 'hypothesis' (cf. Palazzoli *et al*. 1980) which may need to be elaborated or abandoned as treatment proceeds.

Anxious attachment: the pacifists

Here the therapeutic task is to break the psychological link between demandingness and aggression on the one hand and separation on the other. This involves mobilising the counterphobic partner to respond to demandingness with firmness or even anger, to move not 'away' nor 'towards' but 'against', to use Karen Horney's (1939) clasification. Paradoxical intervention can be helpful here. Aggression is what is most feared since it leads to separation: for that reason it must be prescribed.

> K was an attractive twenty-eight-year-old nanny whose phobic symptoms started while her parents were on holiday. Her parents, as we shall see, played the role of the counterphobic element in the system. Her symptoms consisted of agoraphobia and a curious fear of looking at herself in the mirror. She was the youngest of three children and the last to leave home. Her parents – who had met at school – were strong pacifists both politically and domestically and believed in the paramount importance of reason in solving problems. K's mother, a counsellor, was very anxious to help her daughter who always seemed to be in some sort of trouble: losing her job, getting robbed, being thrown out of her digs and becoming involved with 'unsuitable' boyfriends. Her father, a quiet man, sided with K when her mother tried to stand up to her, saying that she was being 'unfair' and that he, like K, had had his troubles in his twenties.
>
> At interview the parents, after an initial period of trying to 'understand' K's exasperating behaviour, said that they were at their wits' end. They had done everything they could for her: lending her money, arranging jobs for her, allowing her to live in their house, but still she was unhappy and dissatisfied. Now she had become 'ill', which was worrying enough in itself: it meant that she exempted herself even more from being considerate and responsible. At this point K's behaviour was reframed as an attempt to 'help' her parents by remaining dependent and thus sparing them from the pain of losing their last child. The father perked up and at the following session reported that K's symptoms had improved and that they were all feeling more cheerful. Her irresponsible behaviour continued, however. By reframing her behaviour as 'helpful' the basic family ideology of

avoidance of anger had not been challenged. K still evoked distant concern and understanding in response to her intolerable demandingness. The secret alliance between the daughter and father against the mother, the centrality of the mother–daughter relationship and her assault on the parental couple (her symptoms had started when the parents went away alone together on holiday) had yet to be tackled. In a subsequent session, therefore, K was told that she now had to help her parents some more: she must do something to them that was so outrageous that her father would have no option but to put his foot down, to punish her, even to involve the law. The family then laughed and revealed that K and her boyfriend had recently used her parents' house while they were away for the weekend, and that they had taken her father's car and smashed it. He had been furious and as a result K had agreed to move out and was now living in a 'squat' on her own. Her mother was very worried about this and felt it was unsuitable and unhygienic. She was encouraged by the therapist to continue to worry about K.

Although this case is atypical in that the counterphobic part of the system consisted of a parental couple it illustrates the point that we are dealing with a phobic-counterphobic *system*, rather than any specific family constellation. The father's anger and his daughter's demandingness were reframed as attempts, in their different ways, to 'care' for each other. This enabled them to stay in touch while they became more separate. The mother, to some extent, was held by the therapist until the father and daughter were able to give up their secret alliance and so make some space for her between them.

The collusive marriage: the Oxbridge graduates

In these collusive marriages each member takes over part of the other's psychological functioning. The wife holds the anxiety while the husband is apparently caring and responsible. One of the mysteries of marital pathology is to identify the difference between this and the normal division of psychological labour that occurs in healthy families. A key issue seems to be that of flexibility. In pathological families the partners seem stuck in their respective roles and much of their interpersonal work has to do with maintaining this system. Thus if one partner departs from the expected position the other may subtly manoeuvre him back so as to maintain the status quo. This means that changes achieved in individual sessions, whether behavioural or psychodynamic, may later be undermined or nullified by the family system. In marital therapy with phobics, the aim is to unlock the projected parts of the self: to uncover the counterphobic's anxieties and difficulties, to help the phobic patient to be in touch with the coping part of herself. It often takes a crisis, either naturally occurring, or therapeutically generated, to achieve this.

In the case of the Oxbridge graduates this happened spontaneously under the stress of an initial psychiatric consultation. They had two children of five and three, the younger of whom was adopted. Her agoraphobic symptoms started soon after she had an abortion. She had been agonised by the decision to have this abortion, but had finally decided on it as she felt she could not really cope with the demands of the children she already had, especially her adopted daughter towards whom she often felt frighteningly aggressive. Both of them were science PhDs and had been hardworking children of striving working-class families. She, as a child, had always felt outshone by her elder sister in attractiveness and liveliness. She had clung first to her mother and then to her books. Her father was remote and suffered from anxiety. The husband was a reliable-seeming, phlegmatic man who had patiently tolerated his wife's anxieties. After taking the history at the first interview the comment was made that it must have been a difficult year for both of them. To the interviewer and the wife's surprise, the husband suddenly started to cry and then to speak of his father's death which had happened earlier in the year. He had not been able to cry about this before, because, he said, he did not want to upset his wife who had enough troubles of her own. He went on to say how sad he felt that education had separated him from his father and that he had only realised this when it was too late. His wife – who had never seen her husband cry before – could then add that she felt alienated from *her* father and together they seemed to have discovered that men can be vulnerable and show their feelings.

In this case the technique seemed simply to involve giving the husband a chance to speak for himself and not always to be speaking for, and feeling responsible towards, his wife. It is not usually as simple as this. In the case of the *steeplejack's wife* it was only when the intrepid husband was given the task of answering the telephone to his interfering mother-in-law that he had to admit he too had fears: he would far rather he had been asked to climb the Post Office Tower than tackle her!

The precipitating change: the divorced train driver

Change implies both gain and loss, even when it involves the 'happy events' which provoked the onset of phobic symptoms in the patients in this series: marriage, having a baby, children getting into university, promotion, planned emigration. In these phobic systems the negative aspect is denied by common consent. The patient is then left feeling guilty about the anxieties and resentment that change evokes in her. Her spouse, on the other hand, his ambivalence safely located in his wife, cannot see what she is making such a fuss about.

Therapeutic work has to be directed towards achieving a shared acceptance of the anxieties and difficulties aroused by the change. The counterphobic spouse has to be 'taught to worry' by the symptomatic patient.

A West Indian train driver in his thirties, a part-time all-in wrestler, developed hypochondriacal fears centring around his genitals for which he had been extensively investigated. His symptoms, which also included mild agoraphobia, had begun soon after he set up house with a new woman. At first he resisted the idea that he had any worries or problems other than his symptoms. Later he confessed that he had been deeply hurt when his two children who initially had come to live with him and his cohabitee had returned to their mother after a quarrel with their 'stepmother'. When the couple were seen together his cohabitee appeared to be strong and competent. She was also divorced: a nurse who had brought up her three children on her own. She said that this had not been difficult as she had learned to fend for herself after her father had died when she was ten. The therapist challenged her strong façade and directed the patient to discover what she was really feeling underneath. She began to cry and said how much she wished that her 'husband' would protect her and in particular to help her cope with her fifteen-year-old son who was out of control and in trouble with the law. The patient then decided that he would take his 'stepson' to wrestling. At the next session they spoke more openly about their difficulties in living together, their hopes and anxieties about the change. Later they decided to marry and began saving for a flat.

Escalation: the secondary school teachers

In order to de-escalate, the normal balance of symmetry and complementarity has to be re-established (cf. Bateson 1973). At some point in the evolution of the symptom, it was suggested, a shift occurs from 'normal' reassurance which, by negative feedback, has an anxiety-reducing effect, to 'runaway' whereby the more the patient asks for reassurance from her spouse, the more anxious she becomes. To reverse this 'catastrophe' (Woodcock and Davies 1980) two things must change. First, the wife must learn to trust her husband again, and, paradoxically, this can only be achieved by his showing some sign of weakness. This will reassure her that when he does offer her his strength it is real and not counterfeit. Second, her demands for reassurance must be seen by him *as* demands (or better, requests) and not as intolerable attacks, or a swamping insistence on symbiosis.

The secondary school teachers provide a good example. The wife, who was the patient, came from a difficult background in which her father, of whom she was very fond, had died when she was in her early teens, leaving her with a mother and elder sister who were in strong alliance. As she began to be interested in boys she developed fears that she might magically contract VD, but these disappeared when she met her husband at college. He was a cool, controlled, strong-seeming man in whom she had complete confidence. He came from a Jewish background and had to wrench himself away from an overpowering mother, who appeared to despise her henpecked husband. He prided himself on his independence and scorned middle-class aspirations. After leaving college the couple went to a developing country for a year, during which time they were constantly in each other's company. When they returned to England her symptoms of hypochondriasis and agoraphobia returned. Around this time they got married. A major part of their interaction consisted of her confiding her worries to him and of his trying to reassure her that there was 'nothing' wrong. He found her infuriating but never showed it. However, he took to disappearing for a few hours which would add to her sense of panic. Direct efforts by the therapist to persuade him to reveal anxieties were met with a stonewalling intellectualising scepticism. It was suggested that it might be harder for him to let her look after him than it would be for her to relinquish her fears. At the next session they related how he had got completely drunk at a party and had started crawling round the floor. Neither she nor their friends had ever seen him like this: he had to be put to bed 'like a baby'. Further work involved rationing her to two 'symptom sessions' per day, at which she could be sure that he was genuinely sympathetic and caring. A marked improvement followed and they decided to move back out of London to their home town after she had been offered a promotion there. However, about eighteen months later she made contact again, saying that her fears had returned and asking to be referred for help locally.

The compulsory marriage: the frightened violinist

In many cases described, the symptoms have been of relatively recent onset. Here, cure may be a reasonable goal, as the marital relationship is still pliable enough for considerable change. In long-standing cases the couple's mode of relating may have set hard, with the symptom firmly embedded in the matrix of the marriage. In these cases, more modest aims and prolonged work are necessary, and the therapist must be prepared to remain – to some extent – part of the system (cf. Chapter 5). Only thus can the fire of the wife's anxiety be drawn, the therapist-husband be freed from his enmeshed detachment. The couple fear that without symptoms their marriage will fall apart, and excessive therapeutic zeal will be met with an equal-and-opposite resistance or breaking off. The aim is to make the marriage feel more voluntary by encouraging shared enjoyment and pleasure on the one hand, and the open expression of hostility and irritation on the other. The therapist must be prepared to contain the anxiety that will be aroused by this change. Another danger is that the compliant husband may start to try and please the therapist in the same way that he has acceded to his wife's demands.

The frightened violinist had been an outpatient for many years following a manic episode in her early thirties. She was always accompanied by her husband, a research chemist. Just as her two children were leaving home to go to college, she began to develop moderately severe agoraphobia symptoms. Her husband had 'rescued' her in her teens from an overbearing, ambitious father who was determined that his daughter should become a famous musician. Her husband was everything that her father was not: calm, quiet, understanding. He coped with his wife's worries by adopting a professional role, treating her like a patient, never getting angry and offering himself as a kind of resident nurse-co-therapist to her outpatient psychiatrist. On one occasion there was a long discussion about whether it was a 'good thing' for him to do all the shopping for her. With prompting from the therapist, the husband reluctantly admitted that often this was the 'last thing' he felt like doing when he got back from work. He then tried to manoeuvre the therapist into giving him a *dictat* (rather as his father-in-law would have done) either not to do the shopping because it was bad for his patient-wife, or to go on doing it because it was 'good' for her. Instead they were given the rather obvious, but to them intensely puzzling, instruction that she was to ask him to do the shopping, and he was to refuse, but *only* if he really didn't feel like doing it.

DISCUSSION

I will give two general conclusions from the cases I have described. First, in some cases of agoraphobia and other phobic syndromes the spouse – or a significant other such as parent, boyfriend or doctor – may play a key role in the maintenance of the symptoms, thus contributing to a *phobic-counter-phobic system*. Second, successful treatment can result from trying to alter this system, rather than by concentrating on the symptomatic individual alone.

This takes us into the difficult area of aetiology. Family theories of mental illness are numerous but have tended to founder on the question of specificity. If a specific family constellation is to be accepted as an aetiological agent for a particular illness – in this case phobic syndromes – then a number of negative conditions must be fulfilled. If, for example, families can be found with the illness but without the constellation, or conversely there are families with the constellation but without the illness, then the constellation can be neither a necessary nor a sufficient cause for the condition. Thus have Hirsch and Leff (1975) cast doubt on family theories of schizophrenia. Recently Minuchin has claimed that there is a specific pattern of enmeshment in families of children with psychosomatic disorders such as anorexia nervosa (Minuchin *et al.* 1978). However, this pattern can be found in many families without a psychosomatically ill member, and has been shown not to be present in about half of a group of psychosomatic families (Loader *et al.* 1980).

Perhaps, as discussed in the previous chapter, proponents of family factors in adult mental illness should settle for more of a modest role therefore, viewing families as stressors and perpetuators of pathology rather than as aetiological agents as such. Hoffman's (1971) use of the concept of deviance amplification is a good example of such an approach, and is the one followed in this account of the development of phobic symptoms. The role of the family therapist would then be one of deviance reduction, aiming to uncouple the ill member and the homeostatic system so that both can change, either spontaneously or with further outside help.

CONCLUSION

The model of agoraphobia put forward here is a developmental one, based on a series of sequential stages. At each of these there is a choice of pathways which – depending on environmental conditions – will lead the individual closer to, or further from, becoming ill. I have focused particularly on the patient-to-be's spouse who, by denial of his own anxieties, may augment his wife's fears and so push her on towards illness. The illness is not *caused* by the husband's personality, but without it the outcome might have been different – marital breakdown or a chance for the wife spontaneously to overcome her difficulties. The marriage-plus-illness becomes the compromise by which the couple manage to control fears that have dogged them since childhood. Each is trying to escape – but to do so each needs the other. Therein is the paradox of the marriage. By being together they run the risk of evoking those old feelings of anger and demandingness that were so terrifying; but only by being together can those feelings be avoided. Therein too lies the promise of change. Each sees in the other their own mirror-image, also vainly struggling to escape from its shadow. If she can accept her husband's weakness, his denied anxieties – and if he is brave enough to reveal them – she may come to realise that she too has a hidden aspect, a strong side, and with it can start to overcome her fears.

Part III

Literature and psychotherapy

Literature and psychotherapy
An introduction

As Marcus (1974) suggests (see Chapter 8), every psychotherapeutic case-history is, in a sense, a 'fiction' – a story wrought collaboratively by patient and therapist from the raw materials of memory, history, dreams, transferential relationship and theoretical perspective. The urge to weave meanings out of experience seems fundamental to human psychology (see Chapter 2) – perhaps because stories enable experience to be organised satisfyingly and can lead to successful predictions about the future behaviour of ourselves and others. Both analytic and family therapies involve the discovery or rediscovery of personal stories, an owning of one's past. A similar impulse to organise inchoate experience into meaningful and satisfying patterns underlies the artistic impulse. Literature and psychotherapy make comfortable bedfellows. The three essays in this section explicitly take literature as their starting point, drawing parallels between the process of literary creativity (whether writing or reading) and the psychotherapeutic experience. The specificity and uniqueness of the artistic image provides a model for the analytic interpretations, their aesthetic 'rightness': a validation that stands alongside scientific attempts to provide a firm grounding for psychotherapy.

Chapter 10

The language of psychotherapy
Metaphor, ambiguity, wholeness

INTRODUCTION

Psychoanalysis has two faces. One is public, outer, claiming a place in the mainstream of scientific medical culture. The other is the reverse: private, inner, courting the arts rather than the sciences, but conscious as it does so that this may, by the procrustean rules of our cultural divide, disqualify its outer aspirations (cf. Chapter 12). This ambiguity has internal and external repercussions. Critics have seized on the outer surface of psychoanalysis and sought to show that it does not measure up to the rigorous standards expected of a true science. Farrell (1981), for example, invokes a psychology of common sense like Jane Austen's as an antidote to Freudian metapsychology. Psychoanalysts and their supporters often feel confused by this mis-comprehension and have been tempted to retreat into their esoteric world, claiming as they do so that critics such as Farrell, with little direct analytic experience, have missed the point. They might, before disappearing into their consulting rooms, also remark that it is the very breakdown of common-sense solutions to their problems that drives people to seek help; that what we call 'common sense' is a complex and mature psychological state, one certainly not possessed by infants and small children; and that Freud's stated aim of therapy, 'where it is, there ego shall be', might be seen precisely as an attempt to replace the uncommon and unbridled sensation of neurosis with the common sense of normality.

The main internal repercussion of this ambiguity in psychoanalysis is that it no longer has an agreed and secure theoretical base. For Freud this was biological determinism. Dissatisfied with this, 'outer'-oriented analysts like Bowlby have turned to information theory and ethology for a basic discipline while more inner-oriented theorists have looked to linguistics.

The linguistic case was succinctly put by Rycroft (1966) who wrote:

> It can indeed be argued that much of Freud's work was really semantic and that he made a revolutionary discovery in semantics, viz. that neurotic symptoms are meaningful disguised communications, but that owing to his

scientific training and allegiances, he formulated his findings in the conceptual framework of the physical sciences.

The aim of this chapter is to compare poetry and psychoanalysis. Its context is the view – one that Freud started with and to which he eventually returned (Bettleheim 1982) – that psychoanalysis, whatever its scientific aspirations, is fundamentally a linguistic or interpretive discipline, primarily concerned with meaning rather than mechanism.

My thesis is that the workings of poetry and psychoanalysis are comparable because both communicate mainly by metaphor. Susanne Langer (1951) has called this metaphorical mode 'presentational symbolism'. This is based on images, is personal, emotive and in it apparently incompatible elements may coexist. She contrasts this with 'discursive symbolism', the everyday language of common sense and science. These correspond roughly to Freud's primary and secondary processes (Rycroft 1968).

My aim is to show that psychoanalysis does make sense, not common sense perhaps, but poetic sense. I shall concentrate on three aspects of presentational symbolism: *metaphor*, *ambiguity* and *wholeness*. Other features of poetic language – humour, memorability and creativity, for example – will not be considered. I am well aware that a bridging attempt such as this runs a double risk: on the one hand of offending analysts and psychotherapists with its obviousness, on the other of annoying sceptics with its imprecision.

The discussion is based on a work by the American poet Robert Lowell (1959) describing his stay as a patient in a mental hospital near Boston University (B.U.). One verse has been omitted.

Waking in the Blue

The night attendant, a B.U. sophomore,
rouses from the mare's nest of his drowsy head
propped on *The Meaning of Meaning*.
He catwalks down our corridor.
Azure day
makes my agonized blue window bleaker.
Crows maunder on the petrified fairway.
Absence! My heart grows tense
as though a harpoon were sparring for the kill.
(This is the house for the 'mentally ill'.)

What use is my sense of humour?
I grin at 'Stanley', now sunk in his sixties,
once a Harvard all-American fullback,
(if such were possible!)
still hoarding the build of a boy in his twenties,
as he soaks, a ramrod
with the muscle of a seal

in his long tub,
vaguely urinous from the Victorian plumbing.
A kingly granite profile in a crimson golf-cap,
worn all day, all night,
he thinks only of his figure,
of slimming on sherbet and ginger ale –
more cut off from words than a seal ...

These victorious figures of bravado ossified young ...

After a hearty New England breakfast,
I weigh two hundred pounds
this morning. Cock of the walk,
I strut in my turtle-necked French sailor's jersey
before the metal shaving mirrors,
and see the shaky future grow familiar
in the pinched, indigenous faces
of these thoroughbred mental cases
twice my age and half my weight.
We are all old-timers,
each of us holds a locked razor.

ANALYSIS OF THE POEM

Unconventional in form, conversational in tone, confessional in content, this poem could almost be taken from a psychotherapeutic session. We have first to remind ourselves that the facts it depicts are also fictions, imaginary constructions. What distinguishes it from a factual description of life in a hospital ward? If we approach the poem as a discursive statement it tells us little that we did not know already, certainly less than we would learn, say, from Wing and Brown's (1970) descriptions of life in mental hospitals. Similarly, if we approach psychotherapeutic sessions as discursive statements they might seem to be no more that interminable accounts of well-known neurotic symptoms. The task, rather, in approaching the poem is to find and respond to its meaning in the non-discursive mode. The reader must enter a state similar to that required in 'listening with the third ear' (Reik 1948) to a psychotherapeutic session: free-floating attention, a state of active receptiveness, or negative capability, in which a meaning can emerge – evoked by, but not the same as, the surface, or factual meaning. In the poem, an artefact, each image is chosen to evoke these deeper meanings and is the end result of a previous selection by the poet from his own consciousness. In the psychotherapeutic session the therapist and patient together have to learn to select out the significant thoughts, images and feelings, and separate them from the less meaningful.

I shall now pick out five images from the poem for discussion. The first, coming in the second line, is the 'B.U. sophomore's 'mare's nest of his drowsy head'. This sounds at first like a simple descriptive metaphor based on the hair/mare chime in which the student's head is compared with a horse's, conjuring up a young man's long mane. Then we realise that there is no horse, that a mare's nest means something purely imaginary, a nest for a mythical beast like a unicorn. So we are led from the thought 'boy's head'– 'horse's head' into his head where we find his dreams (night-mares) which are, like a mare's nest, impossible and wonderful. This then becomes a metaphor for the setting of the poem – a madhouse – perhaps also for the poem itself, for the Meaning of its Meaning (one of whose authors, I. A. Richards, was a literary critic who had once planned to be a psychoanalyst). The image 'mare's nest of his drowsy head' becomes a hook which, by imposing the field-force of metaphor, can draw out a string of associations, just as a strong magnet will hold up a chain of nails. This process is clearly similar to Freud's suggested method for the analysis of unconscious material in psychotherapeutic sessions.

Next we come to the image of Stanley as a seal. We have already been prepared to think about water mammals when Lowell turns his heart near the start into a harpoon, and the idea recurs in the unquoted stanza in which an inmate is described as being 'redolent and roly-poly as a sperm whale'. There is another faint reference to amphibiousness when, towards the end, the poet talks of his 'turtle-necked French sailor's jersey'. The jump from silent-man-in-the-tub to seal, or perhaps seal-in-zoo, is not far. From there we are taken to thoughts of the hospital as an aquarium ('in the blue') in which rare beasts are kept, to the idea of the inmates as prey that can be harpooned, and again to the poem itself, which becomes a spear with which painful, 'agonized', feelings can be lanced.

Lowell's seal man – like Ted Hughes' animal folk and even Freud's 'Rat-Man' – is a modern example of the search for animal parallels with man, for correspondence between the natural and the human order. Aesop's animals – or the astrological bestiary – are men-in-beasts, emblems on to which specific human moral qualities have been projected: the cunning fox, the proud ambitious frog, the delicate stork. These contemporary poets seem to explore the contrary theme of beast-in-man. Pre-modern man, searching for control of the natural world, endows it with human qualities. Modern man, knowing in a sense more of seals than souls, searches for truth in the natural order that might illuminate his own uncertainties.

The search for the biological basis of human nature is a central element in the psychoanalytic quest – Rycroft (1966) has described psychoanalysis as a '*biological* theory of meaning'. This takes us on to the next metaphor, contained in the line 'makes my agonized blue window bleaker'. Here the poet links the azure (heavenly blue) of the sky with that of his own eyes (agon-eyes), contrasting its brilliance with his dejection. The use of the body and its sensations as a reference point is, like animal parallels, a recurrent poetic theme. George Herbert, 400 years before Lowell, similarly linked the heavenly bodies and his own:

> Man is all symmetry
> Full of proportions, one limb to another,
>   And all to all the world besides:
> Each part may call the furthest, brother:
> For head with foot hath private amity,
>   And both with moons and tides.

When Freud said that 'ultimately the ego is a body ego' he was making a similar point. Poetic metaphor depends on evoking a specific image or feeling in the reader. Even when the content of the poem is apparently abstract the sound and rhythm produce particular sensations in the listener. The same is true of psychotherapeutic experience which is always concrete, based on specific thoughts, feelings, images or memories. Ella Sharpe (1950) has described how the apparently abstract remarks made by patients in therapeutic sessions can often be linked to specific bodily experience which may have occurred in childhood. The patient who says he has 'wandered off the point' may be referring to feeding difficulties as an infant; the person who is always 'messing things up' may be talking about problems of sphincter control. Similarly, the man who is on the 'fringe of things' may have difficulties with penetration, and the woman who is preoccupied with her 'depression' may be speaking of the female genitals. This unconscious metaphor-making is not so far removed from the medieval poet who speaks of his 'gentle cock', 'which every night it percheth him/In my lady's chamber' (Gardner 1972).

A fourth group of images in the poem cluster around the words 'petrified', 'granite', 'ossified'. Petrify and ossify are obvious plays on words. An 'azure day' is brilliant and jewel-like, but hard as lapis lazuli. These images evoke thoughts of the inmates as fossils: solidified, turned to stone, set. This convergence of images on a central point or meaning is analogous to Freud's concept of overdetermination. This is based on the idea that symptoms and dreams can arise from a multiplicity of unconscious elements, each of which has its own 'level'. Freud was fond of geological metaphors for the unconscious. Another might be a nuclear model in which a central thought or phantasy – in the poem the idea of fossilisation of specimens within a museum – organises around itself a cluster of words and images at varying distances from the core.

From fossils and hardening we are led inevitably to thoughts of death. This is evoked dimly by 'azure' which takes us heavenward, and by the dark crows on the fairway, which might symbolise death. Stanley's obsession with his figure reflects a whole cultural attitude towards ageing and a desperate attempt to deny it through slimming; the men are mummified in their passive resistance to growing old. This leads on to the final metaphor 'each of us holds a locked razor'.

This image of frozen violence reverberates back through the poem, from the blunt edges of the metal shaving mirror to the blue windows of the start. What began as a personal image, 'my heart is sparring for the kill', has become a general metaphor for the human predicament echoing perhaps Pascal's 'we travel under sealed orders', and the idea of the hospital as a metaphor for a sick society to which we can all respond. Lowell's private pain, generalised in this way, can be shared and so lessened.

METAPHOR AND TRANSFERENCE

Transference is central to present-day psychoanalysis, and distinguishes it from other 'talking cures' such as counselling, cognitive therapy and behaviour therapy. The idea of transference is that the patient re-experiences '*in vitro*' with the therapist the unconscious assumptions, emotions and desires that underlie his general behaviour and which ultimately derive from his childhood. Once made conscious, these can be understood, modified, transcended. Strachey's (1934) concept of the 'mutative interpretation' puts together transference, symptoms and childhood experience in one formulation that sees a common pattern running through each. The basis of transference then is finding similarities, analogies and parallels between the therapist–patient relationship and these external and early situations. The impersonal context of analysis aims to maximise the visibility of such patterns and structures.

The task of the therapist is pattern-recognition. In this his own reactions are vital: he has to enter a *transferential mode* in which he reads the patient's unconscious responses to treatment as a metaphor for earlier and outer reactions. The process is very similar to the movement that occurs in reading a poem, in moving by metaphor from its outer surface to the deeper meaning.

Transference and metaphor mean the same thing (Pedder 1979). Metaphor comes from Greek and transference from Latin but the sense is identical: meta/trans/across – phor/fereo/to carry: both mean to 'carry across'. Metaphor carries across or links apparent dissimilarities: fact and phantasy, inner and outer, personal and public. It contains what Paul Ricoeur (1979) calls a 'split reference' to truth and fiction, like the Majorcan storytellers who preface their tales by saying 'it was and it was not'.

Transference may be thought of as a special type of metaphor in which early childhood feelings are carried across into the relationship with the therapist. Like the poetic metaphor, the transference relationship is both a fact and a fiction, both is what it seems and is not. The therapist is mother, lover, persecutor – and a professional trying to understand and help. Crows on the petrified fairway are symbols of fear and death – and dark birds on a frozen golf course.

From this perspective we can see why it is that the underlying parental relationships revealed through transference are not literally true. One patient, for instance, stated that he had at times feared it would be impossible to end therapy without the death of the therapist or himself. This related to an intense ambivalent relationship to his father. While it was probably true that he had hated his father and wished him dead many times as a child, it was also untrue he had never lifted a finger to hurt him, and in fact loved him deeply. To say that he wished to kill his father was as true and untrue as to say that each of us carries a locked razor. This point is well made by Laplanche and Pontalis (1973):

> When Freud speaks of the transference repetition of past experiences, of attitudes towards parents etc., this repetition should not be understood in the literal sense that restricts such actualisation to really lived relationships. For one thing, what is transferred, essentially, is psychic(al) reality – that is to say, at the deepest level, unconscious wishes and the phantasies associated with them. And further, manifestations of transference are not verbatim repetitions but rather symbolic equivalents of what is being transferred.

This raises two important questions. First, what is the nature of 'psychic reality'? Second, what is meant by 'symbolic equivalents'? Both these topics have been the subject of prolonged psychoanalytic debate and it is well beyond the scope of this chapter to tackle them in any depth. I shall confine myself to some brief comments that follow from the perspective I am advocating.

The 'psychic reality' revealed in transference takes the form of an image that occurs to the therapist or patient. This has to be agreed on by both – it has to feel 'right' or 'true'. It is a shared reality that is neither entirely private to the patient, nor is it a general feeling that would be applicable to any other person or moment. What is experienced in the transference is not an 'Oedipus complex', say, but a specific feeling: for instance, that either the therapist or the patient might die. Although the image may feel as though it was 'out there' waiting to be found, rather as some poets have described 'discovering' their poems, their job being simply to write them down, in fact it is called into being by the relationship between patient and therapist. This is perhaps what Bion (1962) was referring to when he said that 'psycho-analysis is that primitive type of communication that requires the presence of the object'.

A similar process is at work in creating 'poetic reality'. We may summarise Lowell's poem by saying that each of us has the potential for violence, but it is in the image of the locked razor that this thought comes alive and becomes the basis of a shared meaning. Every reader will make something slightly different of this, each contributing to a common pool of personal meanings. The metaphor, standing transitionally (Winnicott 1971) between the entirely unspoken private thought and the generalisation, is poetic and analytic truth. Eliot (1975), mixing his metaphors, compared the result of this metaphorical process to an alloy produced by the poetic enzyme, a seachange that 'transmutes personal and private agonies into something rich and strange, something universal and impersonal'.

A consequence of this viewpoint is that analytic theory becomes not so much a body of objective knowledge as a set of rules and guidelines for interpreting transferential metaphors. Theory and therapy are intimately linked – theory is a language for describing the experience of therapy. Musical theory or poetic criticism have a similar relationship to their arts. Innovations in analytic theory – the contemporary preoccupation with narcissistic disorders, for example – are similar to innovations in musical or poetic form: a new language is created which enables new territory to be explored.

This equation of transference with poetic metaphor-making is at variance with Jones's (1916) classical analytic view of symbolism. He viewed 'true symbolism' as the product of repression – so this would be revealed in the transference symptoms and dreams; while poetry would be an instance of sublimation, symbolism only in what Jones calls 'its widest sense'. In Rycroft's (1968) discussion of the Jones paper he proposes that symbol-formation be seen as a general psychological function, not as an expression of psychopathology. In line with this, I would argue that the capacity to respond to poetry and comprehend transference depends on the development of 'imaginative competence' (cf. Chapter 4). This faculty evolves in the course of childhood, starting with the linguistic and imaginative freedom of the toddler and young child in which phantasy and reality are not yet separated, and continuing into adolescence with the development of the autonomous imagination.

In describing this process Trilling (1950) quotes the eighteenth-century philosopher Vico: 'Poetry is the primary activity of the human mind. Man, before he arrived at the stage of forming universals, forms imaginary ideas ... before he can articulate, he sings: before speaking in prose, he speaks in verse; before using technical terms he uses metaphors, and the metaphorical use of words is as natural to him as that which we call "natural".' Trilling goes on to suggest that 'psychoanalysis is a science of metaphor ... it makes poetry indigenous to the very constitution of the mind. Indeed, as Freud sees it, the mind is in the greater part of its tendency exactly a poetry-making organ.'

These themes can now be illustrated by some clinical examples.

As a workday instance we may take a patient – a young woman who had been in therapy for some time following repeated self-mutilating episodes – who began a session by commenting in a rather attacking way that there were never any personal papers on the therapist's desk and wondering if any other doctors used the room. This remark could have had a number of meanings: a complaint that the therapist himself was too impersonal, or a disparaging wish to change to one of the other doctors. However, it soon became clear that the true significance of this was the feeling that material discussed in the sessions was 'cleared away' each week, and that the patient was complaining that her sessions were not frequent enough. This emerged when she said how she often felt depressed in the middle of the week but the therapist was not there, and the feeling had passed by the time the session came round. This then linked with her present sadness at being separated from her father who lived abroad, and with the feelings of anger that he never really listened to what she said when they did meet. This then connected with memories of blankness she had experienced during long separations from her parents as a child when they went away on business trips.

The initial transferential percept was the empty desk which then became a metaphor which linked in feelings at a number of different levels: other aspects of the transference, anger and sadness towards her father and childhood memories of separation and depression.

In the Lowell poem the slow pace and sparse diction evoke the poet's desolation and separation from life. In the same way the tone and manner in which the patient brings material provides a metaphorical key with which patient and therapist may unlock the past.

An example comes from a patient, one of whose presenting symptoms included a conflict over homosexuality. After he had been in treatment for some time it became apparent that, although bringing plenty of 'interest-ing' information, particularly dreams, he was in some way controlling the sessions, simultaneously holding back and offering his 'material' as though to excite and stimulate the therapist. Knowing that the patient had at times as a lonely adolescent had sexual encounters with older men in which he felt special and powerful, the interpretation was offered that therapy had become a kind of psychic *fellatio* to which he had been driven by fear and loneliness just as he had been in his teens. In the next session he said how shocked he had been by this comment which he had visualised literally. He then linked this to feelings of exclusion he had experienced when he saw his parents kissing and holding hands as a child, and his envy of his mother for her passive power over his father whom he wanted all to himself. The discovery in his teens of the power of his penis to attract men had then given him a feeling of triumphant retaliation for this exclusion which he had reproduced with his therapist, and in which he was unconsciously identified with his mother. In this sequence he had moved from personal distress and intense shame and controlling dependence on the therapist, to a universal biological experience – of being a helpless child, feeling excluded and envious, of wanting to be loved. His distress, in Eliot's word, had become impersonal. After this there came an interesting shift in his attitude towards his mother. Near the beginning of treatment he had described a dream which, he said, summed up their relationship. He was standing by the door of his house trying to leave, but he could not because she was holding his testicles. She had him by the balls. After this sequence he went back to the dream and now its metaphorical significance had changed: he felt that she was cradling him in a gentle, protective way. He was then able to admit a similar change had occurred in his attitude towards therapy.

A change of perspective like this is an essential part of the psychotherapeutic process. As treatment progresses a patient's metaphors change level or deepen, giving a richer and more varied set of possible responses, resonances and relationships. The first patient I mentioned had a dream that expressed this neatly. She dreamed that she was flying in an aeroplane that was likely to crash. Suddenly she found she was in another plane flying higher up and so more safely. She had moved on to a 'higher plane'. A similar change can occur in the appreciation of art or poetry as the reader increases in experience and maturity. The process could be seen as an increase in an individual's inner *valency*, offering a greater range of options for connection and combination. Bion's (1962) concept of 'attack on linking' reflects the reverse of this, whereby an individual diminishes his valency, as a defensive and retaliatory manoeuvre.

Psychotherapy moves from the contemporary experience with the therapist, to childhood and back by a double shift. First, the transference metaphorically stands for childhood feeling: the patient simultaneously excites and frustrates the therapist – this is what he did to his homosexual partners in his teens and what he imagined his mother doing to his father as a child. Behind this are his feelings of exclusion and loneliness, and the rage and wish for revenge that they evoke in him. These childhood images, derived from Oedipal theory, then become a metaphor for his current relationships including that with the therapist. As a child he had felt trapped by his mother just as he later did by therapy; now he feels protected. This therapeutic circuit parallels that of the development of the neurosis itself. A defective reality has imprinted itself on the developing child. This creates an inner template of phantasy (Bowlby's 'internal working model') by which reality is experienced and controlled. In the development of the adult neurosis this template then actively reproduces the kind of relationships and situations from which it had been passively moulded in childhood.

Therapy involves reawakening and personalising an individual's dead metaphors, the unconscious assumptions by which he lives. These reveal themselves all the time, but especially in symptoms, innuendo, puns, plays on words, dreams and transference. Psychoanalysis provides a set of rules for decoding these metaphors. Sometimes psychoanalytic imagery, if used insensitively, remains lifeless, a set of fossilised clichés – 'the bad breast', 'the Oedipal situation' – an overworked short-hand that has become a deadend. This may also happen in poetry when conventional poetic images – sun, moon, rain, flowers – fail to come alive. In art, aesthetics attempts to evaluate and define artistic truth, to separate the good from the bad and the lifeless. A similar aesthetic is needed in psychotherapy. Therapist and patient may have a strong sense that a particular interpretation is right; this is usually defined intuitively. When an interpretation 'clicks' or 'works' the feeling is often described as a physical sensation of 'rightness' or of illumination, rather as A. E. Housman's test of good poetry was whether it gave him a prickling sensation at the back of his neck.

Ambiguity

The ambiguity inherent in some psychoanalytic concepts has been seized on by many of its critics, for example, Medawar (1975); Farrell (1981). An example is the notion of reaction formation, which holds that any strongly felt psychological attitude may conceal its repressed opposite. The Casanova may be a repressed homosexual, the pacifist a potential murderer and so on. The over-enthusiastic use of this sort of reasoning may occasionally lead to absurdity, or to the closed thinking of which Popper and his followers have been so critical. But there is no doubt that psychoanalysis is close here to a fundamental aspect of human thought that cannot be lightly dismissed (cf. Holmes and Lindley 1989).

Ambiguity and paradox seem to be near the heart of poetic languages. Poetic epigrams, such as 'the Child is Father of the Man' (Wordsworth), 'Damn braces. Bless relaxes' (Blake), or 'I was angry with my friend/I told my wrath, my wrath did end./I was angry with my foe;/I told it not, my wrath did grow' (Blake), have made the leap from literature to psychology without difficulty.

The most explicit critical statement of the importance of ambiguity in literature has come from William Empson (1953) who claims that 'the machinations of ambiguity are among the very roots of poetry'. A central notion is that of the coexistence of opposites. This may apply at the level of a single word: for example the Latin word *altus* which can mean both high and deep. Freud used this point to illustrate his contention that in the unconscious there are no negatives, and that at the level of the unconscious opposites are not incompatible, any more than they were for Catullus when he wrote '*Odi et amo*'. Empson extends this by showing that poetic language itself has ambiguity built into it. This is true even at the level of adjectives and adverbs, since each qualification of a noun or verb can imply the opposite of that qualification. Thus we commonly suspect that the patient who is *very* sorry that he is late may in reality be far from sorry. Empson (1953) ingeniously shows how a negative may imply the very thing that it denies. In Pope's couplet:

Expatiate free o'er all this scene of man;
A mighty maze! but not without a plan.

We are compelled by the grammar to consider the possibility that there just might *not* be a plan – why else mention that there is one, and use the convoluted double negative? It comes as little surprise to learn that an earlier version had read

A mighty maze, and all without a plan.

Similarly Keats'

No, no: go not to Lethe ...

takes us straight there.

The concept of an 'earlier version' is a linguistic expression for the activity of the unconscious. It is the ambiguousness of language that enables us to notice the unconscious meanings that slip through the bars of logical thought. In trying to reconstruct what may lie behind a dream or phantasy or slip of the tongue we are always searching for the 'earlier version', the poetry that escapes with the prose.

An important aspect of this is the ambiguity created by the sound of words. Psychoanalysis, like poetry, is a spoken language. Assonance or dissonance, the play between sound and meaning, are crucial elements in poetry. In *Waking in the Blue*, Lowell uses 'ow' and long o sounds throughout – drowsy, sophomore, bravado, pound, old, razor – creating an atmosphere of timelessness evocative of mental-hospital wards. In psychotherapy and psychoanalysis the patient's tone of voice – angry, self-pitying, childish – often provides vital information. Bateson's 'double bind' hypothesis is based on the discrepancies that can exist between the content of a message and the tone in which it is delivered.

Ambiguity in language is normally avoided by context, which is indicated by grammar and sense. Psychoanalysis sees a symptom as inherently ambiguous, a necessary compromise between inner need and outer constraint, rather than as something to be got rid of. The aim of therapy might be said to be to find a context – usually a childhood context – in which the symptom makes sense, and so loses its ambiguity. The use of paradox in family therapy is another example in which there is a search for a different context for the unwanted problem. Once found this becomes the symptom's 'positive connotation' (Palazzoli *et al.* 1978): for example, an adolescent's delinquent behaviour may be seen as an attempt to bring warring parents together through worry. Similar shifts of contexts – seachanges – occur in psycho-analysis so that 'weakness' may come to be seen as healthy vulnerability, 'failure' as a necessary rebellion and so on (cf. Chapter 7).

An important aspect of ambiguity in psychotherapy is the idea of recon-ciliation of opposites, or integration, to use a Jungian term. It is implicit in

Freud's writing (Rieff 1979) and is to be found in the concepts of reconciliation, compromise, sublimation, in his image of the horse and rider as a
model for the healthy relationship between unconscious and conscious, and
his ironic prescription of the replacement of neurosis with 'ordinary human
misery' as the aim of treatment. The impulse to reconciliation is implicit in
Lowell's poem title which balances an ambiguity in the meanings of the word
blue: blue in the sense of depressed, and blue in the sense of constant (true
blue), the blue of the sky and the 'azure day'.

WHOLENESS

The idea of the harmonious resolution of ambiguity leads on to a third
important characteristic of aesthetic languages and one that is part of Freud's
description of the primary processes. This is the quality of wholeness or
Gestalt (Köhler 1929). A poem or a piece of music or even a picture may
have a narrative drive that is more or less important but we also require of it
that it should exhibit coherence, be a whole, in the sense that every part fits
with every other part.

There are several characteristics of this quality of coherence. First, each
part of the whole points to and in some way 'contains' every other part. We
can usually identify the whole of a symphony or poem from a single phrase.
This quality is related to 'style' or 'tone' and is distinct from content. This
characteristic can be compared with the holograph, a type of image that can
be produced by a laser in which each part contains in reduced detail the
information present in the picture as a whole. A second quality associated
with wholeness is timelessness. A picture has no particular 'direction' and is
thus extra-temporal in that it does not insist on being 'read' in any order. The
same is partially true of a poem in that the ending is informed by the
beginning (this is obviously also true of prose and secondary processes) but
the opening of the poem is also reflexively influenced by what is to come. A
third and perhaps paradoxical feature of wholeness derives from what Blanco
has described with reference to the unconscious as its being a series of
'infinite sets' (Pribram 1981): that is, there is no end to the elements that the
wholeness encircles. In the interpretation of a poem there are a number of
meanings and interpretations that apply, each of which may have its own
level, and none of which need be incompatible. Between the surface of a
work and its deep meaning there is an infinite series of layers.

These three characteristics, interconnectedness, timelessness and limitless-
ness, are all important elements in the psychotherapeutic process. The second
patient mentioned above once remarked that 'psychotherapy is based on
sound ecological principles – everything is recycled, nothing wasted'. He
was referring here to the principle that the therapist is primarily interested in
pattern and process, rather than goals. He is, or should be, concerned with
every aspect of the process that is created between himself and the patient,

whether the patient is a little late or a little early, whether he initiates the end of the session or leaves it to the therapist, the manner and tone in which the story is told. The patient may naïvely expect the truth to be found in the distant past, in the content of his story; the context and manner of its telling are equally revealing. They tell what the patient has made of what he is made of. It is sometimes said that the whole of treatment is 'contained' in the first session, and the theme of a particular session is often to be found in the patient's opening remarks or initial expression. Much of the art of therapy consists in finding the connections between apparently unconnected elements within a session, of finding a single thread or nuclear theme, a phantasy or affect that summarises the hologram. An example of this would be the notion of primal phantasies such as the primal scene which reflect an individual's fundamental view of the male–female relationship expressed in bodily sexual terms. From this basic equation a whole series of subsidiary relations can be deduced: the person's attitude towards his own body, that of the opposite sex and so on. Edelson (1975) has likened this to Chomsky's concept of a 'deep structure' to language from which, by transformational grammar, a potentially infinite series of sentences can be generated. Patients frequently express surprise at a therapist's capacity to remember the detail of past material, but this too is a consequence of the mission to find an holographic organising principle by which apparently disconnected elements may be understood and so remembered.

The idea of timelessness is well-established in psychotherapy, most notably in dream-interpretation, in which the elements of the dream may be read in any order, whatever the narrative flow of the dream itself. An important consequence of this feature of aesthetic language is that it adopts a rather different approach to causality than that demanded by logical se-quencing. It is not that childhood traumata *cause* adult neuroses, but rather that both are connected in a psychological circuit or mental structure. In psychoanalytic short-hand this circuit would be described in terms of a particular phantasy.

This links also with the concept of over-determination. One senses that Freud was never entirely happy with his observations that many factors and phantasies underlie a particular symptom or element in a dream. His rational scientific training taught him that one event should have one unambiguous cause. The concept of over-determination is a rather uneasy attempt to retain the idea of unitary causation by postulating a single higher cause – over-determination – that embraces the observation of multiple causation. The idea of wholeness on the other hand suggests that multiple and non-incompatible relationships are an inherent property of the poetic and psycho-therapeutic modes.

If poetic and psychotherapeutic truth is inherently infinite this is not, however, a justification for the seeming endlessness of some analyses. There is no clear relationship between the number, frequency and duration of psychotherapeutic treatments and the eventual result. Perhaps we should echo Baudelaire and admit that analyses, like poems, are never completed, only abandoned.

A final aspect of the wholeness of aesthetic language comes from the etymological link between wholeness and healing. The explicit goal of psychotherapy is to heal the patient. A healing function is also implicit in poetic activity. This is how W. H. Auden (1963) formulated one of what he called the 'dogmas of his art':

> Every beautiful poem represents an analogy to the forgiveness of sins; an analogy not an imitation, because it is not evil intentions which are repented of and pardoned but contradictory feelings which the poet surrenders to the poem in which they are reconciled.

The wholeness of the poem heals. Psychotherapeutic treatment also involves the surrender of the patient to the treatment in the hope that contradictory feelings will be reconciled. As Marcus (1974) puts it, the patient tells, at the outset, an incomplete story, which, by the end of treatment, has changed:

> because the narrative account has been rendered in language, in conscious speech, and no longer exists in the deformed language of symptoms, the untranslated speech of the body. At the end, at the successful end, one has come into possession of one's own story. It is a final act of self-appropriation, the appropriation by oneself of one's own history.

CONCLUSION

The aim of this chapter has been to look for points of similarity between poetic and psychotherapeutic activity. The fact that it is possible to make such a comparison at all has been used by some to argue that psychoanalysis is an 'art' rather than a science and so, in our science-based culture, to question its status and validity. This has led at times to a defensive, self-justificatory and rather sterile attitude in psychotherapeutic research, a preoccupation with 'outcome' and a neglect of process. I would argue rather that a broader view of the mind and imagination can point to fundamental psychological mechanisms: an approach that embraces both poetry and psychoanalysis may reveal fundamental ways of thinking that any general psychology would also need to take into account.

The question remains whether the categories I have described – metaphor, ambiguity, wholeness – are themselves any more than metaphors or whether they can be directly related to working psychophysiological models of the mind. It is beyond the scope of this chapter to consider this in detail but some suggestive findings may be mentioned. For example, there is good evidence to suggest that the brain itself is organised holographically. Lashley's classical ablation experiments support this, and modern studies of the neurophysiology of vision have showed that, instead of single cortical receptor neurones suggested by Hubel and Weisel's original work, there are a cascade of cortical neurones which respond, like harmonics, to a single retinal stimulus (Pribram 1981) (cf. Chapter 2).

Pribram and Gill (1976) have argued that Freud's distinction between the primary and secondary processes corresponds with modern computer-based ideas about brain functions, which can be divided broadly into those concerned with energy processing and those concerned with information handling. The former are the primary processes – the imaginative activities we have been considering in this chapter. They propose a model of thinking in which the primary processes make an array of crudely defined images, stimulated by the sensory input, but based on the state of the memory-store. The secondary processes then select among this array and develop them further. Both poetry and psychoanalysis would, on this model, be concerned to alter the internal state of the organism (its 'fictions') so as to enlarge the range and valency of the array which would lead to more effective adaption via the secondary processes. The capacity to handle metaphor and ambiguity would then reflect the extent of interconnectedness of information, and its availability in the memory-store. This approach is consistent with recent work on unconscious perception which shows that the perceptual impact of a stimulus is greatly influenced by the subject's internal emotional state (Dixon 1982).

Another important point of scientific contact is with the findings of modern ethology (Hinde 1982; Bateson 1981; Bowlby 1969), which suggests that adult primates need to be highly skilful in social interaction if the group is to survive. The evolution of imagination has enabled individual members of the group to understand one another's feelings, and so to fulfil the essential co-operative functions of nurturing, reproduction, defence and so on. Hazlitt anticipated this when he emphasised the importance of the 'sympathetic imagination', quoting Cleopatra: 'He's speaking now, or murmuring "where's my serpent of old Nile?" ' as an example of imagination's myriad mirrorings as Shakespeare imagines Cleopatra imagining Anthony imagining her.

A poem is a specialised device for the communication of imaginative feeling. As Auden (1963) said, poetry provides no programme for action; it offers a deliberate escape from the adult necessities of action and decision. Bronowski (1978) echoed this when he said that a poem is so arranged that 'it positively discourages you from deciding which of its imaginary actions (which of its possible meanings) you like best and should follow'. In this sense poetry enriches, but does not guide. Psychoanalysis works in a similar way. No action is suggested or encouraged. The therapist remains involved, but neutral. In this will-less atmosphere of neutrality and deliberate unreality the imagination can flourish. The patient can experience his own and others' feelings – especially those that are central to his 'biological destiny' (Rycroft 1966) – and this may lead him to act in a more coherent and integrated way, which in turn may lead to better adaption and group survival.

Chapter 11

Discovery in the practice and teaching of psychotherapy

It is difficult to capture and convey the essence of psychotherapy. The living shared experience which constitutes the psychotherapeutic encounter – 'that primitive form of communication which requires the presence of the object' (Bion 1962) – is necessarily elusive. Psychoanalytic theory on the whole has a tendency to pass over this difficulty and to concentrate more on the content of treatment rather than its underlying structure. The aim of this chapter is to focus on the psychotherapeutic method itself, the core element of which, I contend, is the process of *discovery*. The main function of the therapist is to create conditions in which discovery can take place. The nature of these discoveries is always uncertain. If, as is sometimes the case, therapists see their task as revealing known truths to patients, they have become dogmatists and have failed in their mission. I shall illustrate this particular account of the psychotherapeutic method by three non-psychotherapeutic examples – one scientific, two literary – and a final section explores how these literary analogies may inform the teaching and supervision of psychotherapy.

The point of these comparisons is not to elevate the status of psychotherapy (even if that were necessary) from a treatment to a creative art, but only to acknowledge that writers (and scientists) do in some ways face problems similar to those faced by psychotherapists. This applies both to the primary activity of writing (Wordsworth's 'emotion recollected in tranquillity') but more especially to secondary attempts to give an account of the creative process itself. Since, in addition, writers by definition are likely to have special literary skills, any description they give of themselves at work should be of interest to self-reflective psychotherapists who wish to teach their craft. This comparison may also help to illuminate the complex nature of psychotherapeutic interaction and to help understand the activity that underlies the therapist's apparent passivity.

I shall start with an incident which occurred in supervision:

A postgraduate student came with the report that she had suddenly noticed a great change in her patient. Both patient and therapist were attractive young women in their late twenties. The patient had had a disturbed and difficult background: she was an illegitimate child whose mother had only married when she was ten. She had never really accepted her stepfather and half-siblings, and left home after a row with her mother – who was a doctor – over a boyfriend. Two marriages had followed and her depression, which was the presenting problem, coincided with the birth of her first child. The therapy proceeded with a transference of compliance and covert rivalry, eagerly noted and interpreted by the therapist – who was stimulated by the patient and enthusiastic about the treatment – but with no real feeling of change.

Then, suddenly, in the session before the supervision, came the break in the deadlock. The patient arrived wearing a dress, for the first time. She began to speak of her envy of her colleagues at work – she was an actress – and of how she longed to look and carry herself like them. The therapist had mentioned at the start of the session that she would be away soon and the patient then went on to speak of her envy of the therapist, of her feeling of anger and abandonment about the break, and to remember similar experiences as a child when her doctor-mother left her to go to work, and later to go on holiday with her new husband.

In discussing what might have happened the therapist suggested that she might have been preoccupied with preparation for her forthcoming psychiatric examinations (hence the break) and so perhaps had been less anxious to *help* her patient. She had – to use a phrase deployed by E. P. Thompson (1982) in a different context – 'leant off' her patient, and in doing so had created the conditions in which *something new could happen*.

THE PSYCHOTHERAPEUTIC METHOD

I begin with this rather commonplace anecdote because it contains within it the key ingredients of what, in this account, constitutes the psychotherapeutic method: that is, an attempt to create conditions within which a therapeutic *experience* can occur, which can then be identified and understood. There are four sequential elements in this process, as described below.

1   Structure

Dynamic psychotherapy may appear to the uninitiated as a vague, inconsequential activity. In fact a prerequisite of successful psychotherapy is a definite structure. This consists first of the setting itself – the regularity of time and place; second, the consistency of the therapist's personality and posture – non-revealing, non-directive, empathic, warm but non-possessive; and third, of the theoretical orientation that informs his or her questions, interventions and interpretations. This containing structure, firm but not rigid, allows feelings to concentrate, especially those between therapist and patient, just as the strong walls of a crucible are an essential for a chemical reaction to proceed. One patient described this structure as a 'tennis wall' against which he could bounce his feelings, knowing that they would be returned in a predictable way, but often at a new angle. The same patient commented that after three years of therapy, 'I have changed so much but you [the therapist] seem to have remained exactly the same as when I first walked in.'

2 Space

A structure, or boundary, automatically defines a *space* within which the therapy can take place. The concept of space in therapy has been discussed by several authors in recent years (e.g. Green 1975; Pedder 1979). In the example I have given it was the movement from *concentration* to *relaxation* or 'leaning off' that created the space that allowed change to take place when the therapist became preoccupied with her exam. She stopped trying too hard. Perhaps the most potent form of psychotherapeutic space is silence. The therapeutic dialogue differs radically from 'normal' conversation in that it contains a large number of pauses, silences and lulls. In these, therapists adopt a posture of active listening in which they are attending both to the patient and to their own inner world whose 'contents' (the tʰerapist's countertransferential phantasies) are often a guide to the state of the patient. This may lead to a comment or interpretation, followed by another silence in which the patient may identify his or her *own* inner space and its contents. Thus there is a sequence of silence (space)–comment (structure) that clears a new space allowing for the emergence of the third step in the psycho-therapeutic method: discovery. It is essential that therapists be able to attend to and understand their own inner world. The development of this capacity is a necessary part of training for psychotherapy whether this is through supervision, training group, or personal therapy.

3 Discovery

Given structure and space (a crucible and its chamber) and the reactants of therapist and patient, the conditions are set for change: something new can now happen in the safety of the therapeutic laboratory. Initially this will be the revelation of unexpected or unwanted feelings, private thoughts and phantasies, forgotten emotions, hidden patterns. As therapy proceeds these feelings come to focus more and more on the therapeutic process itself, the transference. A central aim of therapy is to allow this process of discovery to happen. Several psychoanalytic writers have looked at this aspect of therapy. Bion (1962) called the creative faculty of the mind, inhibited in neurosis but released in therapy, the 'α-function'. Winnicott speaks of 'learning to play' (Winnicott 1971) and Malan (1979) (cf. Chapter 7) of the 'leapfrogging' which follows a correct interpretation: a sequence of interactions in which both patient and therapist alternately build on what the other has said.

I prefer the term discovery to the more usual 'insight' for a number of reasons. First, true insight has to be differentiated both from insight in the psychiatric sense of not being psychotic and from mere intellectual insight. Second, the notion of insight often arrogates the therapist: insight is what therapists 'have' and what they 'give' to their patients. Third, discovery is a dynamic term and therefore emphasises the importance not of insight as such, but the *acquisition* of insight. The patient is helped as much by the emotional experience that accompanies discovery as by the insight itself. Discovering is as important as what is discovered. This, in my view, follows from the general aim of psychotherapy which is to enhance the *autonomy* of the patient (Holmes and Lindley 1989). The imaginative leap required for discovery contributes to the development of *imaginative competence* (cf. Chapter 3) which is a precondition of autonomous action.

This is not to argue that *any* act of discovery is necessarily therapeutic. The central vehicle of change in analytic therapy is transference. It is the uncovering of feelings about the treatment and the therapist – *transferential experience* – that makes insight come alive. Only through transference is the patient likely to experience how his 'internal parents' can continue to influence feelings and actions long after childhood has been left behind. This leads to greater autonomy both because of the inherent spontaneity of the autonomous imagination and because the internal world, once discovered, no longer becomes a determining (although still a limiting) influence on action.

There is perhaps a paradox inherent in this account: therapy arranges for the predictable emergence of the unexpected. The psychotherapeutic method is a known structure that, through the play of space and structure, fosters the discovery of unknown feelings.

4 Description

The fourth element is the language and theory in which this process is described. This includes both the private shared language with which patient and therapist come to communicate, and the theoretical language with which therapists 'think' and which links them with their colleagues and psychotherapeutic tradition.

The argument of this chapter is that these four linked elements form, like the repeated steps of a dance, the essential pattern of the psychotherapeutic method. They are to be found both at the level of the individual session and also in the overall trajectory of the treatment. This approach places *discovery* at the heart of the psychotherapy. In view of the continuing debate about psychotherapy's uncertain status as an art or science (e.g. Glass 1984) it may be of interest to compare the psychotherapeutic method with descriptions of scientific and artistic discovery.

SCIENTIFIC DISCOVERY: MEDAWAR

I turn first to one of psychoanalysis's severest critics: P. B. Medawar. Despite his hostility to psychoanalysis he has much to say that is of interest to the psychotherapist who wishes to understand and teach his craft (Medawar 1984). The scientific method, as the Popperian Medawar sees it, is based on the 'hypothetico-deductive' system. In this, hypotheses are subjected to critical experiments in which they may be falsified. Where then do hypotheses come from? Here is Medawar's answer to that:

> Every discovery, every enlargement of the understanding, begins as an imaginative preconception of what the truth might be. The imaginative preconception – a 'hypothesis' – arises by a process as easy or as difficult to understand as any other creative act of mind; it is a brainwave, an inspired guess, a product of a blaze of insight. It comes *anyway* from within and cannot be achieved by the exercise of any known calculus of discovery.
>
> (Medawar 1984; italics added)

The giveaway in this passage is the dismissive 'anyway'. Medawar, in common with many creative thinkers, both artistic and scientific, probably does not wish to examine his imaginative capacity too closely for fear of inhibiting it. In my view psychotherapy *is* a method – a 'calculus' – which creates conditions under which personal discovery may occur. The nature of these conditions may well be structurally similar to those governing artistic and scientific discovery.

For Medawar the essence of the scientific method is the interplay between hypothesis and experiment:

> The dialogue I envisage is between the possible and the actual, between what might be true and what is in fact the case – a dialogue between two voices, the one imaginative and the other critical.

In the scientific method the hypothesis is tested via the experiment, against reality. In psychotherapy reality is reviewed, in the session, against discovery. The painful reality of the patient's distress or difficulty is seen in a different light as hidden feelings are discovered. The past cannot be altered, but it can be reinterpreted and so re-experienced. In science the hypothesis proposes, the experiment disposes; in psychotherapy reality proposes, the discovery disposes. Therapy is about what a person makes of what he or she is made of. One aim of therapy is to release creativity – the same creativity which, for Medawar, is integral to scientific innovation. This is not necessarily creativity with a capital 'C', associated with any tangible artifact, but merely a sense of inner freedom and so an enlarged possibility for autonomous choice, action and enjoyment. The structural elements I am putting forward are precisely that 'calculus of discovery' whose possibility Medawar dismisses with such ease.

The sequence I have described, structure-space-discovery, is not arbitrary. My argument is that it is a fundamental pattern that underlies certain creative, imaginative and therapeutic activities. In support of this I shall turn to two writers who have been especially interested in the workings of their own imagination.

ARTISTIC DISCOVERY: HEANEY

The first example is the contemporary Irish poet, Seamus Heaney. He contrasts two important elements in poem-making (Heaney 1980). These are what he calls *craft*, i.e. mechanical skill in metre, rhyme, etc., and '*technique*' which is more akin to our term 'discovery' since it is about getting discovered feelings into words and down on paper. A similar distinction applies in psychotherapy: it is quite possible to be theoretically proficient in the rules of psychotherapy – creating the proper setting, making the right interpretations – and yet for nothing significant really to happen with the patient. This is pure craft, empty without discovery.

Conversely, therapists who are all discovery and no craft may engender powerful feelings in themselves and their patients that they cannot really turn to therapeutic advantage. The transference may become too intense, and the patient may break off, or the therapist may become forgetful, and inconsistent, missing sessions or not telling patients about breaks – all resistances engendered by discovery without craft. This is Heaney:

> I think technique is different from craft ... Learning the craft is learning to turn the windlass at the well of poetry. Usually you begin by dropping the bucket halfway down the shaft and winding up a taking of air. You are *miming the real thing* until one day the chain draws unexpectedly tight and you have dipped into waters that will continue to entice you back. You'll have broken the skin on the pool yourself.
>
> At that point it becomes appropriate to speak of technique rather than craft ... It involves the discovery of ways to go out of the normal cognitive bounds and *raid the inarticulate: a dynamic alertness* that mediates between the origins of feeling in memory and experience and the formal ploys that express them ... Technique entails the *watermarking* of your essential patterns of perception, voice and thought into touch and texture ... That whole creative effort of the mind's and body's resources to bring the meaning of experience within the jurisdiction of form. Technique is what turns, in Yeats' phrase, 'the bundle of accident and incoherence that sits down to breakfast into an idea, something intended.'
>
> (Italics added)

Several phrases in this passage can be applied to psychotherapy.

'Miming the real thing'

Students often start out by a kind of miming of therapy often based on an imitation of their own teacher, supervisor or therapist. It is very important in supervision to accept this phase, but also to help the student to mark the moment when the 'real thing' occurs. It is often important too to learn to *fail*. The student in supervision mentioned earlier had had a previous patient who had suddenly broken off treatment, probably because of the intensity of the therapeutic atmosphere. This failure had taught her not to try so hard next time.

'Raid the inarticulate'

Psychotherapy is always working on the inside edge of confusion and chaos, on or near the borders of an abyss. The teacher has to help the student not to run away from confusion but to live with it, to accept and understand it. Simple techniques for escape from confusion are sometimes invaluable. Often students say in supervision what they 'really' felt about a session but were somehow unable to communicate directly to the patient. The supervisor's job will be to question why the students had been unable to express the thought during the session itself, and to give them the courage to do so in future sessions.

'Dynamic alertness'

This is yet another attempt to describe that state of negative capability, free-floating attention, or unfocused awareness that is essential to creative therapy and yet so difficult to achieve. It is this that creates the space that is needed for the patient's self-discovery to happen.

'Watermarking'

This image has potent implications for therapy. Patients are struggling to identify their feelings, to find their own voice. For Heaney this struggle takes the form of an internal dialogue. In therapy the dialogue is with the therapist, but the aim of therapy should be to initiate a dialogue which, after treatment ends, patients can continue to have with themselves.

The poet starts by using the voices of his poetic 'parents', the literary tradition he inherits. When he finds his own way to voice his feelings he has broken free, incorporated his past, but extended it. Patients undergo a similar struggle first with their internal parents and later with the therapist.

Heaney goes on to quote his own poem:

The Diviner
Cut from the green hedge a forked hazel stick
That he held tight by the arms of the V:
Circling the terrain, hunting the pluck
Of water, nervous, but professionally
Unfussed. The pluck came sharp as a sting.
The rod jerked with precise convulsions
Spring water suddenly broadcasting
Through a green hazel its secret station.
The bystander would ask to have a try
He handed them the rod without a word
It lay dead in their grasp until nonchalantly
He gripped expectant wrists. The hazel stirred.

The diviner's forked stick stands metaphorically for poetry – the vehicle through which feelings can be located, mediated, controlled. The technique of psychotherapy does the same job, often seeking the salt water of tears in the session. In the poem there is an important formal relationship between the sought water and the sap of the stick: a 'green hazel' finds 'spring water': poetry conjures up the feelings that it describes. A similar arrangement applies to the 'green stick' of transference which permeates the whole of the psychotherapeutic relationship: therapy is designed to bring back, or 'broadcast' buried feeling through the creation of transferential experience – but in a controlled and so modifiable form.

Another theme that comes out in this poem is the debilitating power of the expert. The supervisor has to be careful not to induce feelings of helplessness in the student by boasting his or her own prowess.

Heaney goes on:

Technique is what allows the first stirring of the mind round a word or an image or a memory to grow towards articulation ... The crucial action is pre-verbal, *to be able to allow* the first alertness or come-hither, sensed in a blurred or incomplete way, to dilate and approach as a thought or a theme or a phrase. Robert Frost put it this way: 'a poem begins as a lump in the throat, a homesickness, a lovesickness. It finds the thought and thought finds the words' ... technique is more vitally and sensitively connected with that first activity where the '*lump in the throat*' finds '*the thought*' than with 'the thought' finding 'the words'.

(Italics added)

'To be able to allow'

This is another version of the 'space' step in the sequence I have described. A mental 'leaning off' is needed for the origins of a poem to be captured; a similar process is needed for patients to find their feelings and therapists their interpretations in psychotherapy.

The 'lump in the throat' finds 'the thought'

This emphasis on technique rather than craft is reminiscent of Winnicott's (1971) dictum – we help our patients more by giving back to them what they have told us than we do by clever interpretations. This is the basis of Rogerian therapy and the converse of the *furor therapeuticus* that can afflict some highly theoretically sophisticated therapists.

ARTISTIC DISCOVERY: PROUST

I move on now from the muscular cadences and rhythms of Heaney to the deliciously smooth prose of Marcel Proust. I make no apology for quoting from what must be one of the most famous passages of self-observation in modern literature. Proust (or his protagonist) is handed a cup of tea by his mother. In it he dips a *petite Madeleine*. This teacake immediately arouses in him a memory. But of what?

> I put down my cup and examine my own mind. It is for it to discover the truth. But how? What an *abyss of uncertainty* whenever the mind feels that some part of it has *strayed beyond its own borders*: when it, the seeker, is at once the dark region through which it must go seeking, where all its equipment will avail it nothing. Seek? More than that create. It is face to face with something which does not exist so far, to which it alone can give reality and substance, which it alone can bring into the light of day.
>
> (Proust 1941; italics added)

This would do – were it not for Proust's slightly overblown style – as a description of the anxiety that the psychotherapy student (and the patient) may feel when first confronted with the area of uncertainty which they have to enter: as the panic which both may feel when 'the history-taking has to stop'.

Something new has to happen. But how to make it? In the following passage Proust describes the phase of structure or concentration that delineates space into which a memory or feeling can come. The function of the therapist at this stage is, by creating the setting, by facilitating remarks, to help build that structure or container that the patient needs.

> I decide to attempt to make it [the memory] reappear. I retrace my thoughts to the moment at which I drank the first spoonful of tea. I find again the same state illumined by no fresh light. I compel my mind to make one further effort; ... I clear an *empty space* in front of it. I place in position before my mind's eye the still recent taste of that first mouthful, and I find something start within me, something that leaves its resting-place and attempts to rise, something that has been embedded like an anchor at a great depth; I do not know yet what it is, but I can feel it mounting slowly;

I can measure the resistance, I can hear the echo of great spaces traversed.

(Italics added)

The next passage describes the moment of discovery of the memory (it reminds him of the teacake his aunt gave him as a child in the village of Combray). The link between the present and the past is the taste of the teacake. This, like transference, is the connection that allows the memory to surface. The transferential moment is a living experience in the session (the patient's angry response to the therapist's announcement of her holiday) that can provide a bridge to the significant past (the absence of the patient's mother). The key phrase in the passage that follows is the 'magnetism of an identical moment'. There is a movement from concentration to relaxation and then, under the pull of this magnetism, to discovery.

> Will it ultimately reach the clear surface of my consciousness, this memory, this old, dead moment which the *magnetism of an identical moment* has travelled so far to importune? I cannot tell now that I feel nothing, it has stopped, has perhaps gone down again into its darkness, from which who can say whether it will ever rise? Ten times over I must assay the task, must lean down over the abyss. And at such time the natural laziness which deters us from every difficult enterprise, every work of importance has urged me to leave the thing alone, to drink my tea and to think merely of the worries of today and of my hopes for tomorrow, which let themselves be pondered over without effort or distress of mind. And suddenly the memory returns.
>
> (Italics added)

My final quotation is perhaps the most famous of all, and justly so. This is partly because of its sheer beauty, but also because it describes so clearly the movement from depression and ruination through memory to recollection and reparation that is the essence of therapy. Another important aspect of this passage is its clear sexual imagery. Proust describes a 'vast structure', filled with a tiny drop of 'essence'. This may be seen as a concrete and bodily expression of the regenerative power of intercourse. We remind students that ultimately the 'ego is a body ego' (Freud 1921) and that sexual metaphor will probably apply at some stage to the process of therapy:

> When from a long-distant past *nothing subsists*, after the people are dead, after the *things are broken and scattered*, still, alone more fragile, but with more vitality, more unsubstantial, more persistent, more faithful, the smell and taste of things remain poised for a long time, like souls, ready to remind us, waiting and hoping for their moment amid the *ruins* of all the rest; and bear unfaltering, in the tiny and almost impalpable drop of their *essence*, the *vast structure* of recollection.
>
> (Italics added)

CONCLUSIONS

I have tried to demonstrate an underlying sequence which is fundamental to successful psychotherapy and to relate it to other creative activities. A theory of the psychotherapeutic encounter itself is just as necessary as 'formal' psychodynamic theory (cf. Goldberg *et al.* 1984). The literary parallels I have tried to draw provide some validation of the four-stage model and in particular of the part played by creativity in the psychotherapeutic process.

I will now draw some conclusions about how this approach may inform the teaching and supervision of psychotherapy. The teacher has one overall and a number of specific tasks. The overall task of the trainer is to act first as 'midwife', then 'health visitor', and later as 'tutor' to the treatment: to help trainee and patient to create and sustain a living therapy with a boundary and character of its own. The trainer must be familiar with the lifecycle of a therapy on a broad scale – the phases of starting, symptom loss, transference neurosis (positive and negative), resistance, depression, reparation, illusion-ment–disillusionment, grief, loss and acceptance. He or she must also be aware at a micro-level of session-to-session issues of lateness, absence, silence, overtalkativeness and other details of therapeutic rhythm.

Some of the more specific tasks of the trainer may be derived from the account I have given of the psychotherapeutic method. These include:

1 Helping the therapist to find the right *level* at which to do therapy. Students, and patients, can tolerate very different distances from 'the abyss'. There always has to be some confusion and anxiety, but not more than each can cope with.
2 Identifying what therapist and patient have *left out*. Therapy always involves a 'raid on the inarticulate' and the supervisor needs to point to areas which remain unspoken or are conspicuous by their absence.
3 Knowing the importance of *failure*. Most students (and all teachers started off as students) have had important failures when they were, to use Heaney's words, in the 'miming' phase of learning to do therapy. The inevitable mistakes that students make often provide rich opportunity for understanding more about themselves and their patients.
4 Knowing how to create conditions in which '*something can happen*'; knowing when to concentrate with firm limit-setting and probing questions, and when to back off and so create an 'empty space'. The rhythm and tact of this balance constitute the true art of therapy. The supervisor has to be able to help the overcontrolling student who is all concentration and no space at one extreme, and at the other the trainee who is all space and letting things happen and so is overrun by the patient. The supervision session often creates a 'second-order transference' between trainer and trainee, which reflects this clinical relationship between student and patient.
5 Helping the student to recognise and voice *transferential experience* when it occurs. This is perhaps the most important and the most difficult skill to

impart. Students have to learn to recognise the *metaphorical* nature of the material their patients bring.

The following is an example in which the patient taught the student to think metaphorically. The patient complained that her chair was always stuck right in the corner of the room. One day she arrived to find it, by accident, moved nearer to the therapist. She became very excited and began to tell him how she had always felt trapped and stuck away as a child and how angry she was that, as she saw it, her parents had not bothered to help her out of the 'corner' of her misery.

Transference is a special form of metaphor involving the carrying over of feelings and emotions from one situation to another via 'the magnetism of an identical moment'; these moments are often turning-points in therapy. They reveal in an inescapable way the nature of the patient's internal world and the distortion it imposes on their view of contemporary reality. At the same time these transferential moments bring with them the affect which, like Proust's lost memory, may otherwise continue to haunt but elude the patient.

6 To find a *shared language* with which to reflect on and describe what is happening.

It is hardly necessary to add that these six ways in which the teacher can help the trainee parallel those in which, with luck, dynamic therapy may help the patient.

Chapter 12

Two cultures, two nations
The implications for psychotherapy

INTRODUCTION

In the opening scenes of Evelyn Waugh's novel *Scoop*, William Boot, nature
correspondent of the *Daily Beast*, famous for such lines as 'feather-footed
through the plashy fen passes the questing vole ... ', is summoned from his
remote country seat to the metropolis. The newspaper's proprietor, Lord
Copper, has been tricked by the brilliantly scheming Mrs Algernon Stitch into
appointing Boot war correspondent to the Civil War in the remote country of
Ishmaelia. Copper brooks no refusal; every time Boot protests that his
speciality is nature, not war, he doubles his salary. Boot goes, and eventually
returns a hero, having, through sheer naïveté and luck, got the story which
eluded the sophisticated Fleet Street journalists. But he was the wrong Boot
all along. Mrs Stitch's protégé was Courtney Boot, the fashionable novelist.

Memories of this plot came to mind when I opened, with excitement and
some anxiety, Joan Raphael-Leff's letter of invitation to give the third *British
Journal of Psychotherapy* annual lecture. Had they got the wrong person?
What could a rural refugee, only partially assimilated into the mainstream of
psychotherapy, have to offer that would be relevant or interesting? But then,
like Waugh's readers, I abandoned myself to the Oedipal reverie of the
changeling, the naïve younger brother, who, with the help of the good fairy,
outflanks the corrupt patriarchal order. Tempering this phantasy with reality,
I began to think that perhaps there *was* something to be said for a view from
the periphery, a rural worm's-eye view of urban psychotherapy. I reminded
myself that Waugh had also made a move from London to the West Country,
that *Scoop* marks the transition from the witty chronicler of the gay young
things of the 1930s to the more serious concerns of his later novels; that
psychotherapy might need, if not a barefoot view, at least a gum-Boot as well
as a Gucci.

To continue in this homespun vein, I sometimes view a psychotherapy
session as a tangled skein of wool in need of unravelling. The first task is to
find a loose end and to work back from that to the main theme of the session.
My themes in this chapter are *assimilation*, *envy* and *inequality*. As in a

session, I shall be approaching them from a number of different angles – first literary, then sociopolitical, finally clinical. Talcot Parsons, a psycho-analytically trained sociologist, saw the social function of psychotherapy in terms of the assimilation of alienated individuals into the mainstream of society (Parsons 1951); this view of the role of psychotherapy has to be reconciled with the Kleinian understanding of the part played by envy in preventing the assimilation of good experiences.

The issue I am preoccupied with in this chapter is the problem of how envy may be overcome and assimilation achieved, when the inevitable helplessness of infancy is reinforced by real material deprivation; and whether psycho-therapy has sufficient *outsight* to face this issue.

MOVING HOUSE

The 'loose end' that formed the starting point of this talk was an article entitled *Moving House* which appeared in the *London Review of Books* written by a Mr H, an English Lecturer. In it he described his marital difficulties, depressive breakdown, and subsequent psychiatric treatment (Hyde 1988). He attributed the onset of his illness to the rise in house prices in the South East. Feeling that his house was 'inadequate' he had sold it but had then been trapped by rising prices which made it impossible for him to afford another. I was astonished to read that his psychiatrist had not only firmly told the patient that all forms of psychotherapy were useless, but also offered to solve the problem by selling him *his* house. This prompted a letter to the *L.R.B.* in which I wrote:

> The author's account of his psychiatric breakdown is a sad reminder of the separation between the 'two cultures', psychoanalytic and medical, which so handicaps British psychiatry today. Anyone with a modicum of psycho-analytic training would have seen Mr H's anxiety about his house as more to do with his relationship with his wife and inability to value himself than with the monetary value of his property.
>
> His psychiatrist's offer to sell him *his* house reveals at best a complete unawareness of the phenomena of transference and countertransference; at worst, it was, like his denigration of all forms of psychotherapy, highly unethical. It was a relief to read that the house sale, if not the treatment, fell through.
>
> (Holmes 1988)

There was an ironic postscript to this story to which I shall return, but this clash between 'English' and 'scientific' psychiatry had reawakened memories of the 'two cultures' debate which broke out in the 1960s between the novelist-scientist C. P. Snow (Snow 1959) and the literary critic F. R. Leavis (Leavis 1962), and led me to reread their work, hoping to throw some light on the continuing debate between biological psychiatry and psychotherapy.

I shall first consider Leavis, because his work has interesting parallels with psychotherapy. The 'Leavisite' approach had an impact on literary and cultural thought which lasted half a century, stretching from his first championing of T. S. Eliot's *The Waste Land* in the 1920s, until the seismic shifts in political and cultural life in the early 1970s led to the gradual eclipse of Leavisism as a dominant paradigm in literary criticism.

For Leavis, the critic approaches the text in the same way as the analyst responds to the patient's material; and on the basis of this he makes a judgement, analogous to an interpretation:

> A judgement is personal and spontaneous or it is nothing ... The form of a judgement is 'This is so, isn't it?', the question asking for confirmation that the thing *is* so, but prepared for an answer in the form, 'Yes, but ...', the 'but' standing for correction, refinements, precisions, amplifications. The judgements may be 'value-judgements' but they are in intention universal.
>
> (Leavis 1975)

Leavis is straining here with the problem that good criticism is always a personal response to the text, but this emphasis on individual response undermines the critic's claim to authority and universality of judgement. The critic is in a similar position to the analyst who 'knows' his perception of the case is 'right', but lacks any absolute criterion by which to establish his correctness. Somehow he has to hold to this view while knowing that alternative formulations, both within psychoanalysis and from different psychotherapeutic approaches, can be shown to be no less convincing or therapeutically effective.

Leavis' solution to this problem was to endow the critic with a special discriminatory sensibility which, in relation to the novel, meant considering only a small number of selected authors – Austen, Eliot, Dickens, James, Lawrence and Conrad – as inheritors of the 'great tradition' and more or less dismissing the rest as being of secondary value. A similar tendency towards exclusivity can be observed in some psychoanalytic circles. The critic then becomes a member of a Coleridgean 'secular clerisy', a defender of the Faith, an arbiter of taste not in the ephemeral dilettante sense, but as one who *knows* what is good and bad, what is valuable and what is dross.

Leavis' social vision is in the tradition of enlightened individualism, where the critic occupies a special place within the university and society in general; his job is to defend standards and values in a secular world characterised by moral chaos. Leavis saw literature as a 'third realm', neither public nor private, creating an invisible community between writer, reader and critic to all responding to 'the black marks on the pages': 'a product ... of human creativity' with 'an essentially collaborative nature' (Leavis 1975).

There are parallels here with Winnicott: the concept of culture as occupying a transitional space between private and public: words on the page, like a transitional object, coming to life as an act of primitive creativity; the essential *value* of the psychoanalytic encounter in its creation of an 'invisible community of two' to use Philip Rieff's phrase (Rieff 1979); learning to read a text, like 'learning to play', a vital ingredient in any culture.

In Winnicott and other independent psychoanalysts we see the convergence of the Romantic tradition with psychoanalytic thought, a breaching of the careful barriers put up by Freud against Romanticism in his quest for scientific credibility and his fierce rejection of German mysticism (Turner 1988).

Leavis' approach, then, continues the Romantic tradition of creativity, individualism and a nostalgia for a pre-industrial past. He harks back to a community of artisans, based on the neo-medievalism of William Morris and the early socialists. At the same time he rejects the Marxist ideals of a classless society and espouses individualism and defiant *in*equality, quoting Lawrence:

> We are all different and unequal in spirit – it is only the social differences that are based on accidental material conditions. We are all abstractly and mathematically equal, if you like. Every man has hunger and thirst, two eyes, one nose and two legs. We're all the same in point of number. But spiritually there is pure difference and neither equality nor inequality counts.
>
> (Leavis 1962)

Lawrence's distinction here between the social and spiritual defines a territory vacated by religion that psychoanalysis has increasingly come to occupy. The emphasis on the primacy of individual experience prefigures psychoanalytic rejection of the headcounting and statistical obsessions of contemporary scientific psychiatry. At the same time it opens the way for a social vision in which, in Rieff's startling phrase: 'psychoanalytically speaking, there were free slaves in Athens, as there are enslaved citizens in Manhattan' (Rieff 1979).

We must now return for a moment to the English lecturer and his psychiatrist. Following my letter, *both* of them contacted me. The psychiatrist telephoned and in a friendly but reproving way pointed out that I had made the elementary clinical mistake of only listening to the patient; that he was in fact quite sympathetic to psychotherapy and employed nurse therapists on his wards; that this patient had been extraordinarily difficult and that, as a psychiatrist, what he needed was support from psychotherapy, not ill-informed public criticism. Not long after this the patient then wrote to me saying that he was planning to publish an account of his illness and the treatment he had received, enclosing a draft account of what had happened between himself and the psychiatrist over the house.

What was at issue here, it seemed to me, was an overwhelming theme of envy. The patient found it unbearable that the psychiatrist should earn more than he did, should live in a larger house and should be in a position of power over him. The psychiatrist in turn may well have felt a twinge of envy at a patient who had the licence to be so unreasonable and demanding. Both seemed to blame their wives, implying that it is women who stimulate men's envy, and showing how demandingness is projected into the envied breast and then attributed to it. The patient ended touchingly with the acknowledgement of his 'psychotic bit' which:

> never goes away altogether and I'm still stuck, to a certain extent, in the world of the Freudian id, which does not know time and space. A bit of me wants to believe that it can go back to the past, to the little house where we were happy; the rest of me knows that this is a sentimental fiction; so I'm split.
>
> (Hyde 1988)

At this point I shall follow the patient in his regressive wish to return to the past to a world apparently free from envious destructiveness which could not be contained within the psychiatric system and had spilt out into the external world of literary debate.

> Mr H was undoubtedly a difficult patient. Let us consider instead the case of Miss E. There are no hints here of psychosis or self-harm. Miss E is an attractive, comfortably off twenty-two-year-old, lively and intelligent: an ideal training case for psychotherapy perhaps. She lives in the country with her kind but ineffectual and hypochondriac father. Her mother died when she was ten, and her much older sister married several years ago. The precipitant of her seeking 'treatment' was the marriage of her governess and companion, Mrs W. Miss E felt inexplicably troubled and bereft by this, despite the power and status of her parentified role in relation to her elderly father. She has no boyfriend or lover and has vowed that she will 'never marry'. She has a 'therapist', a Mr K, a man in his forties, with all the features of what Bollas (1986) calls a 'transformational object'. He is strong, detached, slightly mysterious; available for a variety of transferential perceptions as brother, father and lover; taking a benign interest in his 'patient', but well able to resist her manipulations. He is sensitive immediately to the latter, principally her tendency to matchmake and meddle in the affairs of other young people and to try to pair them off.

EMMA

Readers will have realised that this 'patient' is none other than Emma Woodhouse, living in the village of Hartfield, whose 'case-history' forms the basis of the mistress-piece of Leavis' Great Tradition, Jane Austen, who remained single and arranged many marriages for her characters in her novels. Emma's 'therapist' is Mr Knightley, her brother-in-law, who discusses her case in 'supervision' with Mrs Weston:

> 'There is an anxiety, a curiosity, in what one feels for Emma. I wonder what will become of her.'
>
> 'So do I,' said Mrs Weston gently, 'very much.'
>
> 'She always declares she will never marry, which, of course, means just nothing at all. But I have no idea that she has yet ever seen a man she cared for. It would not be a bad thing for her to be very much in love with a proper object. I should like to see Emma in love, and in some doubt of a return; it would do her good.'

I have suggested that there is a parallel between the psychoanalytic moral view and the Leavisite notion of literature as the basis and bastion of moral development in a secular world. Let us follow Emma's progress through the book with a psychodynamic eye, starting with the notion of mild deprivation, of therapeutic abstinence, of the fact that, as Kohon (1986) puts it 'the analysand will have to reconcile himself with the fact that the primary object will never be found again', seeing Emma's difficulties and character-disturbance partly in terms of a delayed mourning for her dead mother, partly a consequence of the Oedipal short-circuit resulting from this bereavement so that she becomes the mother of the house without having to face, and overcome, envy.

Emma's disavowed sexuality is projected into her socially inferior protégé, Harriet Smith, an orphan who is a friendly, attractive but rather simple girl, without apparent depth. Emma mistakenly decides that Harriet and the local curate, Mr Elton, would be ideal partners. Emma starts to paint Harriet's portrait and when Elton comes to watch she imagines her plans are developing nicely. But it is the painter, not the painted whom Elton desires. Emma's authorial exemption (paralleling Jane Austen's) is challenged. She discovers she is object as well as subject; when Elton proposes to *her* she is furious, not least because it confirms what Knightley has insisted all along. But this disappointment leads to a reconciliation with Knightley and, with his help, the beginnings of an appreciation of inner differentiation between her envious 'vain spirit' and her stage-of-concern 'serious spirit'. At the same time she begins to experience the stirrings of sexuality when, at a dance, she sees Knightley in a new light:

> 'Does my vain spirit ever tell me I am wrong?'
>
> 'Not your vain spirit, but your serious spirit. If one leads you wrong, I am sure the other tells you of it.' ...
>
> 'Whom are you going to dance with?' asked Mr Knightley.
>
> She hesitated a moment, and then replied, 'With you, if you will ask me.'
>
> 'Will you?' said he, offering his hand.
>
> 'Indeed I will. You have shown that you can dance, and you know we are

not really so much brother and sister as to make it at all improper.'
'Brother and sister! – no indeed.'

This moment of awakening sexuality has profound consequences for Emma. She begins to emerge from her omnipotent narcissism, and to face the problems of rivalry, competition, envy and jealousy which she has hitherto avoided.

An important point of similarity between psychotherapy and 'English', in the Leavisite sense, is the way in which change and self-knowledge can grow out of apparently trivial events – a session which starts a few minutes late, a bill wrongly paid, a slip of the tongue – which, acting as sudden unexpected windows into the unconscious, reveal key issues in a person's life. Like the beat of a butterfly's wing which, according to chaos theory (Langs 1989), can change a whole pattern of prevailing weather (cf. Chapter 15), mutative moments are often built on apparently minor episodes around which plot and character crystallise and turn: Proust's petite madeleine; what happened or did not happen in Forster's *A Passage to India* in the Marabar Caves; and, in *Emma*, the Box Hill episode.

A picnic, to be held at Box Hill, is agreed upon by the Hartfield gentry. The movement from house to open air, from village to open country, is an important backdrop to this momentous episode in Emma's moral development. Feelings are loosened, the reins of respectability relaxed. Emma's parentified status has hitherto shielded her from rivalry and competition, but now she begins to experience intense discomfort in relation to Jane Fairfax, a talented but enigmatic young woman, secretly engaged to the eligible Frank Churchill with whom Emma has had a flirtation. Jane Fairfax is, like Harriet, an orphan but lives with her grandmother, and with her aunt, the kindly but rather dim Miss Bates.

Emma proposes a Victorian parlour-game based on quotations; Frank Churchill conveys her suggestion to the assembled company:

'She only demands from each of you, either one thing very clever, be it prose or verse, original or repeated; or two things moderately clever; or three things very dull indeed; and she engages to laugh heartily at them all.'
'Oh! very well,' exclaimed Miss Bates; 'then I need not be uneasy. "Three things very dull indeed." That will just do for me, you know. I shall be sure to say three dull things as soon as ever I open my mouth, shan't I? (looking round with the most good-humoured dependence on everybody's assent). Do not you all think I shall?'
Emma could not resist.
'Ah! ma'am, but there may be a difficulty. Pardon me, but you will be limited as to the number – only three at once.'
Miss Bates, deceived by the mock ceremony of her manner, did not

immediately catch her meaning; but, when it burst on her, it could not anger, though a slight blush showed that it could pain her.

Emma's barb has struck home; Miss Bates is momentarily humiliated. But why is this tiny moment of aggression so significant? Emma has no mother and a useless father. For her, there is no one to contain and transmute her Oedipal stirrings of sexuality and rivalry. Jane Fairfax, adored by her aunt and grandmother, loved by Frank Churchill, admired by all for her beauty and talent, arouses Emma's envy, her rivalry, awakening in her an awareness of her own mother's absence, perhaps, too, feelings of anger towards her dead mother, all of which fuel her subtle but psychologically deadly attack on Miss Bates.

But if Emma can own these feelings she can change. She can abandon her narcissism ('one thing very clever') and accept moderation, even dullness. Knightley is at hand to help with this. His rebuke – 'it was badly done indeed!', especially because 'she is poor' – leaves Emma mortified and speechless:

How could she have been so brutal, so cruel, to Miss Bates! How could she have exposed herself to such ill opinion in anyone she valued!

We see here the beginnings of the depressive position, the stage of concern:

Time did not compose her. As she reflected more, she seemed but to feel it more. She never had been so depressed.

The novel now moves speedily to its climax. Emma discovers that her protégé Harriet has designs on Mr Knightley and believes her feelings may be returned. Threatened with the loss of the loved object, Emma feels the full force of desire for the first time. Suddenly, in the famous phrase:

It darted through her with the speed of an arrow, that Mr Knightley must marry no one but herself

awareness of desire, the possibility of loss, of envy, of her *position* in relation to Harriet and Miss Bates opens her to the self-knowledge she has hitherto avoided.

It was this knowledge of herself which she reached. She was ashamed of every sensation but the one revealed to her – her affection for Mr Knightley. Every other part of her mind was disgusting. With insufferable vanity had she believed herself in the secret of everybody's feelings; with unpardonable arrogance proposed to arrange everybody's destiny.

Emma begins to reconcile herself to the conviction that she has lost Knightley for ever; and the beginnings of some sort of calm descend upon her with this acceptance of loss, of banishment from a longed for country:

Consolation or composure could be drawn from the resolution of her own better conduct, and the hope that, however inferior in spirit and gaiety might be the following and every future winter of her life to the past, it would yet find her more rational, more acquainted with herself, and leave her less to regret when it were gone.

But help is at hand to alleviate the misery of this painful maturity, to move her on through the pricked bubble of her narcissism, in the shape of the English weather, so vital a metaphor of shifting feelings, such an important aspect of life in the countryside:

> The weather continued much the same all the following morning; and the same loneliness, and the same melancholy, seemed to reign at Hartfield; but in the afternoon it cleared; the wind changed into a softer quarter; the clouds were carried off; the sun appeared; it was summer again. With all the eagerness which such a transition gives, Emma resolved to be out of doors as soon as possible. Never had the exquisite sight, smell, sensation of nature, tranquil, warm, and brilliant after a storm, been more attractive to her. She longed for the serenity they might gradually introduce.

Emma is at last ready to receive Knightley. She no longer *possesses* him; he is no longer a phantasised brother, father, an extension of her needs and controlling desires. He appears diffident, uncertain, *different*. She can approach him, for the first time, as an equal. A space exists between them intimating uncertainty and mystery, but also creativity, possibility. Using metonymy they can speak at last of what is on both their minds, through a reference to the impending marriage of Frank Churchill and Jane Fairfax. The possibility of marriage, prefigured in the reader's mind throughout the book just as the Oedipal situation prefigures mature sexual longings in the course of psychological development, can declare itself at last as Emma and Knightley take a turn in the garden:

> They walked together. He was silent. She thought he was often looking at her, and trying for a fuller view of her face than it suited her to give. And this belief produced another dread. Perhaps he wanted to speak to her of his attachment to Harriet; he might be watching for encouragement to begin. She did not, could not, feel equal to lead the way to any such subject. He must do it all himself. Yet she could not bear this silence. With him it was most unnatural. She considered, resolved, and, trying to smile, began –
> 'You have some news to hear, now you are come back, that will rather surprise you.'
> 'Have I?' said he quietly, and looking at her; 'of what nature?'
> 'Oh, the best nature in the world – a wedding.'

The book ends of course with the wedding between Emma and Knightley:

> The wedding was very much like other weddings, where the parties have
> no taste for finery or parade ... But in spite of these deficiencies, the wishes,
> the hopes, the confidence, the predictions of the small band of true friends
> who witnessed the ceremony, were fully answered in the perfect happiness
> of the union.

As psychotherapists, we can't help hoping for happy endings for our patients
and ourselves. We too are 'a small band of true friends' who know that what
counts is not finery or parade, but moral strength and maturity, often based on
suffering overcome; we know too that this development cannot be forced, but
must be allowed to emerge from a silence, spontaneously, playfully, within
the trajectory of the analytic setting.

THE TWO CULTURES

It is usually unwise, and certainly unfair, to accuse a writer of what they have
not said, of what has been left out. And yet, as psychotherapists, it is
precisely such gaps in our patients' narratives that interest us.

Alongside the great psychological insight and accuracy of *Emma*, is there
perhaps not something wrong, something missing? For a start, by staying
within the formula of 'happy-ever-after' Austen leaves unexamined what
happens *after* marriage and, if the analogy is accepted, Emma ends up
marrying her analyst! If Mr Knightley is Emma's transformational object, so
too, in *Middlemarch*, is Dorothea's Mr Casaubon. Fifty years on from Jane
Austen, a George Eliot or a Gustave Flaubert could take marriage, and a
disastrous one, as a starting point for the exploration of sexuality, fulfilled
and unfulfilled, and the possibilities both for growth and destruction which
the accommodation and compromise entailed in real relationships produce.

Another silent area in *Emma* derives from the fact that it was written and
published during the Napoleonic wars, in the aftermath of the French
Revolution, and yet no hint of these momentous events are to be found
anywhere in the book. The little community of Hartfield remains isolated and
insulated from the world stage, as indeed it may realistically have been: the
historical and political context is never allowed to disturb the tranquillity of
the gardens and houses where the action is played out.

Third, there is the problem of Jane Austen's restricted class palate, the fact
that her observations are confined to a small section of society. As Raymond
Williams puts it:

> Neighbours in Jane Austen are not the people actually living nearby; they
> are the people living a little less nearby who, in social recognition, can be
> visited. What she sees across the land is a network of propertied houses and
> families, and through the holes in this tightly drawn mesh most actual
> people are simply not seen. To be face-to-face in this world is already to
> belong to a class. No other community, in physical presence or in social

reality, is by any means knowable. And it is not only most of the people who have disappeared ... it is also most of the country, for the rest of the country is weather, or a place for a walk.

(Williams 1973)

Jane Austen for all her sensitivity and moral integrity appears never to question a world that is in some respects incestuous; neglects social and political reality; and is confined in its concern to the problems of a particular and numerically limited social class. And this brings us back to the 'two cultures', to Leavis and Snow, and for our purposes to contemporary psychotherapy – at which these charges could also, with at least some justification, be levelled.

Leavis, it will be remembered, was defending values, discrimination, individualism, the complexity of culture, against what he saw as the crassness and moral irrelevance of science. Against this, Snow, I had thought, was defending the aesthetic value of science: arguing that the second law of thermodynamics was no less a thing of beauty than a Grecian urn. But on rereading Snow I discovered that his real message, put with a certain banality, was a social and political one. He was struggling against the marginalisation and isolation of the intelligentsia – against Pascal's 'we die alone', or Conrad's variant 'we live, as we dream – alone' to make a point about the transformational power of science to overcome poverty, inequality and injustice:

Each of us is solitary. Each of us dies alone: alright, that's a fate against which we can't struggle – but there is plenty in our condition which is not fate, and against which we are less than human unless we do struggle. Most of our fellow human beings for instance are underfed and die before their time. In the crudest terms, *that* is the social condition. There is a moral trap which comes through the insight into man's loneliness: it tempts one to sit back, complacent on one's unique tragedy, and let the others go without a meal.

(Snow 1959)

Snow was thus trying to link the problem of the 'two cultures' – the division between arts and science – with that of the 'two nations' – the rich and the poor – described by Disraeli in his novel *Sybil* (1845).

Looking back on the Leavis–Snow controversy, and also considering the implications of the debate for psychotherapy, we might conclude that each is both right and wrong. Leavis is right because of his emphasis on the importance of the individual; because he resists the melting down of differences into a featureless mass of humanity which can be shaped by social forces; because he champions creativity and truth as central values in any culture. He is wrong because of his inherent élitism; because in the end the 'English' which he advocates is based on a nostalgic wish to return to a preindustrial Arcadian past that is irretrievably lost; because of his cultural snobbery and refusal to contemplate ideas that are not consistent with his outlook.

Snow's faults lay in his simplistic approach to the complexities of psychological and political reality. But he was surely right in his vision that without science there could be no solution to the problem of the 'two nations'. And he was surely correct when he sensed the limitations of a culture which represents no more than the interests of a particular class; correct too in his realisation of the need to go beyond *Emma* (and for our purposes *beyond* psychotherapy as it is currently practised) to a wider vision:

> What happens in *Emma* ... is the development of an everyday un-compromising morality which is in the end separable from its social basis ... it is in this sense that Jane Austin relates to the Victorian novelists who had to learn to assume ... that there was no necessary correspondence between class and morality ... that cultivation, in its human sense had to be brought to bear as a standard *against* the social process of civilisation ... Jane Austen provided emphasis which only had to be taken outside the park walls, into a different social experience, to become not a moral but a social criticism.
>
> (Williams 1973)

What, it might be asked, has all this to do with psychotherapy? This return to Jane Austen, to Leavis and Snow, has in part been a parable: an attempt to illuminate an ambivalence within psychoanalysis and psychotherapy about its status as a science or an art; its social role; and its position as a source of moral or social criticism.

Freud, as everyone knows, began his career as a medical scientist and medicine was the Trojan horse with which psychoanalysis infiltrated the citadel of science. Medical science, while providing a vehicle for psycho-therapy, also embodies, through social medicine, an implication of universal applicability which psychotherapy has yet fully to embrace. Jane Austen's awareness of the need for 'cultivation', for honesty, for self-knowledge and acceptance, for personal growth, for unmanipulative personal relationships, for respect and tolerance, for mature sexuality even, could if 'taken outside the park walls' become a morality with the potential for social trans-formation. So too the values of psychotherapy – its emphasis on autonomy, on the importance of intimacy in relationships, on the necessity for dealing with loss by grief and mourning, its acknowledgement of destructiveness and the possibility of transmuting hate into something positive through the use of a containing object (whether this is a parent or an institution) – have universal applications which society neglects at its peril (Holmes and Lindley 1989).

TWO NATIONS: 'ADAPTING OUR TECHNIQUES ... '

Given that hope, we can now come on to some of the problems associated with a widened availability of psychotherapy, bearing in mind Melanie Klein's contrast between the effects of excessive and superable envy:

When envy is excessive, the infant does not sufficiently build up a good object, and therefore cannot preserve it internally. Hence ... he is unable to establish firmly other good objects in his inner world. But in children with a strong capacity for love the relation to the good object is deeply rooted and can, without being fundamentally damaged, withstand temporary states of envy, hatred, or grievance ... when these negative states are transient, the good object is regained time and time again.

(Klein 1957)

Let us set against this Freud's confidence in the possibility of a widened availability of psychoanalysis:

One may reasonably expect that at some time or other the conscience of the community will awake and admonish [society] that the poor man has just as much right to help for his mind as he now has for the surgeon's means for saving his life ... the task will then arise for us to adapt our techniques to the new conditions.

(Freud 1919)

But the challenge of 'adapting our techniques to the new conditions' is far from simple. For once outside the park walls, psychotherapy encounters problems previously only encountered in symbolic form. 'The poor' do make a brief appearance in *Emma*. Just as Emma is beginning to experience sexual attraction for the first time and is flirting with Frank Churchill, Harriet, her sexual alter-ego, while out walking, is frightened by a group of rough, dirty gypsies, who demand her purse. Fortunately, Frank Churchill arrives in the nick of time and she is rescued. The gypsies have more psychological than social significance here and represent not the real dispossessed, but rather an expression of fears of defloration, dirt and dispossessed sexuality.

What is the attitude of psychotherapy towards poverty? And what are the psychological implications when real deprivation reinforces envy? Do we, like Jane Austen, say, ironically perhaps, but emphatically:

Let other pens dwell on quiet and misery. I quit such odious subjects as soon as I can.

Or in E. M. Forster's statement of this ironic dismissal:

We are not concerned with the very poor – they are unthinkable and only to be approached by the statistician or the poet.

A first necessity is to distinguish poverty as a reality from what Neville Symington, who ran a free-at-the-point-of-delivery psychotherapy service in Camden for many years, called 'delusions of poverty in middle-class patients' (Symington 1980). Here emotional poverty, which is no less real, has to be separated from material deprivation, and may require different psychotherapeutic responses.

Consider Sheila Ernst's account of an analysis in which:

> My analyst wore a suit, lived in a large house in a middle-class suburb with a neat garden, had a wife who didn't work and a spotless child who went to private school. I still don't know what his assumptions were about women's role or what he thought about my attempts to combine being a student with taking most of the responsibility for the house and my small step-son, and being a trade union activist ... He was not oppressive in the blatant way that feminist writers on therapy have documented. He didn't try to seduce me, tell me I should use make-up or dress differently, accuse me of being incapable of real love because I didn't have orgasms.
>
> The oppression lay in *who he was*, the questions *he didn't ask* and the material *I didn't present*. It lay in the way I felt when I arrived at his house on my bicycle and he drew up in his large car; in the sense that I had that he must see his wife and family and home as normal and my household as a sign of my abnormality. To be cured would be to be capable of living like him.
>
> (Ernst and Goodison 1981)

Are we not dealing here with questions which could be dealt with in the transference, with a cultural rather than a material gap between patient and analyst? And are Ernst's complaints not merely a denial of Chasseguet-Smirgel's (1985) double difference: the difference between the generations, and the difference between the sexes? Could they and similar demands for a democratic psychotherapy not be seen in terms of envy, of a false search for:

> A balm for our wounded narcissism and a means of dissipating our feelings of smallness and inadequacy. This temptation can lead to our losing the love of truth and replacing it with a taste for sham.
>
> Chasseguet-Smirgel 1985)

Chasseguet-Smirgel sees a preoccupation with poverty, with dirt, as part of a regressive envy-based perversion in which authority and leadership are denied. She connects the psychology of sadism with the politics of the French Revolution, the origins of which lie in the wish to escape the 'paternal order':

> The pervert will attempt to give himself and others the illusion that anal sexuality (which is accessible to the little boy) is equal and even superior to genital sexuality (accessible to the father) ... In reality, in order to have a genital penis and to procreate, it is necessary to grow up, to mature, to

wait, whereas faeces are a production common to adult and child, woman and man. The two differences between the sexes and between generations are abolished at the anal level. Time is wiped out.

(Chasseguet-Smirgel 1985)

Chasseguet-Smirgel sees it as the job of psychotherapy to help patients to develop a necessary patience, so that the Oedipal task of discovery and acceptance of the 'double difference' can be successfully undertaken. But there is another difference, which psychotherapy is itself in danger of denying – the difference between the classes. And Chasseguet-Smirgel, however perceptive in her account of envy, has little useful to say about how social change comes about. Unlike Winnicott, she cannot see the constructive aspect of hatred (Turner 1988). For her, the little boy who points to the unclothed Emperor is always regressively wanting to abolish differences, to see the powerful as no more than naked babies like himself, and from this perspective psychoanalysis seems inescapably linked to the established order, to stability, differentiation and hierarchy. But the psychobiological realities of growth and development can be used as a cloak for social differences which are often arbitrary and mutable. The progressive potential of medical science, by this sleight of hand, is perverted so that moral criticism is reduced to biological inevitability.

The theoretical and technical problems which confront analytic psychotherapy if it is to become more widely available and yet remain true to itself are formidable, and are often underestimated by its enthusiastic champions. For example, in a study of the referral process for psychotherapy from a deprived inner-city group practice to which I was attached, and where there was a strong ideological bias towards positive discrimination for the underprivileged, I found that working-class patients formed only about one-third of those who were referred (as opposed to the two-thirds that would have been statistically representative), and of those finally taken on for psychotherapy by experienced therapists (as opposed to medical students) only one in eight were from the working class (Holmes and Lindley 1989).

Here is an example of one of these cases and of the technical problems posed by attempts to overcome the 'two nations' in psychotherapy.

The patient was a man of twenty-eight taken on for weekly analytic psychotherapy. He had been brought up in the East End of London in conditions of emotional and material poverty. After leaving school he had worked for a while in a printing firm. When he was eighteen his mother, who had been ill for many years, died of cancer. He became very depressed, gave up work, and refused to leave the house where he lived with his father, a cantankerous respiratory cripple. A visiting psychiatrist diagnosed schizophrenia, probably wrongly, and prescribed monthly injections of a major tranquilliser. The young man continued with these for three years, but remained confined to his house. One day he had a violent row with his father, and left to live in another part of the city. Through the Social Services Department he was housed in a bed-and-breakfast hotel, and eventually referred again for psychiatric help because of his obvious depression. As I got to know him it became clear that his whole world-view was based on mistrust and suspicion. 'How can you expect me to trust anyone?' he ranted. His father was a 'bastard', the psychiatrist who gave him the injections 'ought to be locked up', the social workers were 'no good' and kept offering him flats that were 'unsuitable': everyone let him down, kept him waiting, didn't care. I tried to listen patiently to these tirades, and at first had no difficulty in empathising with his plight. I attempted, with little success, to steer the patient's thoughts to his mother's death and the anger and disappointment it had left him with. Feeling burdened by the bleakness and emptiness of the patient's life (as I perceived it) and that the patient needed more than could be offered in once-weekly sessions, I thought that it might be helpful if he were, in addition to his sessions, to attend a Day Hospital. The patient suddenly became furious. 'How can you make suggestions like that?' he shouted. 'You don't realise how difficult it is for me even to come here to the hospital to wait in the waiting-room, let alone go into a new situation with strangers.' I replied that perhaps he felt he was being passed on or got rid of, just as he may have felt abandoned when his mother died, and that perhaps *this* was what had made him so angry. The patient lost his temper: 'You middle-class bastard, you don't give a damn about me, sitting there with your well-paid job, your nice wife and kids, your comfortable home in the suburbs. What do the likes of you know about the way I live – in a damp room with no money, noisy neighbours, no job, walking the streets in the freezing cold?' (it was a bitter November day). 'You're just doing your job, waiting to go home, you don't care about me one bit.'

The force of this outburst was shocking. The attack had hit home, leaving me speechless and feeling inadequate. In the end I replied that while I accepted the validity of what the patient had said, I also felt that he was using his misery in a self-destructive way. The patient's no doubt accurate perception of my concerns for my own life should not be a justification for inertia, or become a way of avoiding the need to find a future and to free himself from a paralysing attachment to his dead mother. The patient missed the next two sessions, but, rather to my surprise, did return, and work continued. Eventually he began to attend the Day Hospital and, while remaining on the fringes of 'normal' society, became less depressed and paranoid, survived the untimely death of his older sister, and formed a tenuous relationship with an ex-patient.

The Klein-influenced American psychoanalyst Robert Langs is critical of the way in which therapists behave differently with 'clinic patients' (equivalent to our NHS or Social Services-funded psychotherapy departments) compared with those they see in private practice. In his view, 'frame violations' are much more likely to occur: cancelled or changed appointments, sudden changes of tack, referrals (as in this case) to other agencies and he links these to the observation that drop-out rates are much higher among poor patients in free facilities than for middle-class patients seen in private practice (Cheifetz 1984). From this perspective my inability to interpret, tolerate and transmute the patient's rage, emptiness and envy led to the frame-violating Day Hospital referral, which in turn merely reinforced his deep sense of rejection and injustice rather than helping him to face and overcome it.

No doubt my failure to interpret his envy *was* partly based on my own unanalysed guilt and envy, avoided by the easy privilege of the therapist's position, just as Emma could avoid envy and guilt through her parentified position. But it must also be acknowledged that there was a real basis for his envy, one that could certainly not be overcome by analytic therapy alone. This leads on to an important unexplored lacuna within psychoanalytic psychotherapy. For Freud, countertransference was the blind spot which meant that therapists, no less than patients, must subject themselves to analysis. Roustang (1980) and others have pointed to a further blind spot within this blind spot, one often collusively shared with the analyst's analyst: the 'unanalysable transference' to psychoanalysis and Freud's ideas themselves. My concern in this chapter has been with a third area of potential blindness within analytic psychotherapy, located at the boundary rather than the focus of our field but, like peripheral vision, none the less central for all that. This is a lack of *outsight*, an unawareness of the social position of therapy, without which psychotherapy remains confined within *its* park walls, limited in its capacity to address the psychological problems of the poor, or to tackle the interplay between material and psychological deprivation.

CONCLUSIONS

But what, even given outsight, is to be done? We know that simply to take psychoanalysis, unmodified, out of the consulting rooms and into the community mental-health centres, the GP practices, the psychiatric hospitals just does not work, any more than it would have worked if Jane Austen had been asked to centre her novel on the gypsies rather than the owner-occupiers of Hartfield. We know this at a practical level – the problems encountered by the community mental-health movement in the USA in the 1970s, of which Robert Langs is so cogently critical and which we are now trying to emulate in this country (cf. Part IV), show that. We also know it at a theoretical level. We know that assimilation is impeded by envy; and we know that envy is inevitably increased by deprivation and trauma. We also know that we cannot be all things to all men: it is in the nature of the Oedipal situation that by trying to be everything we end up as nothing; only when omnipotence is abandoned, is real potency possible. Only when Emma gives up her meddling, faces her envy and acknowledges her loss, can she make real choices and on that basis form new attachments.

And yet, despite – perhaps even because of – her exclusivity, Jane Austen, as Raymond Williams implies, does have a message which can be more widely applied. Emma's values of honesty, self-scrutiny, her distaste for finery and snobbishness as well as her love of fun and wit, stand against those of the Eltons and the Churchills and, within the community of Hartfield, may even have had a modifying influence. And if we are searching for a contribution from psychoanalysis in the fight against arbitrary inequality and injustice it may also be at the level of values and attitudes, alongside its limited role as a practicable treatment for the few. This is not to argue that psychoanalysis should not be much more widely available; that modified treatments do not have a great deal to offer; or that far more state-funded therapies should not be provided for the less well off. Leaving aside these practical considerations, however, I shall conclude by considering four key themes in which I see the clinical insights of psychoanalysis making a general contribution to the critique of an inequitable society. These are *assimilation*, *pluralism*, *irony* and the *transformational image*.

Assimilation

I have suggested that, from a sociological perspective, the function of psychoanalysis could be seen as a means of integrating outsiders excluded from a dominant culture. Freud's genius was to take his own particular historical and cultural situation as a partially assimilated Jew and to develop a theory and technique that had universal applicability. Psychoanalysis recognises that we are all outsiders, none of us fully assimilated. Freud, as Lacan (1977) realised, saw the contradiction between a culture that is always excluding, which means that the 'I' is *always* a social construct, and the absolute necessity for integration into this socially constructed culture. The ironic transformation which follows from this is that the assimilated, differentiated 'I' acquires a freedom, including the freedom to challenge the values of the assimilating culture. This is Raymond Williams' 'cultivation' which turns a wilderness into a garden; a wild, motherless, omnipotently meddling girl into a mature woman.

Pluralism

The fashionable notion of pluralism is used by the Left as a justification for 'anything goes' absurdities; by the Right as a justification for the status quo – the rich man in his castle and the poor man at his gate remain pluralistically where they are. From a psychoanalytic perspective pluralism involves differences of position; but not of value. Pluralism is consistent with inequality, but not inequity, and its developmental perspective implies that the more differentiated people are, the more equal they become. As Emma's moral development proceeds, she moves from dependency to assume a unique position with her own special value and contribution, equal to, yet different from that of Knightley. Within the analytic setting, the patient comes to accept that there is no absolute distinction between himself and the analyst, simply a difference of role. At another level, acceptance of pluralism implies a lessening of envy so that, for example, psychoanalysis would accept the strengths *and* limitations of its position without the fear, which Freud expressed of, being assigned to the graveyard of 'Methods of Treatment' within psychiatry. Pluralism requires mutual respect between psychoanalysis and other forms of psychotherapy (in contrast to the experience of the English lecturer with whom we started), cross fertilisation between them, and an acceptance of valid forms of scientific influence and evaluation, rather than a Leavis-like wholescale rejection of science.

Irony

The mature ego defence of irony is another central value of psychoanalysis with important general implications.

The ironic vision sees through pretensions and defences – both of patient and therapist – to a deeper level of reality, but at the same time does not belittle the need for defence and protection; it acknowledges human vanity and self-centredness without trying to eliminate them. It is a moral, but not a proselytising vision. In its original meaning the ironist was a dissembler – one the intention of whose words conveyed the opposite of their surface meaning. The Christian slave who told the Roman guard 'I am going to my father's house' was an ironist in this sense. This defensive dissembling later took on further meanings: paradox – a deep truth revealed by apparent surface incongruity – and, in tragic irony, a vision of the way in which people's projects are confounded by events over which they have no control. The patient who became furiously depressed in her sixties when, at the end of a life in which she had waited dependently and expectantly for fun and attention from her hard-working husband when he retired, but whose mother then became ill and had to be looked after, and whose husband and mother then died within a few weeks of each other, needed to be listened to with a sense of tragic irony.

The ironic vision sees and accepts human folly; and in psychotherapy, through the notion of countertransference, it ensures that the therapist's vision is never a fixed Archimedean point, but has always to be questioned. The novelist too can include him or herself and the reader in an ironic self-scrutiny: as, for example, does George Eliot in the following passage, relevant to our theme of whether poverty should be seen by psychotherapists as reality or phantasy:

I am led to reflect on the means of elevating a low subject ... to observe that ... whatever has been ... narrated by me about low people may be enobled by being considered a parable; so that if any bad habits and ugly consequences are brought into view, the reader may have the relief of regarding them as not more than figuratively ungenteel, and may feel himself virtually in company with persons of some style.

The transformational image

Finally, we must consider a fundamental value of psychoanalysis which brings us close to the process of thought itself, to what might be called (Bollas 1986; Langs 1988) the *transformational image*. Change, at both a personal and a political level, often coalesces around an image. In therapy this can be a thought, a dream, a phantasy, an artefact, a transferential moment (as with the patient who shouted), or even a delusion which contains within it all the themes, conflicts and potential with which the patient is struggling. The capacity of such imagery to contain in a concentrated form both love *and* hate, and to act as a pivot around which transformation from bad to good can occur, forms a focus of opposition from psychoanalysis to a contemporary culture which tries to force false choices, divisions and exclusions. I shall end with a brief clinical example of such imagery.

> The patient was a man in his thirties who had come into treatment because of chronic feelings of anxiety and inexplicable outbursts of anger. He had been brought up by a depressed and controlling mother, his father having died when he was two. He dealt with his boredom, anger, fear, exhaustion and rejection by compulsively turning to alcohol, cannabis, and watching films on video, especially if mildly pornographic. He found the early stages of treatment excruciatingly difficult as he tried to avoid the empty space of therapy by attempts to fraternise, control, please or antagonise the therapist. Gradually he relaxed. During a break in therapy he acquired some money and thought he would buy a video-recorder, but, rather to his surprise, he bought instead a large, beautiful dolls' house, unfurnished and empty. He wondered what to put inside it, and then had the idea of filling it with tiny clay erotic figures lying on couches, based on Indian sculpture. This transformation of debased into more mature sexuality, the transferential reference to the therapeutic couch, the acceptance of the empty space of therapy and of his own less crowded mind, was marked by an intensification of his investment in therapy, an improved relationship with his wife, and fewer outbursts of rage.

The words country and city in their origins both imply connections, unity. Country comes from 'contra', against: the landscape that lies against the eye, the essential other that contrasts and complements the self. City comes from 'civitas', community (Williams 1973). This man, like many others, had moved from city to country life, to farming work in search of an 'unspoiled' garden, a mother undiminished by loss, undamaged by envy, hoping she would yield her fruits to him. He saw the city he had left behind as no longer a community, more divided than ever into two nations; he experienced a countryside debased and polluted, his idealised mother-woman's body defiled. Through the transformational image, he was able to acknowledge his own hand in destructiveness, to see how good could come out of evil.

The image which helped him was that of the empty dolls' house which, like therapy, acted as a container within which he could put *all* his impulses, good and bad, and where transformation could take place.

I have described four themes, each of which corresponds to a different psychological level and each of which, like Russian dolls, is contained by the next. The transformational image belongs to the id, but depends on an ego capable of irony; the ironic ego depends on a superego that can accept plurality and differentiation; pluralism requires a society prepared to assimilate the whole variety of experience – art and science, psychiatry and psychotherapy, country and city, rich and poor – a society based not on exclusion and denial, but, as in this chapter, on a search for connectedness and community.

Part IV

Psychotherapy and psychiatry

Psychotherapy and psychiatry
An introduction

The previous chapter ended with a discussion of how psychotherapy might contribute to a better society. The three essays in this section continue this wider theme by looking at the place of psychotherapy within psychiatry. They are based on an 'ecological' model of psychiatric services in which treatments are adapted to and modified by the prevailing geographical and sociopolitical environment. The first two essays are in one sense quite parochial. They originate in my move from a centre to a periphery of excellence, from a London teaching hospital with a long tradition of psychotherapeutic psychiatry, to a small, rural self-contained district run along community psychiatry lines, but without any established psychotherapy service. The promise and problematics of practising psychotherapy in such a setting are described. The recent eruption of market forces into the health service has had an enormous impact on the delicate ecological balance between patient, physician (of which the psychotherapist is a specialised form), and government, and the implications of this for psychotherapy services are discussed. The final chapter indulges in futurism and tries to visualise the changes and challenges which psychotherapeutic psychiatry faces in the approaching millennium.

Chapter 13

The contribution of psychotherapy to community psychiatry – and vice versa

INTRODUCTION

This chapter is based on my experiences as a newly arrived consultant psychiatrist/psychotherapist in North Devon (population 140,000), a predominantly rural district that until 1986 based most of its psychiatric facilities in a large mental hospital in Exeter, nearly forty miles away. When Exeter went 'Italian', services were devolved to local districts. North Devon was given the responsibility for providing comprehensive psychiatric care based on a DGH unit, a Day Centre, two hostels and a small multidisciplinary team. No formal psychotherapy services were included in this plan.

This is a familiar enough pattern, one that can be found throughout Europe and North America. I shall try to chart the movement from the heady days of decarceration to current uncertainties about community care, a state which might be called *post-deinstitutionalism*.

My account is informed by the distinction drawn by the sociologist Karl Mannheim (1936) between *ideology* and *Utopia*. For Mannheim, ideology implies deception, albeit unconscious: a justification used by ruling groups to legitimise their position and practices. Utopia reflects the wish to escape from the dominance of the ruling group by those who lack power, based usually on a negation of the existing order. Both, for opposite reasons, avoid certain aspects of reality: ideology because it is static, Utopia because of its insistence upon continuous change.

Community psychiatry has moved rapidly from Utopia to ideology. In the days when psychiatry was almost entirely based in mental hospitals, the hope of a community-based psychiatry became a Utopian ideal, a means of escape from the repressive, authoritarian structures of the total institution, an ideal society in which the mad were sacred and prejudice overcome. Now that community psychiatry has become the dominant paradigm, it in turn is an ideology in which the problems of the post-institutional era – the uncertain fate of the new chronic sick, interprofessional rivalries, the fragmentation of services, the transfer of resources away from mental illness – are concealed under the banner of normalisation. Utopian longings now take the form of a nostalgic wish to return to the good old days of the mental hospital where, like a medieval village in Merrie England, staff and patients lived harmoniously together. Alternatively, a Utopian dream of unlimited resources is envisioned.

Freud always insisted that the essence of neurosis was a turning away from reality. One task of psychoanalysis is to help people to face reality without the need to repress, deny or distort it. However, it should be noted that psychotherapy itself is not immune from ideological or Utopian aspects, when, for example, it denies the reality of mental illness or the need for drug therapy, or when it offers the false hope of discovering some primal trauma which, once identified, will lead to complete cure.

THE NORTH DEVON EXPERIENCE

I shall now to try to show how the introduction of a psychotherapeutic milieu in North Devon helped community psychiatry to move from ideology-based confusion to a more realistic and effective system of care.

Community psychiatry in North Devon started off in good heart with an optimistic, enthusiastic team, housed in a new, spick-and-span unit. But it was not long before difficulties became apparent. 'Nasty' psychiatric patients were unwelcome as they wandered around the rest of the General Hospital; some had to be transferred back to neighbouring districts which had not progressed so fast towards mental-hospital closure. Confusion and disillusionment began to surface.

The problems experienced by the staff manifested themselves in three main ways: *splitting*, *envy* and *delinquency*. Splits were legion. One consultant was seen as 'bad', another 'good'; one ward was seen as having 'nice' patients, another as having all the difficult ones. There was little respect between the in-patient unit and the Day Centre. Tension and rivalry existed between community workers whose values were vaguely psychotherapeutic or systems-based, and the medical 'pill-pushers'.

At times of crisis, especially with difficult patients, these splits became chasms. When a patient committed suicide the consultants blamed the junior staff or each other. On Ward X the staff complained about consultant A's patients who stayed for 'ever' and 'never' got better, unlike consultant B's; on Ward Y it was the reverse. The community team complained that they could 'never' get hold of the hospital team when they needed to, and vice versa.

Envy was also widespread. The surgeons who had been pressing their claim for new operating theatres for years were appalled to see the opening of a brand new psychiatric block, and there was a prevalent myth that psychiatry had somehow hijacked local funds rather than, as was in fact the case, benefiting from monies transferred from the closure of the mental hospital in the nearby district. Some GPs were dissatisfied with the service and one was heard to complain, echoing Williams and Clare (1981), that compared with ten years ago, there were now twice as many psychiatrists seeing half the number of patients.

Perhaps the most serious problem was a subtle delinquency among a few staff members. The majority were devoted, hard-working professionals but these exceptions easily became scapegoats and seemed to reflect a dys-functional aspect of the whole unit. The delinquency took many forms, from minor examples such as never coming to staff meetings, to more serious infringements.

This was by no means the whole picture. As with a borderline patient, the unit contained areas of normal or even good functioning which coexisted with the problems described. Many of the difficulties were seen as intractable or insoluble and a blind eye was turned to them. Nevertheless, there was a general just-below-the-surface awareness of the atmosphere depicted that led to a discomfort and disillusionment about community psychiatry. Nor was the author exempt from these difficulties. I was often inwardly and sometimes openly censorious of what passed for 'therapy' among some staff members who flagrantly transgressed boundaries by treating patients at irregular hours in their homes, even at times meeting them for a drink in the pub! What passed for 'psychotherapy' was often superficial and half-baked, with frequent 'frame-violations' (Langs 1982) leading to unconscious role reversal between client and therapist. No doubt these criticisms were valid, but a lot of good, supportive work was undervalued by such dismissal. The criticisms added to the general atmosphere of splitting and mistrust, and were partly defensive, since the author's psychoanalytic orientation seemed less immediately appealing than common-sense counselling and behavioural methods or cathartic sessions of emotional release.

The contribution of psychotherapy to community psychiatry

Like community psychiatry, psychotherapy also has an ideology in the triple sense of a set of working models, ideals to be striven for, and, at times, a way of avoiding certain aspects of reality. The values of psychotherapy (Holmes and Lindley 1989) include:

1 An emphasis on fostering *autonomy* so that the patient is no longer in thrall to their illness or difficulties, but can choose to direct their life as they would wish. Unlike community psychiatry, which emphasises external barriers to autonomy, psychotherapy aims to remove internal obstacles, so helping the patient to feel more free in relation to himself.

2 The view that a prerequisite for the development of autonomy is a *secure setting* in which the patient feels *held* and *contained*.

3 A *holistic* approach that takes in the entire field. Psychoanalytically this refers to unconscious and irrational elements, including those of the staff;

from a systemic perspective it means that patients, the institution and the staff have to be considered as a system in which no one element is privileged.

4 An emphasis on *thought* rather than action, and on the need to create a *space for reflection* before change can occur.

5 A *developmental* perspective that recognises the need for differentiation and acknowledges real differences between people, based ultimately on Chasseguet-Smirgel's (1985) 'double difference': the difference between the sexes and the difference between the generations.

It is noteworthy that there has been an 'ecological' (Malan 1963) shift in psychotherapy, mirroring the movement in psychiatry from institution to community. Psychotherapists are increasingly preoccupied with the themes of containment and holding in their patients in the face of splitting and fragmentation, rather than, as in the past, focusing on repression and the need to overcome authoritarian structures, both internal and external.

There are several important implications of this perspective for community psychiatry. The mental hospital provided not just a physical structure but also a 'second skin' (Bick 1988) for patients and staff, analogous to the containing function provided by the mother and the family which is then internalised as the child develops. Community psychiatry finds it physically hard to contain its difficult and disturbed patients. Equally important is the lack of the psychological containment needed to hold together a unit divided into numbers of smaller subunits that communicate badly or not at all with one another, serving patients whose inner and outer worlds are also characterised by fragmentation and splitting.

Second, the holistic psychotherapeutic approach recognises the inevitability of negative feelings towards the mentally ill, both in society at large and in the form of countertransference reactions among staff. It is confusing for administrators or psychiatric workers who, following the ideals of community psychiatry, champion the 'rights' of the mentally ill to be treated just like any other ill patients, to find they meet with hostility in the public and, even more disturbingly, within themselves.

Another source of confusion within community psychiatry derives from the breakdown of the traditional medical hierarchy when patients are treated in the community. There is a movement from role rigidity to role blurring within the small units; at the same time community nurses, occupational therapists, social workers, psychologists and others wish to work as independent practitioners rather than submit to psychiatric hegemony. Mollon (1989) has written of the 'narcissistic perils' which befall practitioners when faced with difficult and disturbed patients armed only with an 'all-you-need-is-love' model that de-emphasises pathology, dismisses the idea that the inner world of the patient may be damaged or distorted, and sees only 'environmental failure', 'problems in living' or 'behavioural difficulties'. Workers

easily become confused and discouraged and begin to loose faith in themselves; they start to take avoiding action rather than face problems (see, for
example, Wilson and Wilson 1985).

With its developmental perspective and emphasis on differentiation,
psychotherapy can help clarify and sometimes resolve some of these difficulties by offering a model of pathology that takes account of the internal
world and at the same time is not dismissible as a medical 'label'. It can also
recognise real differences between practitioners in ability, experience and
training without simply reinforcing existing hierarchies, thereby providing a
path between the 'what I say goes' of traditional psychiatry and the 'anything
goes' of community confusion.

The preconditions for a psychotherapy service

A psychotherapy service can make three main contributions to the work of a
psychiatric unit (Grant *et al.* 1991). First it is a *primary* treatment for a
number of important conditions including mild-moderate depression, some
personality disorders, eating disorders and post-traumatic stress disorder.
Second it is an *adjuvant* to other methods of treatment as in the use of family
therapy in schizophrenia. Third it has a role in the *support, supervision* and
training of staff. The main emphasis in this account, however, is on the
preconditions for the setting up of such a service. It is necessary to create a
culture that is sympathetic and receptive to psychotherapy before a service
can be effective, just as, especially with unsophisticated patients, psychotherapy outcome is improved if treatment is preceded by explanatory
sessions (Beutler *et al.* 1986). Seting up a psychotherapy service within a
culture that is rife with splitting and envy can merely accentuate those
tendencies and runs the risk of being marginalised, or seen as an inessential
'luxury' (Holmes and Lindley 1989).

The first objective in North Devon, then, was not necessarily to start 'doing
psychotherapy', but to create a safe, containing setting, based on mutual
respect, which at the same time recognised the real differences between
workers. Two practical steps were taken to this end. First, two adult
psychotherapist posts were created. One was only two sessions per week, but
setting up this post and the discussions which this entailed, especially with
managers, had an important role in educating and explaining the nature and
necessity for psychotherapists as part of the community psychiatric team.

The second step was the establishment of a Psychotherapy Centre and a
half-day psychotherapy training seminar. These evolved from an analysis of
the work of the Day Centre which showed that it provided a sometimes
muddled mixture of drop-in facility, day care and sessional work. The Centre
was reorganised so that day care continued for three days per week but on the
other two the Centre was used for psychotherapy, providing both a service,
and, through the seminar, staff education and supervision.

A striking feature of contemporary community psychiatry is that, perforce, 'we are all psychotherapists now'. Most mental health workers – community psychiatric nurses, psychologists, occupational therapists, junior psychiatrists – are doing psychotherapeutic work as best they can, often with difficult clients, largely untutored and unsupervised, often with very limited training in psychotherapy. The aim of the seminar is to provide a forum for a multidisciplinary group of community workers which offers education and supervision at least equal in intensity and continuity to the therapeutic requirements of their clients. The seminar offers a model of a secure and regular setting within which anxieties can be expressed and learning can take place. It has also led to increased mutual knowledge and respect between the different psychotherapy disciplines. The analytic therapists have learned about cognitive therapy, and no longer see it as a palliative which ignores deep issues, but as a powerful form of brief therapy. Cognitive therapists no longer view analytic approaches as woolly and interminable, but as the treatment of choice for patients with personality difficulties and long-standing relationship difficulties. On the basis of this, and other, rapprochements it has been possible to establish an integrated psychotherapy service offering a range of therapies, including family therapy, cognitive therapy, analytic therapy and a number of short- and long-term groups (cf. Chapter 1).

There have also been a number of external consequences of the group. Some staff members have left, making way for others more in tune with the prevailing ideology. There is a growing interest in formal psychotherapy training (which the seminar does not aim to replace) and several members have either completed or are undertaking such trainings. A third development has been the recognition of the need for psychotherapeutic work in the rest of the unit, and one of the psychotherapists now runs a staff support group at the DGH unit, which has led to improved morale and reduced splitting among the staff there.

What can psychotherapy learn from community psychiatry?

So far community psychiatry has been depicted as a frail damsel menaced by the dragons of role-blurring and good intentions, saved by the shining knight of psychotherapy. It must be emphasised that the benefits are by no means all one way. Just as community psychiatry needs saving from therapeutic promiscuity, so psychotherapy, like Rapunzel, needs to be released from imprisonment in its ivory tower, to let down its hair a little. The principle that services need to be available to a whole population, not just to a particular section who have the ability to pay, the necessary intelligence or a suitable personality has not yet been fully accepted within psychotherapy. Community psychiatry sees the need for a network of graduated facilities and levels of intervention if the whole range of difficulties and illnesses are to be met (Bennett 1978). Psychotherapy needs to learn from this 'flexible response' and to offer a range of interventions appropriate to the differing psycho-therapeutic needs of a whole population.

This pluralistic approach will mean much greater mutual respect between the different psychotherapeutic schools if psychotherapy is to offer a client/treatment matrix of the kind envisaged by Paul (1967) when he asked 'what treatment, by whom, is most effective for this individual, with what specific problem, and under which set of circumstances?'.

CONCLUSION

This chapter has tried to show how psychotherapy and community psychiatry may mutually benefit one another. Only with a strong psychotherapy presence within the NHS will this be possible. Haunting both disciplines is the issue of evaluation. The basis of psychotherapy is the creation of meanings out of confusion, wholeness out of fragmentation. In the current political climate health workers are now being asked to put meanings not into words but figures. If a community psychotherapy service is to become a reality rather than a Utopian ideal, meeting that challenge must become an urgent task.

Chapter 14

Psychiatry without walls
Some psychotherapeutic reflections

INTRODUCTION

According to Tyrer's (1985) 'hive model', the community psychiatrist is a busy bee buzzing around her patch, restlessly intervening, rehabilitating and monitoring her clients, dancing with and directing her fellow-workers and, no doubt, if it is a self-governing hive, returning to base to serve and service her chief executive, the queen. An entomological image for psychotherapy would be quite different: perhaps a silkworm, endlessly chewing things over, spinning a beautiful but impractical material, occasionally producing an unexpected transformation from grub into moth; or maybe a praying mantis – still, silent, mysterious.

This study is a companion piece to the previous chapter in which the role of psychotherapy within a community psychiatry service was described. It was suggested that the presence of a psychotherapy service could help overcome the fragmentation that is the negative aspect of the post-institutional era. Here again I endorse the need for a strong psychotherapeutic presence within a psychiatric service, but strike a more sombre note, emphasising some of the difficulties of combining a psychiatric and psychotherapeutic role; presenting a case which ended with suicide; and calling attention to the impact on psychotherapeutic work of some of the recent changes in the organisation of the NHS.

DEFINITIONS

We must start with the problem of definitions. 'Community psychiatry' and 'psychotherapy' are vague, baggy concepts to which, like peace and democracy, most people can subscribe, but which, if made specific, often become contentious. Psychotherapy in its wider sense covers the whole range of non-medical and non-social treatments from behavioural-cognitive approaches through systemic and experiential therapies to analytic psychotherapy, while in its narrow sense it refers only to the latter (Holmes and Lindley 1989; Mollon 1991). The perspective of this chapter is that of psychoanalytically-informed psychiatry (Gabbard 1988), trying to bring analytic understanding to bear on the problems of everyday psychiatric work.

Just as, in a psychiatric context at least, psychotherapy is often defined by negation – not drugs or ECT – so community psychiatry is often defined as being non-institutional, non-medical, non-hierarchical, combining an *attitude*, based on the aim of integration and normalisation, with a set of *structures* such as day centres, hostels and community teams. Psychotherapists should beware of this tendency to definition by negation. In adolescence it may be a healthy enough part of identity formation, but if persistent it is usually a sign of splitting and projection of unwanted or feared parts of the self into that which one is not. This process is frequently seen in the attitude of community psychiatric workers and psychotherapists towards psychiatric hospitals, whether mental hospitals or DGH units, and often implies a defensive avoidance of the realities of the disintegration and destructiveness associated with psychiatric illness.

HISTORY

Although the roots of community psychiatry go back to the early nineteenth century, its more recent history has been very much bound up with, and influenced by, analytic psychotherapy (Pines 1991). Early 'neurosis clinics' were opened in the 1920s and 1930s by such pioneers as Hector Munro, Helen Boyle and Hugh Crichton-Miller, all of whom were strongly influenced by psychoanalytic ideas which were then just entering psychiatry. The Tavistock and Portman clinics were founded in the 1930s, as was the Cassel Hospital. One impetus behind these clinics was the need to treat the victims of shell-shock from the First World War. They represent an early example of the attempt to broaden a psychiatric service to cater not just for the severely mentally ill but also for the psychological casualties of social traumata and disasters. The danger is that these services are not seen as complementary, but as competing for attention, time and resources (Holmes and Lindley 1989), leading inevitably to the neglect of one or other group.

During the Second World War the short-lived but influential Northfield experiment was set up by a group of psychoanalytically-minded military psychiatrists, including Bion, Sutherland, Foulkes and Main. Soldiers with psychological difficulties were encouraged, through group discussion, to overcome their shame by considering neurosis as the enemy and to take individual responsibility for their problems, rather than handing them over to a medical-military authority (Pines 1991).

The postwar period saw the development of the therapeutic community movement, associated particularly with the pioneering work of Maxwell-Jones, David Clark and R. D. Laing. The patient was to be 'held' within the community which, as in individual therapy, provided the opportunity for growth and experiment for its members through the experience of 'living-learning'. Some communities developed an Utopian flavour, which, with the projection of all 'badness' on to the past and the outside world, contained the seeds of disillusionment and decay. The need for a balance between nurturance and limit-setting was not always grasped, and a psycho-analytically derived family-developmental model was sometimes inappropriately applied to patients with chronic and possibly organically-based illnesses offering a false hope of cure or redemption. Main's (1957) classic paper 'The Ailment' describes the splitting and dissent created in such communities by difficult borderline patients and how carers project their own difficulties into damaged clients.

THE CONTEMPORARY SCENE

In the face of these and other difficulties the therapeutic community movement has, to some extent, lost its way. The 'community' in community psychiatry now refers less to a therapeutic community than to some notional community 'out there', away from institutions where the patient supposedly lives a 'normal' life, in harmony with and supported by his fellow-citizens. Thus a Utopian ideal has been exchanged for an empty 'normality'.

There have nevertheless been great gains and changes for the better. The institutional era is virtually over. Care has replaced custody. Patients are on the whole treated with dignity and respect and as partners in their own therapy. The stigma of psychiatry has lessened and the role of the psychiatrist has expanded enormously. But there have also been many losses, vulgarisations and obfuscations.

One of the most important of these has been the function of the hospital in attachment and containment. If the institution is seen in entirely negativ: terms, its role as a secure and inviolable 'stone mother' (Rey 1975) with a clear boundary and a containing function within which disability and 'badness' can be held and metabolised cannot be valued. Bion (1988) sees the maternal function as that of introjecting and so containing the growing infant's unmanageable feelings, holding them and transmuting them into a form which, as development proceeds, can then be reintegrated. This maternal function of containment and metabolism is a model for the task of the analytic therapist. Bowlby (1988) sees a similar analogy between the mother who provides a secure base from which the child can explore, and the part played by the psychotherapist.

But contemporary psychiatry is plagued by a blurring of boundaries and by fragmentation. The mental hospitals were able to introject, if not metabolise, the 'bad object' which, even if it festered and stagnated within, was at least securely located. The dissolution of the institutions has meant that this process of introjection becomes much more problematic. Morgan's description of the 'malignant alienation' which often precedes the rare but tragic phenomenon of suicide (Morgan and Priest 1991) within psychiatric units, can be seen as a failure of this introjection-metabolism-reintegration process. The patient's projections, rather than being accepted, are thrown back at her, leading to an escalating spiral of failed introjection in which the scapegoated patient feels more and more isolated and unwanted, while the staff feel increasingly irritated and invaded.

To illustrate some of these points let us take the case of Alison. Her difficulties started unremarkably in her late forties when her husband left her for a much younger woman. For the first year she coped very well, busying herself with looking after her two teenage children, finding accommodation and fighting with her husband's company which she felt had let her down after all the work she had put in as a manager's wife. As a Christian she felt angry with God for allowing this tragedy to happen, especially when she had served him so faithfully for so many years. Then, just before Christmas, she became depressed and despairing and let her GP know that she intended to kill herself. Her GP referred her to a psychiatrist with the question: 'What does one do about someone who appears to have a rational wish to commit suicide; she doesn't appear to be psychiatrically ill and yet she is determined to end her life?'

Alison was seen a few days before Christmas and given a second appointment early in the new year, but as her GP had predicted, made a serious suicide attempt and was admitted to hospital. She soon convinced the staff that her overdose had just been an example of 'silliness'. They felt angry and outraged that she could contemplate killing herself in cold blood, given the dependency of her two children, and were exasperated by her refusal to accept the fact of her husband's desertion and by her insistence that they, the staff, were welcome to their superficial 'modern' relationships but her marriage had been made in heaven and was indissoluble. On the ward she alternated between defiance and compliance, and it was with some relief that the staff let her go home to look after her children. But within a few weeks she again tried to kill herself and was readmitted. This time she remained on the unit for several weeks and, upon discharge, started in once-weekly analytic therapy.

Therapy was difficult and stormy from the start. The therapist soon wondered, given Alison's evident 'borderline' features and apparent complete lack of insight, what he had got himself into. She accused her therapist of depriving her of the one thing she wanted most – death. She insisted, as the transference developed, that she was staying alive simply for his sake, not her own, nor for her children who would be much better off without her, living with their father and his new woman. She resented what she saw as the therapist's attempts to force her to be 'normal' and to accept the shallow values of a society which she rejected. She complained about the lack of reciprocity in the therapeutic relationship and taunted him with the accusation that he was just doing his job and that he would be glad to be rid of her.

Alison was the younger of two children. She had always felt second best in comparison with her older brother who, in her view, her mother had idolised. She described herself as a difficult child who had spent 'half her life' sitting on the stairs – a family punishment in which the worse the misdemeanour, the nearer to the bedroom she had to sit. She had few childhood memories and most were factual rather than affectual. Of her mother she had nothing good to say. She had felt close to her father when he was around (he was a travelling salesman who had died seven years before), but she sensed that her mother resented this. She remembered sitting next to him on the sofa with his arm around her, and how good this felt, and then how he sprang guiltily away when her mother came unexpectedly into the room. Despite considerable academic and sporting potential which her father insisted she put to good use (she had played at junior Wimbledon), she defiantly left school at sixteen and got a job as a secretary. Soon after this she became a strongly committed Christian and the Church then became the focus of her life. She had no real boyfriends until she met her husband in her late twenties, through the church where he was a lay preacher.

Alison's therapy continued for the next eighteen months. For most of the time it felt like a battle: an interminable game of tennis in which she knew that she would eventually wear her opponent down and so 'win'. She remained actively suicidal for much of this time. On one occasion, before a bank holiday, the therapist became convinced that she intended to kill herself and had physically to restrain her (which, she later confessed, she found enjoyable and reassuring) until she could be compulsorily detained. Once again the staff found her irritating as she so rarely opened up with her feelings (any more than she did with her therapist), and would try to 'escape' from the ward in silly, childish ways. She left hospital on extended leave, while remaining on her 'Section'. Her GP found this a suitable arrangement since it made it easier for him to readmit her when necessary and the hospital staff felt that it provided some degree of symbolic containment: the conformist and rebellious parts of her were kept separate by this notional degree of control which she found reassuring and she insisted that she would never kill herself while she remained on a Section.

In addition to her weekly analytic sessions Alison attended the hospital-based Day Hospital three times a week, but complained constantly to her therapist that 'they' expected her to do normal things like join clubs and go out and meet people and try to find new men, when all she wanted was to die. She had one or two brief affairs with totally unsuitable men as if to prove the point. However, she did appear to begin to improve: she played tennis again, slept better and developed some friendships in the village where she lived. But there was little change in the tenor of her therapy and the sessions continued to be a guessing game in which the therapist had to try to imagine what she was really feeling underneath her breezy, compliant manner. She would defiantly challenge the 'rules' of therapy in minor ways, for example by refusing to sit in the chair provided and by sitting on the floor instead. She gave the therapist little opportunity to understand her feelings and dismissed his interpretations as irrelevant speculation. She made it clear that there were only two things she wanted from therapy: permission to die, or to marry her therapist. Since both were impossible she would taunt him with remarks like 'Well, when are you going to get fed up with me and let me do what I want to do?' (i.e. die). Her envy was overwhelming – she envied her husband who had 'got off scot-free', her brother who swanned off on expensive holidays while she was penniless, her daughter who had a boyfriend, her son who got on well with his father, and her therapist whom she imagined as happily married with a satisfying job.

Alison continued to do battle with the hospital and complained to the Mental Health Act Commission about the way her Section was imposed (while at the same time insisting that she stay on it). No amount of interpretation – that she saw the hospital as an uncaring mother into whom she projected all her own envy and resentment and who she was punishing with her 'difficultness' – had much impact. She was not ready to reintroject her 'badness' and the task of the therapy and the hospital seemed to be to continue to contain and to metabolise it. Therapy, for all its problems, was a lifeline for her and special 'babysitting' arrangements had to be made during breaks for her to be seen by other therapists.

Eventually her Section came up for renewal and was rescinded: it was just not justifiable to go on with it in view of her apparently normal mental state and continuing improvement. Immediately Alison started to wean herself off medication. Her behaviour in the sessions became increasingly mute and peculiar. She started to refuse to sit in the waiting area, hiding in the lavatory until the moment came for her session. Christmas, always a difficult time for her when her envy and loneliness were at their height, was approaching. Then her therapist suddenly had to cancel a session at short notice but was unable to contact her in time. Alison arrived at the hospital for her session the next day, went into the consulting room and lay on the couch until she was found by a member of staff who talked to her for a while and arranged an appointment with her therapist next day. But that night she gassed herself in her garage, and was found dead there by her 15-year-old son the next morning.

DISCUSSION

I have described this case partly no doubt as an act of exorcism, but also because it illustrates a number of the difficulties inherent in trying to practise psychotherapeutic community psychiatry.

First, the 'democratic' community psychiatric ideal of patient participation and choice has to be tempered not just with the understanding that people's choices may not necessarily be in their best interests, but that the way they experience reality is profoundly shaped by their inner world. Alison's world was one of rigid contrasts between good and bad, normal and mad, behaving 'well' or 'badly'. She saw the hospital rather as she had experienced her family, with a harsh controlling punitive uncaring maternal aspect (the nurses), fellow-patients who were always favoured like her brother, and an idealised but weak paternal aspect (her therapist). The subtleties of these transferential distortions are not always easy to recognise in the everyday hurlyburly of ward life when considering patient's wishes, demands or complaints.

Second, the staff, including the therapist, through projective identification (Gabbard 1986), were shaped into behaving in a way that at times confirmed Alison's sense of a controlling unfeeling environment, thus laying the seeds of the vicious circle of malignant alienation. Nothing was clearcut and whatever policy was followed it was likely to be wrong. Keeping her in hospital was separating her from her children – the one thing which kept her alive and gave her a sense of purpose. But to discharge her was to ignore the profundity of her despair. From the psychiatric point of view it was hard to decide whether she was suffering from a depressive illness, whether stress had uncovered a borderline aspect to her personality – or both. From the psychotherapeutic point of view one might argue that she was unsuitable for treatment, despite her intelligence, especially for once-weekly therapy, since everything was acted out and there was no glimmer of a self-caring, reflective ego with which the therapist could make an alliance. Weekly therapy was likely merely to excite a need in her for a relationship which could never be assuaged – and yet how could she not be offered some form of therapy? In retrospect it was almost certainly a mistake that her psychiatric consultant and therapist were one and the same person. She correctly sensed that, in his psychiatric role, he was committed to keeping her alive, however much as a psychotherapist he tried to remain neutral, caring for her simply by helping her understand her feelings and behaviour, without any attempt at judgement or control (which would have been an enactment of the maternal trans-ference). The knowledge that he was committed to keeping her alive, even to the extent of physically wrestling with her at the end of a session, gave her the lever that she needed to win her macabre tennis game to the death; and yet, given the available resources, who else would it have been fair to ask to take her on? Or is this an example of how the therapist was shaped by projective identification into playing God: the God that had died for her when her marriage ended?

For most of the time the staff were aware of these difficulties and processes and could guard against being sucked into them. But at moments of stress or temporary disruption of communication the 'thinking breast' (Bion 1988) would stop thinking and, in a somnambulist way, would enact the rejection which she perceived and felt she deserved. At the end she tried to vanish and become the non-person that she was for her mother; this projection was momentarily but fatally enacted by the therapist when he failed to contact her about the cancellation. To keep her mental pain in mind at all times and for her to be aware of this – perhaps the best non-custodial safeguard against suicide (Campbell and Hale 1991) – to recognise it and hold it and not prematurely to hand it back to her became almost impossible at times. Yet when she was not in mind she felt as though she did not exist and her suicide represented in part her rage and despair about this.

A further point concerns the relationship between the concrete and the symbolic. Both individual and social development can be viewed as a movement from the physical presence of an object to its symbolic representation either internally in the psyche, or socially through shared values and their expression in ritual and custom. Alison's difficulties in psychotherapy had much to do with her inability to make this move away from the physical presence of the therapeutic system to its symbolic representation in her internal world. She felt increasing despair and guilt at her inability to 'lead her own life', and remained, as she felt, chained to her therapist. Equally, she could only leave her 'badness' behind for one or two days after her weekly session before she began to feel that she did not exist for her therapist. We can speculate that the same sort of difficulty bedevilled her attachments and development as a child. Similarly, as psychiatric institutions lose their stone walls, sequestration and regulations, it becomes difficult to sustain a notion of unvarying 'care' without the reassurance of its physical expression. Is it possible to build up a matrix of reciprocal duties, responsibilities and obligations that will feel as immutable as the physical presence of the institution? However much we may insist 'the king is dead, long live the king', a royal palace is still needed if an enduring sense of continuity is to be achieved.

Without such systems and structures the opportunities for primitive or perverse modes of being are greatly enhanced. When a recognised structure is in place, such issues as rivalry, envy and the need to regulate both power and nurturance can be properly negotiated. Alison's death might have been less likely if there had been a built-in system of supervision and case-review for consultants or if 'community ward rounds' (Burns 1990) were more firmly established – although both took place intermittently in this case and she still took her life.

THE PSYCHODYNAMICS OF COMMERCIALISM

It is tempting, at moments of failure, to search for an external focus on which to project blame and guilt, just as Alison blamed the failure of her marriage on the decline of morals in modern society. This concluding section perhaps exemplifies this process. Nevertheless I want now to consider how some of the recent developments within the health service may affect psychotherapy and community psychiatry. Psychotherapy, it might be argued, should have nothing to fear from the introduction of market values into health, since 'talk not pills' is what most patients want and should get if money follows patient choice. Similarly, the development of 'quality assurance' into contracting arrangements should in theory benefit psychotherapy since this could be used to foster the development of supervision for psychiatric work, although at present this tends to be managerial rather than psychotherapeutic super-vision. In addition, a market atmosphere is likely to broaden the range of available psychotherapies, to lead to much needed evaluation of different treatments, and to further the development of new forms of therapy which are specifically tailored to the needs and realities of the NHS (see Chapter 15).

It may be, however, that the new god of the market will prove as fickle as the paternalism it replaced was profligate. Underlying the changes are two factors far more powerful than any alleged rationality of the market. The first is simply scarcity: a discrepancy between limited resources and increasing need. The second is a power struggle between the liberal professions, which include psychotherapy, and a managerial class which has hitherto been excluded from the vast amount of resources represented by the public sector. The market atmosphere is inimical to our work as psychotherapists in at least four ways.

1 Confusion

In her classic paper 'Social systems as a defence against anxiety' Isobel Menzies-Lyth (1988) showed how the pain and anxiety engendered in young nurses by exposure to illness and death was avoided by an endless cycle of busyness and change. The confusion brought about by the current changes in the health service can also be seen, at one level, as an avoidance of the inherent difficulty of the work and an attempt at a 'clean break' in the hope of leaving all the problems behind, rather as our patients in North Devon have moved from towns into a rural area in the hope of finding Shangri-La – only to find further disappointment and disillusion.

2 The Draconian regime

There is a punitive aspect to the current changes as though the 'failure' of the welfare state (which is only a partial 'failure' – it is still for the most part 'good enough') must be punished with the iron hand of the market. This is reminiscent of the way in which Alison's lack of a benign parental introject left her at the mercy of a ruthless and primitive superego.

3 Denial of the inner world

As Marx put it, as capitalism succeeds feudalism, 'everything that is solid melts into air'. As we have seen, in place of institutions we have only a notional 'community', in reality a vacuum. The market constantly replaces inner structures with outer appearances. The emphasis is on attractive packaging so that everything is measured by its face value rather than its intrinsic worth. The vogue for 'intervention packages', short-term solutions with a strong cognitive-behavioural emphasis, can lead mental-health workers to echo those exasperated husbands of depressed wives one sees in the clinic who complain 'I can't understand what's wrong with her: she's got a lovely house, a new kitchen, new car – all paid for – and yet still she's not happy...'. Another example was the young man seen recently with severe and complex problems of sexual identity, possibly schizophrenic. He was terrified by the aggressive possibilities of his own body and frightened of homosexuality; he had been advised in his four statutary sessions with an 'early intervention worker' to 'join a sports club so that he would feel more masculine'. No attempt is made to grasp the inner world; surface solutions are offered and the importance of the relationship with the therapist is devalued. Ministerial directives now govern the procedures for discharge of chronic patients into the community and this, too, while perhaps ensuring that patients are less likely to get lost to the system, contains the danger that a set of formal procedures will replace the need for an internalisation of the patient by an individual or institution, an avoidance of the psychological realities of attachment in an ever-shifting kaleidoscope of keyworkers, case-managers and part-time carers.

4 Serving and servicing

Margot Waddell (1989), writing about the dilemmas faced by psycho-dynamically minded social workers, makes a distinction between serving and servicing the client, similar to Wolff's (1971) differentiation of the 'being with' and 'doing to' functions of medicine. She sees much of what social workers are expected to do as a kind of servicing, doing things to their clients, rather as a mother might feed, water, clean and dress her children without being aware of them as people and the impact of her actions on their inner world. The commercial atmosphere in the health service is likely to reinforce this servicing ethos – a sense of controlling, first-come-first-serviced, a ram who services his flock of ewes for a month and then is removed from the conjugal fold. As psychotherapists we need to hold on to the contrary sense of serving as bondsmen to our patients, supplicants in the healing arts. The irony of the current situation is that whereas its declared aim is to increase the sovereignty of the patient and to enhance the professionals' ability to serve, in reality it is likely to create a servicing mentality in which needs are bureaucratised, fragmented and met piecemeal, with little attempt at containment, or metabolism of the enduring reality of persistent pain and loss that are central features of psychiatric work.

CONCLUSION

What are the lessons to be learned from Alison's death? First, the need and value of long-term treatment in difficult cases like this needs to be recognised (Rosser *et al.* 1987). It may well be, for all its shortcomings, that psycho-therapy postponed Alison's death by two years, an outcome which in physical medicine would be considered highly worthwhile. Second, it is important in such cases that psychotherapy and psychiatric management be kept separate, although it is equally essential that the psychotherapist and the psychiatric team maintain good contact. Third, a network of psychotherapeutic (as opposed to purely managerial) supervision is needed for all mental-health workers, including consultants, if the 'stone mother' is truly to be replaced with a living, good-enough system of community care.

The resource implications of these lessons need to be faced. The current reorganisation of the NHS was initiated when the presidents of the Royal Colleges went to the then Prime Minister to describe the underfunding in the Health Service and asked, like Oliver Twist, for more. What they got was not more but a Gradgrinding audit of inputs, outputs and throughputs in which the sounds of pain they represent are in danger of being drowned by the whirring of the accountants' calculators. As George Eliot ironically wrote:

> If we had a keen vision and feeling of all ordinary life it would be like hearing the grass grow and the squirrel's heartbeat and we should risk dying of the roar which lies on the other side of silence.

> (quoted Waddell 1989)

This chapter has described the contrary danger – a death that resulted from the failure of that keen vision and feeling. One of the tasks of the psychotherapist within community psychiatry is to keep her ears tuned to that silent roar, to help her colleagues and patients to be aware of it, and to survive the pain and failures, as well as the satisfactions, to be found in service in the helping professions.

Chapter 15

Psychotherapy 2000

INTRODUCTION: PREDICTION AND THE MILLENNIUM

My aim in this chapter is to consider the possible contours of psychotherapy in the year 2000. It is bound to be proved wrong. Like long-range weather forecasters and economists, psychotherapists are in an 'impossible profession' (Freud 1937), dealing with non-linear and therefore inherently unstable systems, unable to make accurate predictions about the future. But psychotherapists are familiar with uncertainty, and indeed, in the Keatsian sense of negative capability – 'the capacity to be in doubts, uncertainties, mysteries' – actively cultivate it in order to work more creatively. Also, as I shall discuss, the development of chaos theory (Gleick 1988) has now made uncertainty a respectable topic for scientific enquiry.

Psychotherapists should consider why the idea of the year 2000 exerts such a fascination. The notion of a two thousand years since the birth of Christ seems like a solid, rounded, natural phenomenon, but it is in reality an artefact. The Christian calendar was devised in the sixth century by the monk Dionysius Exiguus, for whom the date of the birth of Christ was sheer guesswork (Williams 1985). For Muslims we are entering the thirteenth century, a far less exciting figure. As Carlyle said, action is solid, narrative is linear. The year 2000 is a narrative, a story, fictive – but none the less exciting for all that.

Freud was fascinated by numerology and, being an obsessional, he was prey to irrational fears about numbers. He was convinced he would die at the age of sixty two and became terrified when the last two numbers of his telephone number were sixty two (Pedder 1990). Because they are arbitrary and abstract signs, numbers attract projections of inner mood states. The 'round' numbers may evoke primitive images of sexuality – it is perhaps no accident that bosomy girls appear on Page 3 of the popular press, while male pinups dangle on Page 7. The year 2000 could evoke the many-breasted Hindu goddess of plenty, or alternatively a sterile uniformity of identical zeros.

The year 2000 is not 1984. It is too near for Utopian or dystopian phantasies, more like the day after tomorrow, and yet by looking into the future we are forced to consider that nothing is permanent, that all we hold dear can crumble away. Like Yeats, we may well ask

> what rough beast, its hour come round at last
> Slouches towards Bethlehem to be born?

Millennial phantasies are prevalent; in the brief moment between the ending of the cold war and the onset of the Gulf crisis, the American historian Francis Fukuyama, in a premature orgy of capitalist triumphalism, announced the 'end of history'. The convergence of spiritual and ecological concerns has produced a New Age movement that, however much one may approve its aspirations, has to be compared with the Plymouth Brethren who stood upon hilltops towards the end of the nineteenth century, confident in their calculations that the end of the world was at hand (Gosse 1989).

From a psychotherapeutic point of view the advent of the millennium evokes primitive fears of dissolution and destruction, and compensatory phantasies of power or bliss. A pre-industrial society could balance these fears with images of continuity: the succession of saint's days, the cycle of the seasons and the orderly sequence of birth, maturation, decay and death followed by rebirth provided by the farming year. Continuity was provided not just by the land but by the family, extended both in time and space. Stripped of their religious and agrarian significance, living in a world of almost unimaginable change, no longer constrained by the dead hand of the past, we are free to invest our feast days and millennia with whatever significance we choose: we celebrate the 150th anniversary of the College of Psychiatrists, the half-century since Freud's death and so on. The professional family replaces the village, community, or even the family itself, as the vehicle of celebration and continuity.

This is the context in which I shall now consider the future of that rather ambiguous branch of the psychiatric family, the psychotherapies. I shall discuss first the organisation of psychotherapy, and then the context and themes of psychotherapeutic work.

THE FUTURE OF PSYCHOTHERAPY

A distinction must be made between the state of psychotherapy in general and that of psychotherapy within psychiatry. For psychotherapy itself the 1990s are likely to be a period of both hope and turmoil. Three current and inter-related themes are likely to dominate the next decade: expansion, professionalisation and pluralism.

The 1980s saw a great expansion in psychotherapy and counselling (Pedder 1990). Trainings have proliferated, new forms of psychotherapy have emerged – ranging from the up-and-coming cognitive-behavioural therapy to the wilder fringes, a sub-culture of complementary therapies varying enormously in depth and respectability. The result has been that psychotherapy is available to a far wider spectrum of the population than ever before, but often in a form which would make some of the psychoanalytic pioneers turn in their graves; not necessarily Freud, though, who in 1919 predicted that if the misery of the masses was to be addressed, the 'pure gold of psychoanalysis' would have to be alloyed with the 'copper of suggestion' (Freud 1919).

A consequence of this proliferation will almost certainly be the further professionalism of psychotherapy. An important step in this direction will be, through the United Kingdom Standing Committee for Psychotherapy (a development of the 'Rugby Conferences'), the registration of psycho-therapists, and, more importantly perhaps, the accreditation of psychotherapy trainings. Pedder (1990) has compared this process with the registration of medical practitioners in the mid-nineteenth century which unified a diversity of doctors from the Harley Street grandees to the unqualified provincial physicians and barber-surgeons who served the poor. The call for the registration of psychotherapists goes back at least to the Foster Report in 1971 (Foster 1971), but recently the pace of change has quickened. By the year 2000 it is very likely that an independent profession of psychotherapists will have been established, comprising the main schools and tendencies within psychotherapy including analytic psychotherapy, cognitive-behav-ioural psychotherapy, family and marital therapy, and humanistic approaches.

Whether such developments will lead to greater unity and a raising of standards, or to dilution and 'discreditation by association' of hard-won rigour represented by the tougher and more established trainings is a matter for debate. The psychotherapies continue to struggle to define themselves, and to find ways to delineate their common features and those in which they differ. Freud was in no doubt about the need for a pluralistic approach. In his paper 'Lines of advance in psychoanalytic therapy' (Freud 1919) he called for widened availability of psychoanalysis. He suggested that this would require at least three major modifications in classical analytic technique. First, the therapist would have to become more of a pedagogue, instructing the patient how to lead his life more effectively. Second, therapies would have to become time-limited. Third, therapists would have to be prepared to use 'suggestion', that is the force of their personality, combined if necessary with hypnotic techniques such as deep relaxation, in order to part the patient from his neurosis.

Freud's call for the use of what we would now see as educational and behavioural models of therapy has clearly been realised in the widespread acceptance within psychiatry of brief psychotherapies, as well as cognitive-behavioural approaches including anxiety management. A continuing theme for the 1990s will be that of eclecticism. Patients need a variety of therapeutic approaches if their differing problems, personalities and situa-tions are to be accommodated, but a mishmash of half-assimilated techniques can produce poor therapy and may lead to a backlash of purism. It remains to be seen how much psychoanalysis will be prepared to comprise its standards (especially the 'gold standard' of five-times-a-week analysis) in order to widen its applicability and accessibility.

IMPLICATIONS FOR PSYCHOTHERAPEUTIC PSYCHIATRY

The reverberations of this pluralistic expansion of psychotherapy will have important implications for psychiatry. The neo-Kraepelinians may argue that psychotherapy is a sufficiently trivial pursuit to be left to the psychotherapists and psychologists, and confine themselves to what they see as the real task of scientific psychiatry: the understanding and treatment of the psychoses. This will lead to fragmentation, with psychiatrists running what is essentially a psychosis service, while the psychotherapeutic needs of the population are met by a diverse group of psychologists, private psychotherapists, GP-based counsellors and so on. The alternative is an integrated model of an NHS-based Psychotherapy and Psychological Treatment Service in which psycho-therapeutically-minded psychiatrists, psychologists and non-medical registered psychotherapists work collaboratively, each contributing their own area of interest and expertise, thus providing a 'matrix' of different treatments which collectively can cater for the varying needs and expectations of patients (Holmes and Lindley 1989).

Interprofessional rivalries are likely to intensify as resources diminish. Medical hegemony will continue to be challenged, especially by psychologists and nurses who will be able legitimately to claim more psychotherapeutic expertise than many of their psychiatric colleagues. There will be a great temptation for psychiatry to concede the territory of psychotherapy and to retreat into a narrow bunker of scientism and rejection of all that cannot be quantified. But even a narrowly defined psychiatry will continue to need psychotherapeutic skills in the management of schizophrenics and their families; patients with depressive illnesses for whom antidepressants are ineffective, unwelcome or insufficient; patients with eating disorders in whom medical complications are an ever-present possibility; suicidal patients; those with somatisation disorders; and patients with borderline personality problems or unstable mood-states, who so often gravitate towards psychiatric services and who, on the whole, are so ill-served by them (Margison 1991). Furthermore, community psychiatrists will need psychotherapeutic skills both to help in the understanding of the meaning and content of their patients' illnesses, and to provide symbolic containment and integration in the face of increasing administrative fragmentation.

These shifting professional boundaries are but one manifestation of the economic and political pressures that will shape the pattern of our work by the year 2000. It seems likely, whatever the political future, that the introduction of market forces into the health service, in one form or another, is here to stay. Although we may deplore this move politically (psycho-therapists tend to be on the liberal wing of the psychiatric party), it may, paradoxically, have the effect of raising the status and morale of psycho-therapy. If 'money follows patients', psychotherapy may benefit since it is what many patients want and are prepared to travel distances to get. Hitherto this tendency of psychotherapy departments to serve a wider population than their immediate district has been frowned upon as an example of an inessential 'luxury'. In future they may be seen by managers as useful money-spinners while general psychiatric services are increasingly squeezed. Never-theless psychotherapy departments remain soft targets, vulnerable to cuts if resources diminish.

Meanwhile there will be increasing discouragement of 'analysis intermin-able' as auditors and managers are prepared to fund only the briefer 'validated' forms of psychotherapy. For some this will undoubtedly be a benefit, widening the availability of therapy and concentrating the minds of the therapists. The danger is that it will encourage a form of psycho-therapeutic consumerism whose outlines are already visible, in which 'customers' sample varieties of different therapies, each with its transitory immediate appeal and impact on surface problems – a pot-pourri of anxiety management, psychodrama weekends, cognitive-therapy courses, sessions of self-assertiveness training and awareness programmes, which may act as a defence against facing the central hollowness of the patient's life and the need for an enduring, intimate relationship with a therapist in which trauma, negativity and destructiveness can be accepted and transcended.

The psychoanalytic paradigm of a prolonged, intense, neutral therapeutic relationship, with its potential for long-term benefit but low short-term cost-benefit pay-off, contrasts with the need for validated and realistic forms of psychotherapy for the NHS. The tension between them is unlikely to disappear over the next decade. My hope is that the creative conflict between the two extremes will lead to concessions on both sides. Psychoanalysts will become more flexible, while brief or cognitive therapists will acknowledge the need in many patients for more prolonged, open-ended therapeutic encounters than they currently endorse.

THEMES FOR THE FUTURE

No science operates in a social or cultural vacuum, least of all a part-scientific, part-pedagogic, part-artistic discipline such as psychotherapy. Numerous examples testify to the intimate relationship between technical and cultural change in society and developments in the field of psycho-therapy. Freud's lifework must be seen in the context of the assimilation of the Jewish intelligentsia in the nineteenth century. There is an obvious link between his concept of the death instinct and later elaborations of it by Melanie Klein and others, and the terrible impact of the First World War. The spread of psychoanalysis to the USA and Britain in the 1930s (and its conspicuous absence from the Soviet Union) is a direct result of the rise of Nazism and Stalinism in the 1930s. The development of group therapy in this country derives mainly from the impact of the Second World War on a group of psychoanalytically minded military psychiatrists including Bion, Main, Rickman, Trist and others (Pines 1991). The ideas of cybernetics and the study of communication systems, developed as part of the military effort in the Second World War, laid the foundations for Bateson's work (Bateson 1973) which led on to the development of family therapy in the 1960s. The current vogue for cognitive therapy can be seen as a response to the first oil crisis of the 1970s, and the consequent need for briefer, cheaper forms of therapy.

THE CONTOURS OF THE MILLENNIUM

I shall pick out five themes which are likely to influence the climate of psychotherapy over the next ten years; science, religion, inequality, gender and trauma. I shall suggest in particular that trauma and its sequelae will provide a paradigm for psychotherapeutic work in the coming decade.

The impact of contemporary science and technology

Psychotherapy, like psychiatry itself, is both a science and an art. Scientific developments have undoubtedly had their impact on psychotherapy. Sulloway (1979) described Freud as the 'biologist of the mind'; he showed how Darwinian ideas were an indispensable precursor of Freudian notions of the evolution of the psyche, and the relationship between our adult conscious minds and the 'primitive' instinctual forces from which it has emerged in the course of development. Communications theory and cybernetics provided a language for the development of family therapy. Ryle's Cognitive Analytic Therapy (Ryle 1990) – which is likely to become increasingly popular among NHS psychotherapists over the next ten years – is couched in the language of Artificial Intelligence. John Bowlby's Attachment Theory (Bowlby 1980; Bretherton 1990) which combines ideas from psychoanalysis, ethology and cognitive science, will become increasingly accepted as a psychotherapeutic paradigm.

Although it is now firmly established that psychotherapy is effective, the question of how change comes about remains a central issue for psychotherapy research. Audio and video recording enables the therapeutic process to be studied accurately, and this will continue to be a growth point for psychotherapy research in the coming decade. Sophisticated computer-based methods of analysing the myriad of interactions that take place in psychotherapy sessions are becoming available (Thoma and Kachele 1986), and mathematical models that are adequate to undertake this task are being developed (Langs 1989). Chaos theory (Gleick 1988) which studies the laws which underlie the behaviour of complex systems such as the weather, stock markets, or paroxysmal cardiac arrhythmias, looks like a promising paradigm for psychotherapy researchers to study. For example, the 'butterfly effect' indicates how small differences can have big impacts on outcomes of complex processes; psychotherapists are familiar with the way in which early, apparently trivial, events in a session may have a determining impact on the overall shape of the therapeutic encounter. Chaos theory, through its notion of 'fractal geometry', paints a holographic picture of complex systems, showing how all heaven can indeed be found in a grain of sand, how the close texture of a coastline can be related to its overall shape in an atlas. This is relevant to the psychotherapeutic observation that no one part of a therapeutic encounter is privileged, and that each session in a sense 'contains' the whole of the patient's pathology (cf. Chapter 10). The notion of 'strange attractors' may help us to understand the nodal points that develop in psychotherapy: the recurrent themes and mood-states to which the patient regularly returns, the understanding and overcoming of which often prove to be turning-points in therapy.

The spiritual quest and the search for meaning

At the opposite pole to the scientific aspect of psychotherapy is the hermeneutic project of decoding meanings, the need to deepen understanding and so increase the significance and richness of lived experience. Many authors have seen psychoanalysis and psychotherapy as providing a response to spiritual needs, especially among the intelligentsia and middle classes, in an increasingly secular world. An upsurge of interest in psychotherapy is likely in Eastern Europe, filling the vacuum left by the collapse of Marxist-Leninist ideology. Psychotherapy provides an account of *personal* meanings and a method by which they can be explored and healed that complements the religious impulse. There will be an increasing dialogue between psycho-therapy and religion over the next ten years. The impact of Eastern religion may be particularly significant: Zen Buddhism, for example, can itself be seen as a secularised religion, with its absence of theism, its stress on paradox and spontaneity and its use of breathing techniques, which are now a standard part of psychological methods of anxiety control (West 1990).

How this spiritual dimension to psychotherapy (Cox and Thielgaard 1987) will fit in with the new market economy of the health service is uncertain; but it will remain one of the most important tasks of psychotherapy to be a bastion of human values, of 'being with' the patient as well as 'doing to' him (Wolff 1971) in an increasingly technologised and commercialised medical world.

Psychotherapy and inequality

Despite its increasingly widened availability, psychotherapy within the NHS, the 'YAVIS' image, persists (Holmes and Lindley 1989). The typical patient attending a psychotherapy department may well be between twenty and forty, white, of above average educational achievement, with middle-class aspirations or connections. In themselves, these demographic features are unexceptionable. Perhaps there is more motivation and opportunity for change in younger patients; and since most psychotherapies depend on putting feelings into words they are likely to appeal more to the educated and aspirant. There has been a gradual, but still too hesitant, recognition by psychotherapists that they are not reaching disadvantaged groups. The next decade will see increasing attempts to consider and cater for the psychotherapeutic needs of those who are elderly, the members of ethnic minorities, the unemployed, the poor or those living in isolated communities such as large housing estates or in rural areas. Urgent efforts must be made to train those who are working in these communities in psychotherapeutic skills, and also to learn from such workers about how psychotherapeutic techniques need to be modified and adapted to a less-rarefied environment. An eclectic, broad-based, non-dogmatic approach is indispensable, while holding to the essential psychotherapeutic requirements of a secure, holding environment and a recognition of the role of the unconscious.

The gender question

The need for a new psychology of men has been brought home to me recently by two sets of clinical experiences. The first has been what seems almost an epidemic of young psychotic men passing through our unit. A common theme seems to be the pressure to achieve sexual maturity (at an emotional rather than a physical level) and their failure to do so, with breakdowns in which fears of inadequacy, homosexual panic, a regressive demandingness and at times violence towards their mothers are prominent. Often brought up with weak or absent fathers, this constellation cannot be understood in classical Oedipal terms, but seems based on an infantile fear of the overwhelming power of the mother, reactivated in young adulthood when faced with the possibility of a real relationship with a woman and the lack of identification with a potent father. These emotional problems are often exacerbated by difficulties in finding work in an economy in which unemployment, especially for the unskilled, is endemic.

The second has come from working psychotherapeutically with a number of men married to feminist women in whom there is a conflict between their need to suppress feelings in order to function at work, and wives who expect and demand intimacy and affective liveliness at home. Soldiers, offshore oil-workers, long-distance drivers, salesmen, who travel away from home and who habitually deal with the pain of separation and the difficulties of re-entry into families by repressing feelings of grief and loneliness are particularly vulnerable. There are expected to be emotionally available by wives who are themselves often cut off from traditional intimacy and whose hunger for closeness focuses more and more on their spouses as the strength of traditional family and social networks diminishes. The result of these pressures is often domestic violence and a split-off sexuality in the form of affairs, sexual perversions or sexual abuse.

The 1970s and 1980s were the decades of feminist psychology. By the year 2000 the question of male psychology will have come more and more into prominence. Psychotherapists will play their part in helping to find an answer to the reverse of Professor Higgins' complaint: 'Why can't a woman be more like a man?'

The impact of real trauma

Psychotherapists can be divided into those who emphasise the impact of environmental failure in producing emotional difficulty, and those who emphasise the contribution of the inner world to neurosis and psychological breakdown. As the recent Masson (1985) controversy has shown, Freud belonged at different times to both camps. At first he viewed hysteria as a result of sexual seduction in childhood (rather as he saw the traumata of the Franco-Prussian war leading to battle neurosis), but he later came to think that it was *phantasies* of infantile seduction that were important and universal, rather than their reality.

This debate has continued throughout the postwar period. Authors like Bowlby, Winnicott and Kohut have emphasised environmental failure as a determinant of neurosis, seeing the therapists' role as providing corrective, non-traumatic counterbalancing experience; while in a curious alliance Kleinian and cognitive theorists consider the inner world with its distorted perceptions as the key issue, viewing the therapists' role as one of correcting misperceptions through interpretation or instruction.

The 1980s in Britain has seen an increasing awareness of the impact and sequelae of individual and group trauma. The psychological needs of the survivors of disasters is beginning to be recognised (Garland 1991); so too is the prevalence of the sexual abuse of children and its long-term consequences for mental health (Grant 1991). The recognition of Post Traumatic Stress Disorder (Horowitz 1986) as a psychiatric entity, and its increasing invocation as a basis for compensation claims, is one manifestation of this awareness. Psychosis itself can be considered as a trauma, needing psychotherapeutic skills alongside pharmacological skills, to help its victims and their families cope with its impact (Leff and Vaughan 1983).

The 1990s will see a continuation of this emphasis on the impact of real trauma, but also pay increasing attention to its effects on the inner world:

thus bringing together the two tacks of psychological thought. When the external world fails so decisively as it does when a vessel drowns its passengers or a parent abuses a child, the survivor will initially (and sometimes permanently) be unable to trust the environment which has let him down. External failure will be mirrored in his inner world which 'contains' the memories of the trauma but also internal attachment figures now felt to be unavailable or irremediably unreliable. Excessive use is made in this situation of 'projective identification' (Jureidini 1990) as a defence. Feelings of abandonment and hatred engendered by the trauma, so overwhelming that they cannot be contained, are split off and projected into the environment which is then experienced as hostile and unsafe. A fragmented individual thus faces a fragmented and persecutory world. His phantasies confirm and reinforce his traumatic experience. The traumatised individual sees the world as traumatising and maintains a partial sanity by doing so. Clinical examples of this process are to be found in borderline patients who show unstable mood-states, self-loathing, tendency to split, need to seek help and then be unable to use it, to idealise and to feel persecuted, and whose childhood is so often characterised by the traumata of confusion, abandonment and sexual abuse.

In working with traumatised and borderline patients, psychotherapists are beginning to recognise some of the steps needed if some hope for the future is to be found. The first – and often it is not possible to go much further than this – is the full recognition of the extent of the damage, its disclosure and articulation. Next comes the need to deal with the repressed affect associated with the trauma: the rage, fear and guilt. Then – and this is the most difficult part – coming to understand the long-reaching effects of the trauma: how the mental mechanisms used to deal with it can perpetuate the trauma and continue to influence and distort current relationships, including those with the therapist or therapeutic institution. Difficulty arises because the therapist cannot distance himself from the process, but will inevitably be caught up in it himself, be experienced by the patient as unreliable or even traumatising. This is equally true at an institutional level of hospitals and other psychiatric units that try to work with these patients. Finally there is the possibility of reparation, of making good the damage done both to and by the traumatised individual, the overcoming of guilt and the finding, if not of forgiveness, then at least of acceptance. There is no short cut to reparation and attempts to find one may merely lead to further denial and disillusionment.

In working with traumatised patients a balance has to be struck between firmness and concern, between limit-setting and loving-kindness, aiming to produce a safe container which can survive the disappointments and attacks it will inevitably provoke, and within which growth can take place. Translating these concepts into practical psychiatric care is one of the central tasks of NHS psychotherapy for the year 2000.

CONCLUSION

Concern for the environment is likely to be one of the major political and social themes for the coming decade. Here the psychological processes I have just described can be observed at a social and political level. The earth itself is traumatised. Pollution is based on splitting: unwanted products are expelled into the environment – the atmosphere, the seas, the rivers, Third World countries – at first disowned, later experienced as persecutory. In the 'Gaia hypothesis' (Lovelock 1982) the earth is anthropomorphised (or gynomorphised) as a living mother, spoiled, dying even, through the hostile projections of her omnipotent and greedy inhabitants. The green movement can be seen as an attempt at therapy and reparation: helping the community to face up to the cycle of trauma in which it is trapped.

There are some encouraging signs that, despite an increasing capacity for destruction and disaster, the world community can move, in Bion's (1962) terms, from a fight-flight group to a pairing group. The shape of the year 2000 may depend on whether it can transform itself into a work group. If the 'butterfly effect' is to be believed, the increasing importance of psycho-therapy, both as an art and a technology, not just in medicine and psychiatry, but also in commerce and government, may be a vital factor in that transformation.

Bibliography

Abraham, K. (1924) 'A short study on the development of the libido', in E. Jones (ed.) *Selected Papers*, London: Hogarth Press.

Abraham, K. (1927) *Selected Papers on Psychoanalysis*, London: Hogarth Press.

Adams, B. (1986) Personal communication.

Ahlskog, G. (1987) 'The unanalysable transference: a portrait of Roustang's critique of classical technique', *Psychoanalytical Review* 74: 179–200.

Alexander, F. and French, T. M. (1946) *Psychoanalytic Psychotherapy*, Lincoln: University of Nebraska Press.

Althus, W. D. (1966) 'Birth order and its sequelae', *Science*, New York 151: 44–9.

Ansbacher, H. L. and Ansbacher, R. R. (1958) *The Individual Psychology of Alfred Adler*, New York: Harper & Row.

Auden, W. H. (1963) *The Dyer's Hand*, London: Faber & Faber.

Bakan, D. (1990) *Sigmund Freud and the Jewish Mystical Tradition*, London: Free Association Books.

Balint, E. (1963) 'On being empty of oneself', *International Journal of Psychoanalysis* 44: 470–80.

Balint, M. (1959) *Thrills and Regressions*, London: Hogarth Press.

Barker, C. (1983) 'The psychotherapist', in N. T. Singleton (ed.) *The Analysis of Real Skills: Social Skills*, London: Oxford University Press.

Bateman, A. (1991) 'Psychotherapy with borderline patients', in J. Holmes (ed.) *Psychotherapy in Psychiatric Practice*, Edinburgh: Churchill Livingstone.

Bateson, G. (1973) *Steps to an Ecology of Mind*, London: Paladin.

Bateson, P. (1981) 'The ontogeny of behaviour', *British Medical Bulletin* 37: 159–64.

Beavers, W. and Hampson, R. (1990) *Successful Families*, New York: Norton.

Beech, H. R. and Perigault, J. (1974) 'Towards a theory of obsessional disorder', in H. R. Beech (ed.) *Obsessional States*, London: Methuen.

Beiber, I., Dain, H. J. and Dince, P. R. (1962) *Homosexuality: A Psychoanalytic Study*, New York: Basic Books.

Bennett, D. H. (1978) 'Community psychiatry', *British Journal of Psychiatry* 132: 209–20.

Bettleheim, B. (1961) *The Informed Heart*, London: Thames & Hudson.

Bettleheim, B. (1969) *The Children of the Dream*, London: Thames & Hudson.

Bettleheim, B. (1982) 'Freud and the soul', *New Yorker* March, 52–93.

Bettleheim, B. (1983) *Freud and Man's Soul*, London: Chatto & Windus.

Beutler, L. E., Crago, M. and Arizmendi, T. G. (1986) 'Process and outcome in psychotherapy', in S. L. Garfield and A. E. Bergin (eds) *Handbook of Psychotherapy and Behaviour Change*, Chichester: Wiley.

Bick, E. (1988) 'The experience of the skin in early object relations', in E. Spillius (ed.) *Melanie Klein Today*, vol. 1, London: Routledge.

Bion, W. R. (1962) *Learning from Experience*, London: Heinemann.

Bion, W. R. (1970) *Attention and Interpretation*, London: Tavistock.

Bion, W. R. (1988) 'A theory of thinking', in E. Spillius (ed.) *Melanie Klein Today*, London: Routledge.

Black, A. (1974) 'The natural history of obsessional neurosis', in H. R. Beech (ed.) *Obsessional States*, London: Methuen.

Blanco, I. M. (1975) *The Unconscious as Infinite Sets*, London: Duckworth.

Bloch, S. (1987) *An Introduction to the Psychotherapies*, (2nd edn.), Oxford: Oxford University Press.

Bollas, C. (1986) 'The transformational object', in G. Kohon (ed.) *The British School of Psychoanalysis: The Independent Tradition*, London: Free Association Books.

Bowlby, J. (1969) *Attachment*, London: Penguin.

Bowlby, J. (1973) *Separation*, London: Penguin.

Bowlby, J. (1980) *Loss*, London: Tavistock.

Bowlby, J. (1988) *A Secure Base*, London: Routledge.

Brandt Report (1980) *Independent Commission on International Development Issues North-South: A Programme for Survival*, London: Pan Books.

Bretherton, I. (1990) 'Communication pattern, internal working models, and the intergenerational transmission of attachment relationships', *Infant Mental Health Journal* 11: 237–52.

Brim, O. G. (1958) 'Family structure and sex role learning by children', *Sociometry* 21: 1–16.

Brockman, B., Poynton, A., Ryle, A. and Watson, J. P. (1987) 'Effectiveness of time-limited therapy carried out by trainees: comparison of two methods', *British Journal of Psychiatry* 151: 602–10.

Bronowski, J. (1978) *The Visionary Eye*, London: MIT Press.

Brown, G. W., Bhrolchain, M. N. and Harris, T. (1975) 'Social class and psychiatric disturbance among women in an urban population', *Sociology* 9: 225–54.

Brown, G. and Harris, T. (1978) *The Social Origins of Depression*, London: Tavistock.

Burns, T. (1990) 'Community ward rounds', *Health Trends* 22: 62–3.

Byng-Hall, J. (1980) 'Symptom-bearer as marital distance-regulator: clinical implications', *Family Process* 19: 335–65.

Campbell, D. and Hale, R. (1991) 'Suicidal acts', in J. Holmes (ed.) *A Textbook of Psychotherapy in Psychiatric Practice*, Edinburgh: Churchill Livingstone.

Casement, P. (1985) *On Learning from the Patient*, London: Tavistock.

Casement, P. (1987) 'The experience of trauma in the transference', in *Illusion and Spontaneity in Psychoanalysis*, London: Free Association Books.

Casement, P. (1991) *Further Learning from the Patient*, London: Routledge.

Cawley, R. (1974) 'Psychotherapy and obsessional disorders', in H. R. Beech (ed.) *Obsessional States*, London: Methuen.

Chase, J. and Holmes, J. (1990) 'Family therapy in adult psychiatry', *Journal of Family Therapy* 12: 162–71.

Chasseguet-Smirgel, J. (1983) *Freud Memorial Lecture*, University College, London.

Chasseguet-Smirgel, J. (1985) *Creativity and Perversion*, London: Free Association Books.

Cheifetz, L. G. (1984) 'Framework violations in psychotherapy with clinic patients', in J. Raney (ed.) *Listening and Interpreting: The Challenge of the Work of Robert Langs*, London: Jason Aronson.

Clarkin, J., Frances, A. and Moodie, J. (1979) 'Selection criteria for family therapy',

Family Therapy 18: 391–403.

Claxton, G. (1986) *Beyond Therapy*, London: Wisdom.

Cohn, N. (1957) *The Pursuit of the Millennium*, London: Secker & Warburg.

Coltart, N. (1986) 'Slouching towards Bethlehem...', in G. Kohon (ed.) *The British School of Psychoanalysis*, London: Free Association Books.

Cooklin, A. (1979) 'A psychoanalytic framework for a systemic approach to family therapy', *Journal of Family Therapy* 1: 153–65.

Cooklin, A. (1982) *Family Therapy: Complementary Frameworks for Therapy and Practice*, A. Bentovim, G. Gorrell-Barnes and A. Cooklin (eds), Oxford: Pergamon.

Cooper, A. M. 'Changes in psychoanalytic ideas – transference, interpretation', *Journal of the American Psychoanalytic Association* 35: 77–98.

Cox, M. and Theilgaard, A. (1987) *Mutative Metaphors in Psychotherapy*, London: Tavistock.

Cushna, B. (1966), in B. Sutton-Smith and B. G. Rosenberg (eds) *The Sibling*, New York: Holt, Rinehart & Winston.

Dare, C. (1979) 'Psychoanalysis and systems in family therapy', *Journal of Family Therapy* 1:137–54.

Davanloo, H. (1978) *Basic Principles and Techniques in Short-Term Dynamic Psychotherapy*, New York: Spectrum.

Davies, H. (1980) *William Wordsworth*, London: Weidenfeld & Nicolson.

Dennett, D. (1991) *Consciousness Explained*, Oxford: Oxford University Press.

Deutsch, F. (1957) 'A footnote to Freud's "Fragment of an analysis of a case of hysteria" ', *Psychoanalytic Quarterly* 26: 159–67.

Dicks, D. V. (1967) *Marital Tensions*, London: Routledge & Kegan Paul.

Dixon, N. (1982) *Preconscious Processing*, London: Wiley.

Domhoff, C. W. (1985) *The Mystique of Dreams: A Search for Utopia Through Senoi Dream Theory*, Berkeley: University of California Press.

Dunn, J. (1985) *Sisters and Brothers*, Cambridge MA: Harvard University Press.

Dunn, J. and Kendrick, C. (1982) *Siblings: Love, Envy and Understanding*, Cambridge MA: Harvard University Press.

Edelson, M. (1975) *Language and Interpretation in Psychoanalysis*, London: Yale University.

Eliot, G. (1876) *Daniel Deronda*, London: Everyman.

Eliot, T. S. (1975) *Selected Prose*, F. Kermode (ed.), London: Faber & Faber.

Empson, W. (1953) *Seven Types of Ambiguity*, (3rd edn.), London: Chatto & Windus.

Erikson, E. (1962) 'Reality and actuality', *Journal of the American Psychoanalytic Association* 10: 451–74.

Erikson, E. (1968) *Identity : Youth and Crisis* London: Faber & Faber.

Ernst, S. and Goodison, L. (1981) *In Our Own Hands: A Book of Self-Help Therapy*, London: Women's Press.

Falloon, I. R. H., Lindley, P., McDonald, R. and Marks, I. M. (1977) 'Social skills, training of out-patient groups: a controlled study of rehearsal and homework', *British Journal of Psychiatry* 131: 599–609.

Farrell, B. A. (1981) *The Standing of Psychoanalysis*, Oxford: Oxford University Press.

Ferenczi, S. (1932) 'Confusion of tongues between adults and children', reprinted in J. Masson (1985) *The Assault on Truth* London: Penguin.

Ferenczi, S. and Rank, O. (1925) *The Development of Psychoanalysis*, New York: Nervous and Mental Disease Publishing Company.

Fleugel, J. C. (1921) *The Psychoanalytic Study of the Family*, London: Hogarth Press.

Fonagy, P., Steele, M., Steele H., Moran, G. and Higgitt, A. (1991) 'The capacity for understanding mental states: the reflexive self in parent and child and its significance for security of attachment', *Infant Mental Health Journal* 12: 201–17.

Fontana, D. (1986) 'Mind, sense and self', in G. Claxton (ed.) *Beyond Therapy*, London: Wisdom.

Foster Report (1971) *Enquiry into the Practice and Effects of Scientology*, London: HMSO.

Frank, J. (1973) *Persuasion and Healing* (2nd edn.), Baltimore: Johns Hopkins.

Frank, J. (1983) 'The placebo is psychotherapy', *Behavioural and Brain Sciences* 6 : 291–2.

Freud, A. (1936) *The Ego and the Mechanisms of Defence*, London: Hogarth Press.

Freud, A. (1966) 'Obsessional neurosis', *International Journal of Psychoanalysis* 47: 116–22.

Freud, A. (1969) *Indications for Child Analysis*, London: Hogarth Press.

Freud, S. (1900) *The Interpretation of Dreams*, Standard Edition, vols. 4 and 5, London: Hogarth Press.

Freud, S. (1905) *Fragment of an Analysis of a Case of Hysteria*, Standard Edition, vol. 7, 1–122, London: Hogarth Press.

Freud, S. (1909) *Notes upon a Case of Obsessional Neurosis*, Standard Edition, vol. 10, London: Hogarth Press.

Freud, S. (1913) *The Disposition to Obsessional Neurosis*, Standard Edition, vol. 12, London: Hogarth Press.

Freud, S. (1915) *Instincts and their Vicissitudes*, Standard Edition, vol. 14, London: Hogarth Press.

Freud, S. (1915) *The Unconscious*, Standard Edition, vol. 14, London: Hogarth Press.

Freud, S. (1916–17) *Introductory Lectures on Psychoanalysis*, Standard Edition, vols. 15–16, London: Hogarth Press.

Freud, S. (1917) *Mourning and melancholia*, Standard Edition, vol. 14, London: Hogarth Press.

Freud, S. (1919) *Lines of Advance in Psychoanalytic Therapy*, Standard Edition, vol. 17, London: Hogarth Press.

Freud, S. (1920) *Beyond the Pleasure Principle*, Standard Edition, vol. 18, London: Hogarth Press.

Freud, S. (1921) *Group Psychology and the Analysis of the Ego*, Standard Edition, vol. 18, London: Hogarth Press.

Freud, S. (1923) *The Ego and the Id*, Standard Edition, vol. 19, London: Hogarth Press.

Freud, S. (1926) *Inhibitions, symptoms and anxiety*, Standard Edition, vol. 20, London: Hogarth Press.

Freud, S. (1927) *Fetishism*, Standard Edition, vol. 21, London: Hogarth Press.

Freud, S. (1937) *Psychoanalysis Terminable and Interminable*, Standard Edition, vol. 23, London: Hogarth Press.

Fromm, E. (1960) 'Psychoanalysis and Zen Buddhism', in E. Fromm (ed.) *Zen Buddhism and Psychoanalysis*, New York: Grove Press.

Fry, W. F. (1962) 'The marital context of an anxiety syndrome', *Family Process* 1: 245–52.

Gabbard, G. (1986) 'The treatment of a "special" patient in a psychoanalytic hospital', *International Review of Psychoanalysis* 13: 333–47.

Gabbard, G. (1988) 'A contemporary perspective on psychoanalytically informed hospital treatment', *Hospital and Community Psychiatry* 39: 1291–5.

Gardner, H. (ed.) (1972) *New Oxford Book of English Verse*, Oxford: Oxford University Press.

Gardner, H. and Winner, E. (1979) 'The development of metaphoric competence', in S. Sacks (ed.) *On Metaphor*, Chicago: University of Chicago Press.

Garfield, S. L. (1986) 'Research on client variables in psychotherapy', in S. L. Garfield and A. E. Bergin (eds) *Handbook of Psychotherapy and Behaviour Change*, Chichester: Wiley.

Garfield, S. L. and Bergin, A. E. (eds.) (1986) *Handbook of Psychotherapy and Behaviour Change* (3rd edn.), Chichester: Wiley.

Garland, C. (1980) *The Survivor Syndrome*, London: Trust for Group Analysis.

Garland, C. (1982) 'Taking the non-problem seriously', *Group Analysis* 12: 4–14.

Garland, C. (1991) 'Working with survivors: external disaster and the internal world', in J. Holmes (ed.) *Psychotherapy in Psychiatric Practice*, Edinburgh: Churchill Livingstone.

Gay, P. (1988) *Freud: A Life for our Time*, Oxford: Oxford University Press.

Gedo, J. E. and Goldberg, A. (1973) *Models of the Mind*, Chicago: University of Chicago Press.

Gewirtz, J. L. and Gewirtz, H. B. (1965) in B. M. Foss (ed.) *Determinants of Infant Behaviour*, London: Methuen.

Glass, R. M. (1984) 'Psychotherapy: scientific art or artistic science', *Archives of General Psychiatry* 41: 525–6.

Gleick, J. (1988) *Chaos: Making a New Science*, London: Penguin.

Glover, E. (1956) 'Functional aspects of the mental apparatus', in *On the Early Development of the Mind*, New York: International Universities Press.

Glover, J. (1988) *I: the Philosophy and Psychology of Personal Identity*, London: Allen Lane.

Goldberg, D. P., Hobson, R. F., Maguire, G. P., Margison, F. R., O'Dowd, T., Osborn, M. and Moss, S. (1984) 'The classification and assessment of a method of psychotherapy', *British Journal of Psychiatry* 144: 567–80.

Gosse, E. (1989) *Father and Son*, London: Penguin.

Grant, S. (1991) 'Sexual abuse', in J. Holmes (ed.) *A Textbook of Psychotherapy in Psychiatric Practice*, Edinburgh: Churchill Livingstone.

Grant, S., Margison, F. and Powell, A. (1991) 'The future of psychotherapy services', *Psychiatric Bulletin* 15: 174–9.

Green, A. (1975) 'Orestes and Oedipus', *International Review of Psychoanalysis* 2: 355–64.

Greenberg, H., Mayer, D., Guerena, R. (1963) 'Order of birth as a determinant of personality and attitudinal characteristics', *Journal of Social Psychology* 60: 221–30.

Haffner, R. J. (1977) 'The husbands of agoraphobic women and their influence on treatment outcome', *British Journal of Psychiatry* 131: 289–94.

Haley, J. (1973) *Uncommon Therapy*, New York: Norton.

Haley, J. (1977) *Problem Solving Therapy*, San Francisco: Josey Bass.

Haley, J. (1980) *Leaving Home*, New York: McGraw-Hill.

Hall, A. D. and Fagan, R. E. (1956) 'Definition of system', *General Systems Yearbook* 1: 18–28.

Hall, C. S. (1953) *The Meaning of Dreams*, New York: Harper & Row.

Hare, E. H. and Price, J. S. (1969) 'Birth order and family size: bias caused by changes in birth rate', *British Journal of Psychiatry* 15: 647–57.

Heaney, S. (1980) *Preoccupations*, London: Faber & Faber.

Hinchelwood, R. (1989) 'Therapy or coercion: psychoanalytic considerations on ethics', *Freud Memorial Lecture*, University College London, January.

Hinde, R. (1982) *Ethology*, London: Fontana.

Hirsch, S. R. and Leff, J. P. (1975) *Abnormality in Parents of Schizophrenics: A Review of the Literature and Investigation of Communication Defects and Deviances*, London: Oxford University Press.

Hobson, J. A. (1990) *The Dreaming Brain*, London: Penguin.

Hoffman, L. (1971) 'Deviance – amplifying processes in natural groups', in *Changing Families: A Family Therapy Reader*, New York: Grune and Stratton.

Hoffman, L. (1981) *Foundations of Family Therapy*, New York: Basic Books.

Holmes, J. (1988) Letter, *London Review of Books* 10: No. 18.

Holmes, J. (1991) 'Analytic therapy' in J. Holmes (ed.) *A Textbook of Psychotherapy in Psychiatric Practice*, Edinburgh: Churchill Livingstone.

Holmes, J. (forthcoming) *John Bowlby and Attachment Theory*, London: Routledge.

Holmes, J. and Lindley, R. (1989) *The Values of Psychotherapy*, Oxford: Oxford University Press.

Holmes, R. (1989) *Footsteps*, London: Penguin.

Hopkins, G. M. (1953) *Poems and Prose*, Harmondsworth: Penguin.

Horney, K. (1939) *New Ways in Psychoanalysis*, New York: Norton.

Horowitz, M. J. (1979) *States of Mind*, New York: Plenum.

Horowitz, M. J. (1986) *Stress Response Syndromes*, London: Jason Aronson.

Hudson, L. (1985) *Night Life*, London: Weidenfeld & Nicolson.

Humphrey, N. (1981), 'Four minutes to midnight', *The Listener*, 29 October.

Humphrey, N. (1983) *Consciousness Regained*, Oxford: Oxford University Press.

Hyde, G. M. (1988) 'Diary', *London Review of Books* 10: No. 17.

Jackson, D. and Haley, J. (1963) 'Transference revisited', *Journal of Nervous and Mental Disease* 137: 363–71.

Johnson-Laird, P. (1983), *Mental Models*, Cambridge: Cambridge University Press.

Joll, J. (1979) *Gramsci*, London: Fontana.

Jones, E. (1916) *Papers on Psychoanalysis* (5th edn.), London: Baillière.

Jung, C. (1978) 'Yoga and the West', in *Psychology and the East*, London: Routledge.

Jureidini, J. (1990) 'Projective identification in general psychiatry', *British Journal of Psychiatry* 157: 656–60.

Keithly, L. J., Samples, S. and Strupp, H. H. (1980) 'Patient motivation as a predictor of process and outcome in psychotherapy', *Psychotherapy and Psychosomatics* 33: 87–97.

Kelly, G. A. (1955) *The Psychology of Personal Constructs*, New York: Norton.

Kernberg O. F. (1987) 'An ego psychology-object relations theory approach to the transference', *Psychoanalytical Quarterly* 56: 197–221.

Khan, M. (1983) *Hidden Selves: Between Theory and Practice in Psychoanalysis*, London: Hogarth Press.

Khan, M. and Lewis, K. (1988) *Siblings in Therapy*, London: Norton.

Klein, M. (1950) *Contributions to Psychoanalysis*, London: Hogarth Press.

Klein, M. (1957) *Envy and Gratitude: A Study of Unconscious Sources*, London: Tavistock.

Klein, M. (1969) *Collected Writings*, vol. III, R. Money-Kyrle (ed.), London: Hogarth Press.

Koch, H. L. (1955) 'Some personality correlates of sex, sibling position and sex of sibling among 5 and 6 year old children', *Genetic Psychology Monographs* 52: 3–50.

Koch, H. L. (1956) Some emotional attitudes of the young child in relation to characteristics of his sibling', *Child Development* 27: 393–426.

Köhler, W. (1929) *Gestalt Psychology*, London: G. Bell & Son.

Kohon, G. (1986) 'Reflections on Dora: the case of hysteria', in G. Kohon (ed.) *The British School of Psychoanalysis: The Independent Tradition*, London: Free Association Books.

Kohut, H. (1971) *The Analysis of the Self*, New York: International Universities Press.

Kohut, H. (1984) *How Does Analysis Cure?* London: University of Chicago Press.

Kovel, J. (1985) *Sins of the Fathers*, London: Free Association Books, 1, 113–24.

Kraemer, S. (1991) Personal communication.

Kuhn, T. S. (1962) *The Structure of Scientific Revolutions*, Chicago: Chicago University Press.

Lacan, J. (1977) *Ecrits: a Selection*, London: Tavistock.

Laing, R. (1960) *The Divided Self*, London: Tavistock.

Lakin, M. (1988) *Ethical Issues in the Psychotherapies*, New York: Oxford University Press.

Langer, S. K. (1951) *Philosophy in a New Key*, New York: Mentor.

Langs, R. (1978) *The Listening Process*, New York: Aronson.

Langs, R. (1982) *Psychotherapy: A Basic Text*, New York: Jason Aronson.

Langs, R. (1988) *A Primer of Psychotherapy*, New York: Gardner Press.

Langs, R. (1989) 'The transformation function in the light of a new model of the mind', *British Journal of Psychotherapy* 5: 300–11.

Laplanche, J. and Pontalis, J.-B. (1973) *The Language of Psychoanalysis*, London: Hogarth Press.

Larkin, P. (1955) *The Less Deceived*, London: Marvell Press.

Larkin, P. (1974) *High Windows*, London: Faber & Faber.

Lasko, J. K. (1954) 'Parent behaviour towards first and second children', *Genetic Psychology Monographs* 49: 96–137.

Laufer, M. E. (1982) 'Female masturbation in adolescence and the development of the relationship to the body', *International Journal of Psychoanalysis* 63: 295–302.

Laufer, M. and Laufer, M. E. (1984) *Adolescence and Developmental Breakdown*, London: Yale University Press.

Leavis, F. R. (1962) *Two Cultures? The Significance of C. P. Snow*, London: Chatto & Windus.

Leavis, F. R. (1975) *The Living Principle*, London: Chatto & Windus.

Leff, J. and Vaughan, C. (1983) *Expressed Emotion in Families*, New York: Guilford Press.

Leiderman, P. H. and Mendelton, J. H. (1962) 'Some psychiatric and social aspects of the defence shelter programme', *New England Journal of Medicine* 66: 1149–55.

Lesser, M. and Lesser, B. Z. (1983) 'Alexithymia', *American Journal of Psychiatry* 140: 1305–8.

Levy, D. M. (1935) 'Maternal over-protection and rejection', *Archives of Neurology and Psychiatry* 25: 886–9.

Levy, D. M. (1939) 'Sibling rivalry studies in children of primitive groups', *American Journal of Orthopsychiatry* 9: 205–15.

Lewin, B. D. (1951) *The Psychoanalysis of Elation*, London: Hogarth Press.

Lewin, K. (1973) 'Dora revisited', *The Psychoanalytic Review* 60: 519–32.

Lifton, R. J. (1968) *Death in Life – Survivors of Hiroshima*, New York: Random House.

Loader, P. J., Kinston, W. and Stratford, J. (1980) 'Is there a "psychosomatogenic" family?', *Journal of Family Therapy* 2: 311–26.

Lorion, R. P. and Felner, R. D. (1986) 'Research on psychotherapy with the disadvantaged', in S. Garfield and A. E. Bergin (eds) *Handbook of Psychotherapy and Behaviour Change*, Chichester: Wiley.

Lovelock, J. (1982) *Gaia: a New Look at Planet Earth*, Oxford: Oxford University Press.

Lowell, R. (1959) *Life Studies*, London: Faber & Faber.

Luborsky, L. and Singer, B. (1975) 'Comparative studies of psychotherapies: is it true that "Everyone has won and all must have prizes"?', *Archives of General Psychiatry* 32: 995–1008.

McArthur, C. (1956) 'Personalities of first and second children', *Psychiatry* 19: 47–54.

Mack, J. E. (1981) 'Psychosocial effects of the nuclear arms race', *Bulletin of the Atomic Scientists* 37: 18–23.

Madanes, C. and Haley, J. (1977) 'Dimensions of Family Therapy' (1956), *Journal of Nervous and Mental Diseases* 165: 88–98.

Mahler, M. S. (1963) 'Thoughts about development and individuation', *Psychoanalytic Study of the Child*, vol. 18, 307–24.

Mahler, M. S. (1965) 'On the significance of the normal separation-individuation phase', in M. Schur (ed.) *Drives, Affects, Behaviour*, New York: International Universities Press.

Main, T. (1957) 'The ailment', *British Journal of Medical Psychology* 30: 129–45.

Malan, D. (1963) *A Study of Brief Psychotherapy*, London: Tavistock.

Malan, D. (1979) *Individual Psychotherapy and the Science of Psychodynamics*, London: Butterworth.

Mannheim, K. (1936) *Ideology and Utopia* (trans. L. Wirth and E. Shils), London: Routledge.

Marcus, S. (1974) 'Freud and Dora: story, history, case history', in *Representations: Essays on Literature and Society*, New York: Random House.

Margison, F. (1991) 'Learning to Listen' in J. Holmes (ed.) *A Textbook of Psychotherapy in Psychiatric Practice*, Edinburgh: Churchill Livingstone.

Martin, P. (1977) 'Some implications from the theory and practice of family therapy for individual therapy (and vice versa)', *British Journal of Medical Psychology* 50: 53–64.

Marziali, E. (1984) 'Three viewpoints on the therapeutic alliance: similarities, differences and association with psychotherapy outcome', *Journal of Nervous and Mental Diseases* 7: 417–23.

Masson, J. (1985) *The Assault on Truth*, London: Penguin.

Masson, J. (1989) *Against Therapy*, London: Collins.

Masson, J. (1991a) *Final Analysis*, London: Wiley.

Masson, J. (1991b) *Psychotherapy and its Discontents*, C. Feltham and W. Dryden (eds) Milton Keynes: Open University Press.

Medawar, P. B. (1975) 'Victims of psychiatry', *New York Review of Books* 23 January.

Medawar, P. (1984) *Plato's Republic*, Oxford: Oxford University Press.

Menzies-Lyth, I. (1988) *Containing Anxiety in Institutions*, London: Free Association Books.

Michels, R. (1976) 'Professional ethics and social values', *International Review of Psychoanalysis* 3: 377–84.

Milner, M. (1971) *On Not Being Able to Paint*, London: Heinemann.

Minuchin, S. (1974) *Families and Family Therapy*, London: Tavistock.

Minuchin, S., Rosman, B. L. and Baker, L. (1978) *Psychosomatic Families*, Cambridge MA: Harvard University Press.

Mollon, P. (1986) 'Narcissistic vulnerability and the fragile self: a failure of mirroring', *British Journal of Medical Psychology* 59: 317–24.

Mollon, P. (1989) 'Anxiety, supervision and a space for thinking: some narcissistic perils for clinical psychologists learning psychotherapy', *British Journal of Medical Psychology* 62: 113–22.

Mollon, P. (1991) 'Promoting psychoanalytic understanding in the core professions', *Psychoanalytic Psychotherapy* 5: 151–9.

Morgan, G. and Priest, P. (1991) 'Suicide and other unexpected deaths among psychiatric in-patients', *British Journal of Psychiatry* 158: 368–74.

Muslin, H. and Gill, M. (1978) 'Transference in the Dora case', *Journal of the American Psychoanalytical Association* 26: 311–28.

Newman, C. J. (1976) 'Children of disaster: clinical observations at Buffalo Creek', *American Journal of Psychiatry* 133: 306–12.

Nhat Hanh, T. (1987) *Being Peace*, California: Parallax.

Orlinsky, D. E. and Howard, K. I. (1981) 'Process and Outcome in Psychotherapy', in S. L. Garfield and A. E. Bergin (eds) *Handbook of Psychotherapy and Behaviour Change*, Chichester: Wiley.

Padel, J. (1985) 'Ego in current thinking', *International Review of Psycho-analysis* 12: 273–83.

Painter, G. D. (1977) *Marcel Proust*, London: Peregrine.

Palazzoli, S. M., Cechin, G. F., Prata, G. and Boscolo, L. S. (1978) *Paradox and Counter Paradox*, New York: Jason Aronson.

Palazzoli, S. M., Cechin, G. F., Prata, G. and Boscolo, L. S. (1980) 'Hypothesizing-circularity-neutrality', *Family Process* 19: 3–12.

Papp, P. J. (1976) 'Family choreography', in P. J. Guerin (ed.) *Family Therapy*, New York: Gauden Press.

Parkes, C. M. (1972) *Bereavement: Studies of Guilt in Adult Life*, London: Tavistock.

Parsons, T. (1951) *The Social System*, New York: Free Press.

Parsons, T. and Bales, R. F. (1955) *Family, Socialization and Interaction Process*, Glencoe, Ill.: Free Press.

Paul, G. L. (1967) 'Outcome research in psychotherapy', *Journal of Consulting Psychology* 31: 109–18.

Pedder, J. R. (1979) 'Transitional space in psychotherapy and theatre', *British Journal of Medical Psychology* 52: 377–84.

Pedder, J. R. (1989) 'Courses in psychotherapy: evolution and current trends', *British Journal of Psychotherapy* 6: 203–21.

Pedder, J. R. (1990) 'Lines of advance in psychoanalytic psychotherapy', *Psychoanalytic Psychotherapy* 4: 201–17.

Peterfreund, E. (1983) *The Process of Psychoanalytic Therapy: Modes and Strategies*, New York: Analytic Press.

Piaget, J. (1951) *Play, Dreams and Imitation in Childhood*, London: Routledge & Kegan Paul.

Piaget, J. (1954) *The Child's Construction of Reality*, London: Routledge & Kegan Paul.

Pines, M. (1991) 'A history of dynamic psychiatry in Britain', in J. Holmes (ed.) *A Textbook of Psychotherapy in Psychiatric Practice*, Edinburgh: Churchill Livingstone.

Pribram, K. H. (1981) 'Freud Memorial Lecture', University College London (unpublished).

Pribram, K. H. and Gill, M. M. (1976) *Freud's Project Reassessed*, London: Hutchinson.

Proust, M. (1941) *The Remembrance of Things Past*, vol. 1, *Swann's Way*, (trans. C. K. Scott-Moncrieff), London: Chatto & Windus.

Rachman, S. (1978) 'An anatomy of obsessions', *Behaviour Analysis and Modification* 2: 253–78.

Racker, H. (1968) *Transference and Countertransference*, London: Hogarth Press.

Reik, T. (1948) 'Listening with the Third Ear', *The Inner Experience of a Psychoanalyst*, New York: Farra Straus.

Reps, P. (1971) *Zen Flesh, Zen Bones*, London: Penguin.

Rey, H. (1975) Personal communication.

Ricoeur, P. (1979) 'The metaphorical process as cognition, imagination and feeling', in S. Sacks (ed.) *On Metaphor*, London: University of Chicago Press.

Rieff, P. (1971) 'Introduction', *Freud: Dora – an Analysis of a Case of Hysteria*, New York: Collier.

Rieff, P. (1979) *Freud: The Mind of the Moralist* (3rd edn.), London: University of Chicago Press.

Rogow, A. (1978) 'A further footnote to Freud's "Fragment of an analysis of a case of hysteria"', *Journal of American Psychoanalytical Association* 26: 331–56.

Rollman-Branch, H. (1966) 'The first-born child, male', *International Journal of Psycho-Analysis* 47: 404.

Rosser, R., Birch, S., Bond, H., Denford, J. and Schacter, J. (1987) 'Five year follow-up of patients treated with psychotherapy at the Cassel Hospital for Nervous Diseases', *Journal of the Royal Society of Medicine* 80: 549–55.

Rothschild, L. (1984) *Random Variables*, London: Collins.

Roustang, F. (1980) *Psychoanalysis Never Lets Go* (trans. N. Lukacher), Baltimore: Johns Hopkins University Press.

Russell, B. (1972) *Autobiography* vol. 1, London: Routledge.

Rutter, P. (1990) *Sex in the Forbidden Zone*, London: Unwin.

Rycroft, C. (1966) 'Causes and meaning', in C. Rycroft (ed.) *Psychoanalysis Observed*, London: Constable.

Rycroft, C. (1968) *Anxiety and Neurosis*, London: Penguin.

Rycroft, C. (1968) *Imagination and Reality*, London: Hogarth Press.

Rycroft, C. (1979) *The Innocence of Dreams*, London: Hogarth Press.

Rycroft, C. (1985) *Psychoanalysis and Beyond*, London: Chatto & Windus.

Ryle, A. (1982) *Psychotherapy: A Cognitive Integration of Theory and Practice*, London: Academic Press.

Ryle, A. (1990) *Cognitive Analytic Therapy: Active Participation in Change*, Chichester: Wiley.

Sander, F. (1974) 'Freud's "A case of successful treatment by hypnotism", (1892–1893): an uncommon therapy', *Family Process* 13: 461–8.

Sandler, J. (1988) *Projection, Identification, Projective Identification*, London: Kavnac.

Sandler, J. and Joffe, N. G. (1965) 'Notes on obsessional manifestations in children', *Psychoanalytic Study of the Child* 20: 428–36.

Sandler, J., Dare, C. and Holder, A. (1973) *The Patient and the Analyst*, London: George Allen & Unwin.

Schatzman, M. (1975) *Soul Murder*, London: Allen Lane.

Segal, H. (1991), *Dream, Phantasy and Art*, London: Routledge.

Segraves, R. T. (1982) *Marital Therapy*, New York: Plenum Press.

Shafer, R. (1976) *A New Language for Psychoanalysis*, Yale: Yale University Press.

Shapiro, D. A. (1981) 'Comparative credibility of treatment rationales: three tests of expectancy theory', *British Journal of Clinical Psychology* 21: 111–22.

Sharpe, E. (1937) *Dream Analysis*, London: Hogarth Press.

Sharpe, E. (1950) 'Psycho-physical problems revealed in language: an examination of metaphor', in R. Fliess (ed.) *The Psycho-analytic Reader*, London: Hogarth Press.

Shepherd, M. (1984) 'What price psychotherapy?', *British Medical Journal* 288: 809–10.

Skues, R. (1980) 'Jeffrey Masson and the assault on Freud', *British Journal of Psychotherapy* 3 (4): 305–14.

Skynner, A. C. R. (1976) *One Flesh: Separate Persons*, London: Constable.

Slater, E. and Roth, M. (1969) *Clinical Psychiatry*, (3rd edn.), London: Baillière, Tindall & Cassell.

Slater, P. (1961) 'Towards a dualistic theory of identification', *Merrill-Palmer*

Quarterly 7: 113–21.

Snow, C. P. (1959) *The Two Cultures*, Cambridge: Cambridge University Press.

Sontag, S. (1979) *Illness as a Metaphor*, London: Allen Lane.

States, B. O. (1988) *The Rhetoric of Dreams*, California: Cornell University Press.

Stem, D. (1985), *The Interpersonal World of the Infant*, New York: Basic Books.

Stiles, W. B., Shapiro, D. A. and Elliot, R. K. (1986) 'Are all psychotherapies equivalent?', *American Psychologist* 41: 165–80.

Storr, A. (1965) *The Integrity of the Personality*, London: Penguin.

Storr, A. (1979) *The Art of Psychotherapy*, Oxford: Oxford University Press.

Strachey, J. (1934) 'The nature of the therapeutic action of psychoanalysis', *International Journal of Psycho-Analysis* 15: 127–59.

Sturge, C. (1977) Personal communication.

Sulloway, F. (1979) *Freud: Biologist of the Mind*, New York: Basic Books.

Sutton-Smith, B. and Rosenberg, B. G. (1971) *The Sibling*, New York: Holt, Rinehart & Winston.

Suzuki, D. (1960) 'Lectures on Zen Buddhism', in E. Fromm (ed.) *Zen Buddhism and Psychoanalysis*, New York: Grove Press.

Symington, N. (1980) Personal communication.

Symington, N. (1986) *The Analytic Experience*, London: Free Association Books.

Thoma, H. and Kachele, H. (1986) *Psychoanalytic Practice*, London: Springer-Verlag.

Thomas, D. M. (1982) *The White Hotel*, London: Penguin.

Thompson, E. P. (1982) *Writing by Candlelight*, London: Merlin.

Trilling, L. (1950) *The Liberal Imagination*, London: Secker & Warburg.

Truax, C. and Carkhuff, R. (1967) *Towards Effective Counselling and Psychotherapy*, Chicago: Aldine.

Tudor Hart, J. (1971) 'The inverse care law', *The Lancet* 1: 405–12.

Turner, J. (1988) 'Wordsworth, Winnicott and the arena of play', *International Review of Psycho-Analysis* 15: 481.

Tyrer, P. (1985) 'Neurosis divisible?', *The Lancet* 1: 685–8.

Vygotsky, I. (1966) *Development of the Higher Mental Functions*, Cambridge MA: M. I. T. Press.

Waddell, M. (1989) 'Living in Two Worlds', *Free Association* 15: 11–35.

Waldrop, M. F. (1965) 'Effects of family size and density on newborn characteristics', *American Journal of Orthopsychiatry* 35: 342–3.

Warren, J. R. (1966) 'Birth order and social behaviour', *Psychological Bulletin* 65: 38–49.

Watson, P. (1978) *War on the Mind*, London: Hutchinson.

Watts, A. (1961) *Psychotherapy East and West*, New York: Random House.

Watts, A. (1962) *The Way of Zen*, London: Penguin.

Watzlawick, P., Beavin, J. and Jackson, D. (1967) *Pragmatics of Human Communication*, New York: Norton.

Watzlawick, P., Weakland, J. M. and Fisch, R. (1974) *Change: Principles of Problem Formation and Problem Solution*, New York: Norton.

Weakland, J. H., Fisch, R., Watzlawick, P. and Bodin, A. M. (1974) 'Brief therapy: focused problem resolution', *Family Process* 13: 141–68.

Weiss, R. S. (1974) *Loneliness*, Cambridge MA: M. I. T. Press.

West, M. (1990) *The Psychology of Meditation*, Oxford: Oxford University Press.

Wilkinson, G. (1986) 'Psychoanalysis and analytic psychotherapy in the NHS – a problem for medical ethics', *Journal of Medical Ethics* 12: 87–90.

Williams, P. and Clare, A. (1981) 'Changing patterns of psychiatric care', *British Medical Journal* 282: 375–7.

Williams, R. (1973) *The Country and the City*, London: Chatto & Windus.

Williams, R. (1985) *Towards 2000*, London: Penguin.

Wilson, S. and Wilson, K. (1985) 'Close encounters in general practice: experiences of a psychiatric liaison team', *British Journal of Psychiatry* 146: 272–81.

Wing, K. K. and Brown, G. W. (1970) *Institutionalism and Schizophrenia*, London: Cambridge University Press.

Winnicott, D. W. (1965) *The Maturational Processes and the Facilitating Environment*, London: Tavistock.

Winnicott, D. W. (1971) *Playing and Reality*, London: Tavistock.

Wolff, H. H. (1971) 'The therapeutic and developmental functions of psychotherapy', *British Journal of Medical Psychology* 44: 117–30.

Wolff, H. H. (1972) 'Psychotherapy: its place in psychosomatic management', *Psychotherapy Psychosomatics* 22: 223–39.

Woodcock, A. and Davis, M. (1980) *Catastrophe Theory*, London: Penguin.

Wright, K. (1991) *Vision and Separation*, London: Free Association Books.

Zetzel, E. R. (1966) 'Additional notes upon a case of obsessional neurosis: Freud 1909', *International Journal of Psycho-Analysis* 47: 123–9.

Index